# PRAISE FOR *HERETIC*

*A Lit Hub "Most Anticipated Book Of 2022"*

"*Heretic* is an intelligent and highly entertaining memoir, part cultural history, part personal history. Jeanna Kadlec writes with perspective and poignancy; her writing excavates the ideal of a good Christian woman and reveals it for all it ever truly was, a myth. Kadlec is a captivating storyteller and cultural historian. *Heretic* is both an insight into America's regressive politics and a memoir of astonishing honesty and beautiful complexity. From her life as a good Christian girl to her emergence as a queer woman, Kadlec writes with voice and conviction. *Heretic* is a memoir that employs a coming of sexuality and a coming of womanhood with prose that is empowering and beautiful."

— Lyz Lenz, author of *Godland* and *Belabored*

"Bless this brave, thoughtful, funny, aggravating, nearly triggering book. It made me wish I still believed in the God I knew in my youth so that I could pick a fight with Him. Kadlec provides an astute picture of what it feels like to be born into the maze of a rigid faith, and the twists and turns it takes to find yourself. I wish I had had this book when I was a teenager and am both jealous and so pleased for the people who will have it as an emotional resource to guide them through their own maze. This will hit very close to home for a lot of people."

—Lucy Dacus

"Weaving pop culture, history, and page-turning personal memoir, *Heretic* is a book of incisive, brilliant observation and colloquial, warm humor. Here, an anthropological exploration of power, self-discovery, and the communities we both desire and dismantle; Kadlec bridges past and present to graciously offer a new way forward, a hand to hold, an unforgettable and edifying reading experience you won't want to miss. The best books are often those that energize a reader with a propulsive story, while teaching them something new along the way. This has got it all."

—T Kira Madden, author of *Long Live the Tribe of Fatherless Girls*

"Kadlec is inviting us to reexamine our own lives and reject anything that would restrict us from living as our full selves in favor of a joyful, open, freer path. I've loved Kadlec's work for a long time—she writes with the bold, clear voice of someone who has *been there* and back, and has now settled in to tell you the real deal."

—Literary Hub

"*Heretic* is full of intellect and ferocious emotion, with language so taut that every thread of her narrative—an evangelical upbringing, religious trauma, violence, and queer love—forms a shimmering braid. Kadlec's analysis of fundamentalist belief, placed right up against tales of cartoons, Dungeons & Dragons, and the art of tarot, moved me to tears with its vibrant celebration of hard-won joy."

—Esmé Weijun Wang, author of *The Collected Schizophrenias*

"I can't tell you how happy I am that Kadlec's work exists in the world. *Heretic* is the guidebook I needed for my life. Learning how to overcome harmful systems and find joy and community on our own terms is essential for queer survival, and Kadlec has provided an elegant and astute account."

—Garrard Conley, author of *Boy Erased*

"In this outstanding debut, clear, elegant, and precise as etched glass, Jeanna Kadlec recounts a detachment from her own heart and desires so profound and carefully inculcated that desire for anyone other than God felt like transgression. Her prose is wise and erudite, undergirded by plain speech and an open heart. *Heretic* is a light unto the path of every former evangelical who longs for communion beyond the condemnation and spiritual abuse of the church, and a crucial window for outsiders into what it's like to grow up handed a birthright of original sin."

—Maud Newton, author of *Ancestor Trouble*

"A woman reckons with the religious trauma of her upbringing and embarks on a process of self-discovery in this searing debut. . . . As she recounts her disentanglement from religion, Kadlec weaves a deeply personal narrative with excoriating criticism to unpack the ways in which religious belief is sewn into the fabric of American society. The result provides a poignant story of being born again in a secular world."

—*Publishers Weekly*

# HERETIC

*A Memoir*

# JEANNA KADLEC

**HARPER**

*An Imprint of* HarperCollins*Publishers*

HarperCollins books may be purchased for educational, business, or sales promotional use. For information, please email the Special Markets Department at SPsales@harpercollins.com.

Scriptures taken from the Holy Bible, New International Version,® NIV.® Copyright © 1973, 1978, 1984, 2011 by Biblica, Inc.™ Used by permission of Zondervan. All rights reserved worldwide. www.zondervan.com. The "NIV" and "New International Version" are trademarks registered in the United States Patent and Trademark Office by Biblica, Inc.™

Scripture quotations from the Authorized (King James) Version. Rights in the Authorized Version in the United Kingdom are vested in the Crown. Reproduced by permission of the Crown's patentee, Cambridge University Press.

FIRST EDITION

Library of Congress Cataloging-in-Publication Data has been applied for.

ISBN 978-0-35-858181-9

22 23 24 25 26  LSC  10 9 8 7 6 5 4 3 2 1

**"WHATEVER CAME, SHE HAD RESOLVED NEVER AGAIN TO BELONG TO ANOTHER THAN HERSELF."**

Kate Chopin, *The Awakening*

# CONTENTS

# AUTHOR'S NOTE

## On Genre

While this memoir incorporates research, journal entries, and the findings of retrospective conversations with kith and kin, it's ultimately a constructed narrative of events from my perspective. It's not, nor can it be, wholly representative of any one person. Even the clearest memories are imperfect, rocks shaped by the watery ebb and flow of time.

Some names and identifying details of individuals have been changed to protect their privacy.

## On Terms

The word "evangelical" has meant many things to many people over the years. As of this writing, there is a strong case to be made for its status as the standard bearer of hard-line fundamentalist Protestant beliefs in American politics and popular culture. Because of this, I have chosen, for simplicity's sake, to use "evangelical" as shorthand for contemporary evangelicalism and fundamentalism both. While it's important to understand that there are historical differences between the two, that is not the project of this book.

## On Content

It may be helpful for some readers to know that there are scenes and mentions of domestic violence, substance abuse, sexual assault, and suicidal ideation. Take care of you.

# HERETIC

# 1. IN THE BEGINNING

I DIDN'T PRAY. THERE WAS NOTHING LEFT TO SAY. NOTHING LEFT TO DO BUT down a cup of coffee, slip into my leather jacket, and hop an 87 bus down to the Middlesex County Courthouse to file for divorce. My black cowboy boots thudded heavy on the marble staircase. It felt like a country song, but it was my life: a life I was choosing, even if I was pretty sure this particular choice was going to damn me to hell. Then again, I wasn't even sure I believed in hell anymore. As I walked up to the family court's office on the second floor, "Maneater" was blaring on the radio, greeting all the spouses- and divorcees-to-be alike. "Watch out boy, she'll chew you up."

The well-dressed woman in line ahead of me had brought her own lawyer, which felt like overkill, until I realized that she didn't actually have a copy of the legal marriage certificate—just the flimsy church paper. As if a church holds the same authority as the state. I went through my own manila folder, making sure I had everything: the official marriage certificate, my passport (which had both my maiden name, Kadlec, and my husband's surname, which I had legally added to my own—a compromise for a "progressive" but faithful evangelical couple), and our lease, in case I needed to prove residency in Massachusetts since we'd been married in the Midwest.

*Beware ye who walk in the way of sinners*, my husband had told me mere days before I filed. His efforts to correct my path weren't working: not the silent treatment, or his prayers that I would simply change overnight back to the woman he'd known before. Hence the dispensing of grand statements that began *Beware ye* when we passed by each other in our six-hundred-square-foot one-bedroom Somerville apartment, reminding me of the eternal consequences of my pending decision.

What are decades of devotion compared with one swift fall from grace? I had been teaching *Paradise Lost* to undergraduates that semester—hell, that same week—and the parallel was not lost on me. I had also bitten from a Tree of Knowledge, and, like Eve, couldn't unknow the truth. The life-upending, damning realization that had brought me to the county courthouse, where the helpful clerk was now advising me to pay the extra forty dollars (for a grad student, a tremendous sum) to have the police deliver the papers to my soon-to-be ex-husband, was that I was queer.

*Trust me. You'll want proof that he's been notified*, she said.

The scariest thing wasn't filling in my name as PLAINTIFF in the divorce complaint against my husband, or the fact that I would soon be temporarily living with my best friend (whom I was secretly in love with, and how on earth was I gonna keep *that* hidden?). It was the implication of what this decision meant for someone known for her faith—albeit one nonbelieving friends still felt comfortable shooting the shit about faith and the universe with while smoking and drinking in a parking lot at midnight. Someone who led Bible studies, someone who had spent a lifetime prioritizing a personal relationship with Jesus.

A devout born-again evangelical Christian for, at the time, my entire twenty-five years of life, the divorce would declare publicly, for my faith community from the Midwest to the East Coast to see, that God was not enough for me—that my belief had faltered. Even if trying to suppress my queerness had felt like a kind of death and had driven me to consider taking my own life, I knew these struggles would not matter to my husband, my family, and to fellow evangelicals, to whom it would appear that I was purposefully, belligerently straying from the straight and narrow.

I was leaving the Garden, the evangelical church, and the only version of myself that I had ever known. I was choosing who I wanted to be—but I had no idea who she was.

This had not been the plan.

✝

Where I come from, faith is one of the few centripetal forces that pulls a community together. Most everyone back home goes to Sunday service; it is unusual to know a family in many Midwestern small towns that doesn't. Your actual investment in the faith may vary, but if you want to have a meaningful support system for when life comes at you sideways: get thee to church.

My early childhood was spent in rural Iowa on an acreage surrounded by farms, a twenty-minute drive from "town" (which was, in fact, a village of about 1,800 people). Any social life outside of school revolved around church: Sunday school in the early mornings and seeing if I could tag along later with the junior high kids who were in the youth group my mom led, Vacation Bible School in the summer, and evening potlucks with other church families. My Rush Limbaugh–listening, lapsed-Catholic father didn't participate in organized religion when I was younger, but he didn't stop my mom from taking my younger sister, Jo, and me to the country church that was a short drive from our house.

All our church involvement—reading scripture with Mom before bed, having contemporary Christian music playing in our house and in the car—meant that, despite our attending public school instead of a private Christian school, our framework for understanding the world was ingrained in us at an early age. God created the world. Because we are sinners, he sent his son, Jesus, to die for us. Jesus hung on the cross for our sins. After three days, he rose again from the dead. He ascended into heaven. He is seated at the right hand of the Father Almighty. He will come again to judge the living and the dead.

That's a rough paraphrase of the Apostle's Creed—something I repeated by memory my entire childhood—but it summarizes the Gospels, the "Good News" of evangelical Christianity, and the foundation of the faith I was raised in: believing in Jesus is the way you are "saved" from your own depraved sin, and belief is the only thing that keeps you from the temptations of this world and eternal damnation in the next. And given this extraordinary good news, wouldn't you like to tell other people so that they can be saved, too?

The people of faith I grew up around had an abrasive way of communicating this news of Christ's love. *Why is he yelling, Mommy?* I asked during Pastor Don's passionate sermon one Sunday. Loud enough that other congregants in the pew apparently chuckled, but also loud enough that some of them probably looked snidely at my mom, attending church alone with her two small children. Wondering where the father was. Wondering if the reason for the older daughter's consistent, unruly commentary on the sermons was because of a lack of paternal guidance.

My mom, a dark blond thirtysomething with Kelly green eyes that were no doubt tired as shit from being the primary caregiver, cook, and house cleaner, was doing her best to steward our earthly bodies as well as our souls. When I hear Mom tell this story now, what I hear is an ambivalence that my six-year-old self could already feel between the pastor's angry screeds about sinners and demands for total obedience, and my entire faith that, as a child, had until that point been encapsulated wholly in the gentle children's song: "Jesus loves me, this I know / for the Bible tells me so."

In spite of my pluckiness, I was considered one of the "good kids" at church. My church friends, the other good kids, and I volunteered together in the nursery; we sat together in youth group. While I sometimes struggled to make friends at public school, especially in middle school, at church I was usually part of the in-crowd—if in a Hermione Granger sort of way. As I got older, and my family moved to northern Wisconsin, I remained well liked by youth leaders, even if I was considered rather forward and bossy for a girl. An apt student, I wasn't so keen on the proselytizing and requests that I bring my public school friends to my church, which I found horribly awkward and avoided at all costs, but I did want to know everything I could about what I believed and why. Growing up in the church and being so steeped in evangelical culture from infancy gave me a knack for textual analysis and expressing myself well, honed by my mother's rigorous standards and my own subsequent desire to please and impress authority figures. Before English lit classes taught me textual analysis, how to close-read Shakespeare and Jane Austen and Toni Morrison, I was scrutinizing scripture through what pastors call "exegesis" in Sunday school, digging into the Gospels with questions like *What does this metaphor from Jesus about turning the other cheek really mean? What could he have drawn in the sand to make the Pharisees leave the woman accused of adultery alone? And what do those things mean for my life and how he wants me to live now?* Ask the right questions, and you'll find all the right answers—the ones that explain where and how the elders wanted us to belong.

Becoming a high-achieving, highly observant young teenager also meant that I became ferociously if quietly judgmental of my peers who did *not* take church seriously, particularly the guys. They sat in the back at youth group, barely sang during worship, rarely knew the answers to the youth leaders' questions, and were clearly forced by their parents to be there. Did they even *have* a relationship with Jesus? Were they even *saved?* The fact that my youth leaders still considered the boys to be the natural and future spiritual leaders of the church community simply by virtue of their gender—and not a girl like me, who *cared*—stung, the hurt mixed with a sense of injustice over not being deemed worthy in spite of meeting every task set to me. These early moments of friction began to draw me to feminism before I even had a name for it. But at church, I already knew better than to argue that the girls were treated unfairly, and I kept my opinions to myself.

In part because of how girls were expected to behave, I didn't talk that much about my personal relationship with Jesus, where my faith felt most alive. I filled dozens of prayer journals with our conversations, which felt so close, so real, as if I could hear his voice whispering to me, audible as my parents' voices in the next room. The walks and bike rides I took down to the lake, to Cemetery Island, where it was just me and him and the rustling of leaves and my own tears as I poured my heart out to my savior. In the privacy of nature, or in my own bedroom with my journals, I could escape the rules and surveillance of our big church. I could feel fully safe, loved, held.

So when my mom told me that we were going to be leaving that church with the big youth group and taking part in a church plant—a small group of about forty people from our church who had decided to form a new congregation—where there wouldn't really be a youth group, I wasn't that upset. I was overjoyed that I would get to be at meetings with the adults making decisions about the new church, that I was going to do something *real* for God that wasn't simply working part-time at the local independent Christian bookstore or volunteering in the nursery, as churches assume every woman wants to do. I would get to be in the room where it happened, as it were, even if I, as a teenager, wouldn't be voting on the issues. I was more excited than I'd ever been to serve in what felt like a real, serious, and grown-up way. For the next few years of my adolescence, my mom, sister, and I were up early every Sunday morning to volunteer at the church plant as it slowly grew. I felt like I was in community with adults who truly cared about me and my spiritual growth.

Everything changed one sweltering summer night when I was fifteen. The whole church was at the town's public pool for a mass baptism, complete with moms and dads tailgating with non-alcoholic beverages. Dad was with us, for the first time. We all gathered around the pool, the mood growing somber for the scheduled baptisms. One by one, their arms folded across their chests like corpses, folks were dunked backward then raised out, soaking wet, born again of the chlorinated water that had served as a latrine for toddlers hours earlier.

Moved by the pastor's altar call or the kind of unifying collective feeling that can build up at ritualistic religious events like these—what French sociologist Émile Durkheim calls "collective effervescence"—my dad impulsively jumped in the pool, Wrangler jeans, steel-toe work boots, leather belt, and all. He said the prayer of salvation right there, my mom crying her eyes out and looking on with joy while he accepted Jesus into his heart and effectively converted to evangelicalism.

Folks who regularly attended service with us knew what a big deal this was. Dad never went to church with us; he would be home watching NASCAR and cracking Budweisers before noon. My entire life, we had been that one family at ten o'clock worship without a representative father who everyone else was praying for, the condescension dripping while I watched the other church ladies, the doctors' and professors' wives, ask my mom how my daddy was doing, and would he be joining us next Sunday? when they damn well knew he wouldn't be. Well, here he was, getting baptized, and those same women were coming up to my mom congratulating her now. *The power of a praying wife!* they said.

I was happy for my mom's public recognition and vindication. But skepticism settled over me as I watched the men help my soaking-wet father out of the pool. Even then, I knew that simply saying the prayer of salvation meant jack shit. "Faith without works is dead," the Good Book says,* and I was waiting to see if my dad's newfound belief would be backed up by changes in his behavior at home. Would his drinking stop? Would he learn to control his temper? Would he become more empathetic, a better listener?

In spite of the fact that my dad was what believers call a "baby Christian," the evangelical emphasis on "male headship" in marriage meant that my mom's decades of faith and our years of investment in the church plant were rendered meaningless—my dad was

* James 2:26 (KJV).

now the spiritual head of our household and would get to decide all religious matters, including where we went to church. Uncomfortable with the church plant, where my mom's faith was respected, and, I believe, where some of our fellow congregants were either aware of or suspected what was happening behind the scenes in our home, my dad decided we would attend a different church in town. At the time, Mom, filled with a joy I'd never seen, seemed relieved to pass over the religious reins to my father, something she'd long been praying for, and which was expected of her as an evangelical wife. I felt alone in my silent fury, upset that he got to be making these enormous decisions for our family when he'd barely ever cracked the text that our entire faith was based on. But everyone around me seemed to think that because my dad was a man, God would give him extra support, and he'd do just fine.

Shortly after his baptism, my dad decided to lead our family to the strictest, most totalitarian church around. Most folks in town, both evangelical and otherwise, called it a cult.

This church-cult was called Calvary: Calvary, after the execution site outside Jerusalem where Jesus hung on a cross and died, the cross that it seemed all of us in this church were expected to metaphorically carry and carry and carry and never put down. Emphasis on guilt and suffering and human depravity: *You're literally responsible for the death of the god of the universe.* Less on *Jesus loves me, this I know.* Instability and anxiety were the constant mood in this faith community, furthered by a heightened focus on teachings around God's judgment and wrath. The messaging left little room for questions or individual interpretation, emphasizing how we as human beings are entirely worthless and can find purpose only through service to God.

The senior pastor who drove these messages home was a wiry,

balding fortysomething man who kept his remaining hair extremely long and had a Santa-like beard. With his suspenders and glasses, he was the kind of caricature of a Portland or Brooklyn hipster that *New Yorker* cartoons would eventually satirize—except this was 2003 in northern Wisconsin. In a small town where so many pastors wore conservative, stale suits, he radiated cool and, in that undeniable way so many charismatic leaders are, was wildly clever, able to bend any text to his bidding all while maintaining that he was interpreting scripture the way God intended, which he implied was the *only* correct interpretation of scripture in town. In terms of evangelical trends, Calvary was ahead of its time with the hipster pastor, church coffee shop and bookstore, and jail ministry; barely any other churches in our region were doing those things in the early 2000s, let alone in a town so small.

Calvary was at the extreme end of the evangelical spectrum of most every church I attended growing up: fundamentalist in its theology, politically conservative (which is to say, anti-abortion, anti-LGBTQ+, and opposed to women in church leadership), dedicated to a literal interpretation of scripture, and keen to emphasize our total and wholesale dependence on Jesus. But then, these beliefs, so common among American evangelicals to varying degrees of intensity, have been on our shores since the very beginning and can in fact be traced all the way back to the Pilgrims, the first group of Puritans, who landed in Massachusetts Bay in 1620.*

Listen: repackaging the Pilgrims as well-meaning white folks with pointy hats, buckled shoes, and a turkey craving trying to escape religious persecution is some of the best marketing this country has ever done. The Pilgrims, and later groups of Puritans, didn't

---

* Theologically speaking, the Puritans were strict Calvinists.

colonize this part of North America for freedom. They didn't travel across an ocean because of an idealistic investment in religious pluralism. No. The Puritans came here to establish a supremacist religious theocracy: full stop. To them, England had lost its way. They despised what they saw as the leniency of the Church of England and craved a stricter rule of law. For the Puritans, the church *was* the state, and anyone who didn't believe this could hang. The first waves of Puritans were extreme in their commitment to establishing a purified theocracy, regularly executing dissenters and heretics on the Boston Common—members of the Wampanoag tribe on an ongoing basis, and Quakers as early as 1656, mere decades after the Pilgrims first arrived.

The pursuit of one's own religious "freedom" is a convenient justification for terrorizing others; *this*, not pluralism, is America's real religious and political origin. Eventually, restricted by the Crown, the Puritans were forced to halt the murder of Quakers, who were, after all, their fellow European colonists.[*] Not good for settler-colonialism, if the religious zealots who got here first killed any newcomers who disagreed with them.[†] But as the colonial population grew, so too did powerful new forms of American Protestantism. Ever adaptable, these new, varied Protestantisms no longer executed nonbelievers, but they did continue to perpetuate and

---

[*] King Charles II issued the missives to halt executions of non-Puritans in Massachusetts not only at the behest of Quakers but also in part with an intent toward encouraging Catholic settlement in Massachusetts, as he was a Catholic sympathizer, but this was obviously not successful. Hostility to Catholicism would remain a hallmark of American religious and political life for centuries. To date, we have elected only two Catholic presidents: JFK and Joe Biden.

[†] Executions of Quakers had stopped by 1675. See Carl E. Sigmond, "Quakers Fight for Religious Freedom in Puritan Massachusetts, 1656–1661," Global Nonviolent Action Database, Swarthmore College, March 25, 2012, https://nvdatabase.swarthmore.edu/content/quakers-fight-religious-freedom-puritan-massachusetts-1656-1661.

implicitly conflate those initial theocratic beliefs that hard work meant good citizenship and that obedience to the state was also obedience to God.

The first Great Awakening swept the Eastern Seaboard in the 1730s and 1740s, largely spread through the academic lectures of the Northampton minister Jonathan Edwards (most famous for his sermon "Sinners in the Hands of an Angry God") and the long sermons of the charismatic traveling English preacher George White-field, who popularized the then-new idea of being "born again." While the idea that Christians are given new life by Christ is found in the New Testament, Whitefield's ideas of the necessity of a believer's rebirth had been criticized in England. However, in front of large revivals full of thousands of colonists, it thrived, becoming integral to future iterations of American Protestantism.

One thing can be said for Puritan extremism: it emphasized literacy and education—the kind of academic scripture-studying that I inherently gravitated toward. But as colonial efforts on the frontiers expanded, and as access to books, education, and a more intellectual religious lineage consequently became more limited, it was Whitefield's tradition of charismatic, stadium-style speeches and new Protestant denominations like Methodist and Baptist circuit riders' tent revivals in western territories that won out. The Puritans' emphasis on textual analysis dwindled as their severe tenets were condensed into sound bites and folded into the "simpler, more democratic" faith of the Second Great Awakening, which occurred in the early nineteenth century.* Most tellingly, the Puritans' exploitative, colonial, theocratic insistence on equating hard work

---

* Frances FitzGerald, *The Evangelicals: The Struggle to Shape America* (New York: Simon & Schuster, 2017), 25.

with morality and respectable citizenship was fully absorbed into the American project of citizen-making.

Calvary ran on exploitation. My family was expected to work hard for God, far beyond the intensity of the volunteer work my mother, sister, and I had committed to at our old church plant. We were expected at Calvary whenever the doors were open, as much as was possible outside of work and school obligations. My dad, who was ex-military and had worked in telecom his whole life, worked on Calvary's electrical and internet connections, and anything else the church needed structurally. I got to work in the church bookstore, which went a long way in soothing my frustration with my father's newfound devotion. My parents hosted a home Bible study, which is typically seen as an honor and a sign of pastoral trust in many congregations, until it was abruptly taken away from them, with no warning, for "lack of attendance"—but how could we have been there more than we already were, all day Sunday, every Wednesday night, and other days for volunteering?

While some amount of behavioral monitoring is common within any group of people, Calvary had a heightened level of intercommunity surveillance that trickled down from the senior pastor to the youth leaders to the congregants. Every word trained us to be aware of which way power flowed within the church: as a teenager in the high school youth group, I'd heard tell that the couples in leadership positions needed the senior pastor's permission to have a baby. The assistant pastor would walk up and down the aisles anytime a service was in session, every Sunday morning and Wednesday night, writing in a black, leather-bound notebook, a visible, physical reminder that our leaders were watching. Mom would tell me years later that, during my parents' meeting with the senior pastor during which they were dismissed from their own home Bible study, he had brought out that black book and showed them a page with our family's name on it—notes and dates and records of our behavior, what the pastoral leadership had deemed "the good" and "the bad." Essentially, the pastors at Calvary had been keeping a *Mean Girls*-style burn book with detailed notes on every single member of the congregation.

This kind of surveillance is why organized religion is, historically, so useful for governments. Constitutionally, church and state were technically separate in the United States, but religion was considered vital to policing citizens' morality. Religion was one way to instill shared values, especially in a fledgling nation. These new strains of distinctly American Protestantism blended well with the colonial project of rapid western expansion (and the antihero cowboy identity), which worked together to displace Indigenous peoples in the name of God and to sanctify manifest destiny. This was the insidious theology, trickled down from Puritanism, at work: every American who was observed working hard could be deemed a "good" citizen, or, implicitly, a "good" Christian, and vice versa. And Christ's desire that the Good News be spread (the so-called Great Commission*) could justify all manner of political evils— there's a reason this type of Christianity became a useful religion for states to adopt the world over.

The new denominations that sprung up in the mid-nineteenth century were not necessarily accountable to a rigid internal hierarchy (à la Catholicism) but did create a network of shared values that was clear enough to establish a kind of ranking, from lay people to

---

* "Go ye therefore, and teach all nations, baptizing them in the name of the Father, and of the Son, and of the Holy Ghost: Teaching them to observe all things whatsoever I have commanded you: and, lo, I am with you always, even unto the end of the world. Amen."—Matthew 28:19–20 (KJV)

pastors, that put white men at the top. What we now loosely call the evangelical church evolved across a multiplicity of Protestant denominations, from Puritanism on, in conjunction with the colonization of the west. Religion provided the moral justification for what Isabel Wilkerson calls the maintenance of the dominant caste as the country expanded in population and territory.* The morality codes and systems of behavioral monitoring these new religious movements established were essential for the development of our nation-state and modern evangelicalism.

Teaching believers how to be good citizen-subjects starts early. At Calvary, the youth were policed with just as much rigor as the adults. The modesty of my clothing and behavior, like that of so many teenage girls in evangelical churches, was continually up for discussion among my youth leaders; I was routinely taken aside by older women both privately and publicly for admonishment. On the heels of a particularly painful discussion about my body, the senior youth leader's wife cornered me in front of other people, in a church hallway, Bible in hand, to loudly discuss my dating a guy who went to one of the many Lutheran churches in town. She informed me that since he did not attend our specific church, he was not a Christian, and would I like to bring him in so that she and her husband could talk with him to see if he was a good fit for me? My own parents were not consulted for this conversation, and, even at seventeen, I was agog at the suggestion that anyone who did not attend *our* church in small-town Wisconsin was simply not a real Christian. I had attended enough other evangelical churches and lived in enough other places to find such an accusation ridiculous—an

---

* Isabel Wilkerson, *Caste: The Origins of Our Discontents* (New York: Random House, 2020), 17, 29.

avalanche of public criticism about my body and behavior, set against a seemingly ever-changing set of standards, and now this. So I left Calvary.

After I stopped attending, all my friends in Calvary's high school youth group were explicitly instructed to stop speaking to me. The reasoning they were given by adult youth leaders was that I—who was, again, a seventeen-year-old girl—had been "slandering the church," that I was a bad influence who was not to be trusted. Luckily, my friends and I were high school seniors, and it is difficult to tell teenagers what to do, so some friendships continued, despite the church's best efforts. But leadership's desire to control every aspect of church members' lives, behavior, and relationships—and of course this narrative of singularity and exclusive righteousness around the church itself—was seemingly infinite, and true to the rumors, cultish.

The sexism and criticism—I had experienced those in earlier churches. The consistent emphasis on human depravity and our utter inadequacy without Jesus: this, too, was a familiar teaching in my life, one that my mom had repeated at home over the years. (It is something, to be a six-, seven-, or eight-year-old child and hear your mom tell you that we are nothing without God, that any goodness is found only in him.) But the *intensity* at this church, coupled with the active practice of collective, communal control and shunning (including the pastor actively excommunicating church members directly from the pulpit during Sunday service), sent an earthquake rippling through me from which I never quite recovered.

At the time, I left Calvary knowing that I was angry, that I thought I was right, and not entirely understanding how to articulate either my shifting values or the slights to my admittedly fragile teenage ego. But in hindsight, I also left because the cognitive dissonance was too painful. My faith, which even having been formed by my upbringing in conservative churches had previously felt expansive—like my one most consistent, abundant safety net—had shriveled to a brittle, frayed thing under the care and keeping of this church, steeped in consistent shame. I had sat in one of the front rows every Sunday and Wednesday, devout as ever, but had so absorbed the messages of my worthlessness as a sinner that, even left to my own personal prayer and Bible study, I felt a loss of the grace and love I had thought were inherent in my faith.

The severity of my experience made me realize that this relationship with faith wasn't working for me anymore, but to question how worthlessness, shame, and control were supposed to sit side by side with a belief in unconditional love would have been to question the foundation on which I had built my entire life. Easier to stay in the cognitive dissonance but to seek a space with fewer extremes; easier to try to find ways to justify the dysfunction than to question the rickety bridge I was standing on, lest it collapse beneath me and plunge me into an abyss.

So I ended up back in church (at the church plant) within six months of leaving Calvary—I wasn't yet consciously ready to ask these questions directly, questions that didn't seem to have answers within the Bible. I didn't miss the sermons, but I had actively missed being with other believers. I missed singing collectively in worship. I missed praying with other people. For the remaining duration of my senior year of high school, I attended church alone, the rest of my family unquestioningly still involved in Calvary, my parents too distracted by their own failing marriage to really reckon with why I had left. When I ask them now about that period, neither of them has any recollection of my having left Calvary.

Those last few months of my senior year, I sat in the church plant by myself, and cried Sunday mornings during worship. My faith in

Jesus persisted, but my trust in institutional church leadership had been irreparably damaged, something that would take years, and marrying a pastor's son, for me to fully understand. I'd both witnessed and been on the receiving end of explicit abuses of power by the kinds of authorities who we'd been told were supposed to protect and encourage us, not demean and control us, in Jesus' name.

I did not know that spiritual abuse existed, let alone that I had experienced it. I had no idea how to separate what worked for me from what caused me pain, how to separate God from the church, how to think about what my faith had been and the person I was growing into.

Boston was the birthplace of American democracy, all the Freedom Trail tour guides said—ignoring Philadelphia, I suppose. But they would have been more correct to call it the birthplace of this country's religious fundamentalism.

Though my husband and I did not technically live in Boston proper, but across the Charles River in Somerville, I was in the city at least once a week. Walking up the Park Street subway stop landed you squarely on the Boston Common, that same patch of land where farmers used to herd their animals and where the Puritans executed anyone they deemed a heretic.

By the time we moved to Boston, that kind of fundamentalism within the community and government was long gone, transmuted into a more insidious sort of evangelical control folks in my graduate program denied was present. But didn't they have the same dollar bills in their wallets that I did, the ones printed with "In God We Trust"? That phrase didn't appear on American currency until the religiously zealous President Eisenhower, advised by the evangelical Reverend Billy Graham, signed it into law as our nation's official motto in 1956,[*] two years after Congress officially recognized a fresh addition to the initially secular Pledge of Allegiance: "under God." In elementary school, I dutifully repeated the Pledge of Allegiance every morning; I can still recall each word by heart: "I pledge allegiance to the flag of the United States of America, and to the republic for which it stands, one nation under God, indivisible, with liberty and justice for all." Schoolchildren recite a commitment to a Christian nation, one that was made law by an evangelical Presbyterian president,[†] encouraged by his evangelical adviser. "Out of faith in God, and through faith in themselves as His children, our forefathers designed and built the Republic," Eisenhower said in a 1953 radio address, keen to encourage faith as an antidote to the perceived threat of communism.[‡]

One of the virtues twentieth- and twenty-first-century evangelical Christianity shares with its mother country is its adaptability. For a faith so famous for its stalwartness, it's important to remember that it was born on the frontier, a movement that relies on moving its goalposts, on motivating its base believers toward retaining supremacy by constantly identifying new threats to its survival. First Indigenous peoples. Civil rights. The women's movement. LGBTQ+

---

[*] The law mandated that the "In God We Trust" motto be printed on all paper US currency. In 2011, the US House of Representatives passed a widely bipartisan resolution affirming the national motto. See Jennifer Steinhauer, "In God We Trust, With the House's Help," *New York Times*, November 1, 2011, https://www.nytimes.com/2011/11/02/us/house-of-representatives-affirms-in-god-we-trust-motto.html.

[†] Eisenhower was raised Mennonite. Later in life, his parents became Jehovah's Witnesses.

[‡] William I. Hitchcock, "How Dwight Eisenhower Found God in the White House," *History Stories* (blog), History.com, August 22, 2018, https://www.history.com/news/eisenhower-billy-graham-religion-in-god-we-trust.

equality. Universal health care. Abortion. Evangelicalism perceives the most basic assertions of human dignity as threats to its power, and it uses the language of history and nostalgia to conflate and communicate these fears.

White evangelicals weren't always so blatantly in bed with specific political parties, let alone the Far Right. But it's challenging to pinpoint the precise beginning of the relationship between evangelicals and organized political movements, when the anxiety over the tacit loss of white power first started to materialize. Do you start with the Scopes Monkey Trial—the fight over evolution in schools in the 1920s, in which evangelicals were first satirized and humiliated on a national scale, the trial that saw the subsequent, quiet birth of the Christian private school machine? Do you start with the power couple that is Graham and Eisenhower and their institution of the National Prayer Breakfast in 1953—which is now a Far Right power-broker event that LGBTQ+ people of faith are excluded from? Do you go earlier, to the schisms in Protestant denominations over slavery or even before, into the antislavery Protestant churches that themselves *still* refused to desegregate their sanctuaries, which led to the creation of some of the Black Protestant denominations we know today?

The results of this close relationship between organized evangelicalism and organized politics are dotted throughout American history: the civil rights movement setting off the founding of a wave of new private, all-white Christian schools in the South in response to desegregation, for instance. The legal fights over the right to establish these Christian private schools, *not* abortion (historically a Catholic issue), were what initially galvanized evangelicals en masse toward the Republican Party. To wit: in 1970, three years before *Roe v. Wade*, a staggering 70 percent of Southern Baptist pastors supported abortion to protect the physical *or* mental health of the mother,[*] and in 1971 the Southern Baptist Convention (SBC) came to a denomination-wide resolution supporting legislation that would "allow the possibility of abortion" under a wide number of conditions.[†] They didn't flip sides until well after *Roe* was decided—it was the increasingly unpopular and, of course, illegal practice of segregation that caused white evangelicals to seek out new issues to coalesce under.

During the 1970s, Nixon's "Southern Strategy" was designed to appeal to white voters' racism and capitalize on existing tensions in the South, such as the desegregation of schools and the legal battles over private Christian academies—a fight that white evangelicals were already at the front lines of. The conditions were ideal for Republicans to swoop in and mobilize a deeply angry, insular, *and* highly organized demographic; it wasn't long before white evangelicals became the reliable, religiously motivated base of the Republican Party. It was the anti-Black Southern Strategy that would ultimately make the word "evangelical" indistinguishable from "Republican" while obscuring the explicitly racist goals of its economic policy with talk of "states' rights" and "family values." Republican consultant Lee Atwater later discussed plainly in an interview the goals of the Southern Strategy and what would come to be key conservative and evangelical talking points:

---

* David Roach, "How Southern Baptists Became Pro-Life," Baptist Press, January 16, 2015, https://www.baptistpress.com/resource-library/news/how-southern-baptists -became-pro-life/.

† "Southern Baptist Convention Resolutions on Abortion," Johnston's Archive Baptist Resources, November 7, 2010, https://www.johnstonsarchive.net/baptist/sbcabres .html.

By 1968 you can't say [racial expletive]—that hurts you, backfires. So you say stuff like, uh, forced busing, states' rights, and all that stuff, and you're getting so abstract. Now, you're talking about cutting taxes, and all these things you're talking about are totally economic things and a byproduct of them is, blacks get hurt worse than whites. . . . "We want to cut this," is much more abstract than even the busing thing, uh, and a hell of a lot more abstract than [racial expletive].*

One of the greatest misunderstandings of power is that you can always see it. Certainly, you sometimes can; in particular, on individual levels: a pastor explicitly instructing his flock to shun a person who has left the church is a clear use, or abuse, of power. But power is also often invisible, something that can escape conscious recognition. Power exists in the language we start absorbing from the time we are in our parents' wombs, in the experiences for which there are no words; in who can say what to whom without repercussion. Power is not always solely possessed by certain individuals; it is also the unseen mechanism that informs how we position ourselves every day, how we make decisions in deference to whom—to God, to authority, or even to ourselves.

✢

It would be a grave mistake to believe that the church and state are, or have ever been, truly separate in the United States. "The idea of 'religion and politics don't mix' was invented by the devil to keep

---

* Rick Perlstein, "Exclusive: Lee Atwater's Infamous 1981 Interview on the Southern Strategy," *The Nation*, November 13, 2012, https://www.thenation.com/article/archive/exclusive-lee-atwaters-infamous-1981-interview-southern-strategy/.

Christians from running their own country," Jerry Falwell Sr., the founder of Liberty University, a prominent developer of Nixon's Southern Strategy, and one of the most influential leaders of the early Religious Right, said. These last four centuries have been defined by consistent affirmations of Christian dominance at all costs, now fully championed by the modern-day American evangelical church.

Today, heretics are symbolically executed. Non-evangelicals are punished on a social and civic level: you don't ever have to have stepped foot in a church, let alone left one, to feel the efforts of American evangelicals pressing on your life. There are the obvious newsworthy incidents like Muslim bans and racial profiling at the airport, court cases about bakeries that don't want to do a wedding cake for a gay couple, and government workers who refuse to issue a marriage license for lesbians. There was the early gutting of the Voting Rights Act. But the everyday way the evangelical faith functions to govern and guide communities across the United States is a lot more in keeping with what philosopher Louis Althusser called ideological state apparatuses: via the ostensibly apolitical social institutions (churches, schools) that ultimately function to serve the state in training citizens to be good, obedient subjects.

After I stopped attending church with my husband, filed for divorce, and slowly came out, my Christian community stopped reaching out to me. My college friends, who were my closest friends, and also my most religious friends, wouldn't respond to my emails or texts. One by one, folks dropped off as I reached out, as I said, *Hey, I'm struggling.*

But unlike my leaving Calvary, this was not a coordinated effort. There was no pastor telling my friends, scattered across the country and themselves the products of different churches and denominations, not to respond to me. This was simply their years of evangelical training in action: the accepted practices that, when a fellow believer "falls" into "temptation," you can try to have a corrective conversation, or you can use the power of silence, of shunning. Nonbelievers cannot yet be held to evangelical standards of behavior, but fellow evangelicals must be held to exacting standards, and fellow evangelicals who have known Jesus, heard the Good News, and rejected it? Well, they must be punished.

Because we ex-evangelicals were once insiders, because we speak the language (especially those of us raised in the church from infancy), because we have seen excision and exile enacted on others and have quite possibly helped enforce it, we are immediately aware of when we ourselves are cut off from the Body of Christ. We become witnesses to our own expulsion. Catholics have a more official process and name for this: excommunication. Protestants, and especially evangelicals, like to judge Catholics for a great many things, but you have to give them this: when it comes to leaving the church, at least Catholics will stab you in the front.

*Beware ye who walk in the way of sinners,* my ex-husband had said. He, his family, and my former friends would cast me as the enemy during the final days of our marriage—ceasing all communication, blocking me on social media before I had filed for divorce.

Evangelicalism is defined by fear, any singular threat automatically interpreted as a threat to the whole: fallen Christians, like apples gone bad, pose a risk to the entire batch.

✝

I had moved to Boston from the Midwest with my husband for graduate school, which was supposed to be our joint life ministry: what we were put on earth by God to do in order to help spread the Gospel. The plan had been for me to become an English lit professor; him, chemistry. We were strange outliers in our undergraduate social circle, two Christians interested in the life of the mind who, like Dan Brown's CERN physicist–priest in *Angels & Demons*, believed that faith and science, belief and logic, were not mutually exclusive. We had only to read the history of the church to know that we weren't alone in this calling; Martin Luther himself had been a professor at the University of Wittenberg. However, we faced questions from both sides. Our secular counterparts in academia looked at our faith with skepticism, and our fellow evangelicals tended to look at our intellectual pursuits—particularly mine, a woman's, a wife's—with just as much criticism.

There was one snag in this grand plan: I had gotten into a PhD program, and my husband hadn't. To our evangelical friends who interpreted male headship in marriage and family as the right, God-honoring way to live, the fact that I had been the one to be admitted was an early cause for suspicion. But conveniently, several of the programs that accepted me were in Boston, the land of milk and honey when it came to grad school pickings, with more than one hundred colleges and universities in the region, so that was where we landed. I would start at my program, luckily also my first choice; he would apply again; and eventually, we would be professors together and serve God in academia, setting an example of how to live a life dedicated to the intellect as well as to our faith. We thought we had it all figured out.

However settled my life felt to me, my choices confused my peers. *But . . . why?* one of my earliest friends in my PhD program asked when she first found out I was married. The ice in our coffees was melting in the noonday sun of our window seats at Bloc11, a queer-owned coffee shop in Union Square, and I must have shrank at least an inch in my seat, taken aback by her question and the confidence she felt in asking it. She made unflinching eye contact through the wide tortoiseshell frames, the kind worn by many femme graduate students of a certain age in Cambridge and Somerville in the 2010s.

*You're both so young,* she continued. *Why not move in together?*

*Because it's what we wanted,* was my stumbling answer. I might have said, *Because it was the right thing for us to do,* although I generally tried to avoid explicit God-speak when with grad student friends who I was pretty sure would take it the wrong way. She didn't know what to make of my life choices, but she dropped the subject. Honestly, saying, *We had to get married so we could have sex,* seemed like too much to explain.

By the time I got to grad school, I had plenty of experience with making non-evangelical friends, and I didn't want them to think I was judging them. We just lived by different codes, different moralities, and it would be unfair to ascribe my set of standards to them, since they didn't believe in the same God I did. In this, I differed from my husband and other evangelicals I knew who were comfortable with making others feel judged—and who, consequently, voted accordingly. The way is narrow; few shall find it.

✛

For all the talk of Christ's love, there isn't a lot of compassion or empathy within white American evangelicalism. It's a conditional kind of John Wayne–macho tough love, hewn on nativist individualism, with the belief that the only neighbors worth dealing with are those who can pull themselves up by their bootstraps—and who share your exact values and preferable ethnic background, of course. The same folks who quote 1 Corinthians 13 on Sunday mornings— "Love is patient, love is kind. It does not envy, it does not boast, it is not proud"—consider Black Lives Matter activists to be terrorists, see the election of Midwestern Muslim congresswomen Ilhan Omar and Rashida Tlaib to be a grave threat to national security, and have the audacity to call Jews who oppose Zionist policy anti-Semitic.

In spite of the fact that Jesus said that the second-greatest commandment was to love your neighbor as yourself, "love" has a specific meaning in evangelical Christianity. Believers must demonstrate the purity and truth of one's faith through the abasement of oneself and through one's conformity to "what God wants"—which is to say, one's pastor's interpretation of what the scripture asks one to do. There is little love, compassion, and empathy for individuals within the community, and even less for nonbelievers. In this framework, the only way you can possibly extend compassion to others is to try to introduce someone to the only way you can access compassion, which is through a personal relationship with Jesus, perhaps mediated through church leadership. The result is unyielding chains of judgment and criticism in an effort to fall in line and compel others to fall in line, a knowledge that obedience—not love—is the primary mechanism through which one demonstrates that one has received Christ's love—which is, the gift of salvation from eternal damnation ("the tyranny of heaven,"* Milton's Satan calls it).

This gap between obedience and empathy has had devastating consequences, centuries in the making, for our country. On January 6, 2021, the day of the Capitol insurrection, much was made

---

* John Milton, *Paradise Lost*, 1.124.

of the Christian imagery that accompanied the anti-Semitic Nazi swastikas, the nationalist Trump flags, and the Daniel Boone frontiersman cosplay. The fascist insurrectionists brought an enormous cross as well as a gallows in their attempt to overthrow American democracy and kidnap and execute members of Congress like Congresswomen Omar, Tlaib, and the outspoken, beloved Latina socialist Alexandria Ocasio-Cortez.

Questions like *How is this their God? Do they not know that this is not Christianity?* were everywhere on social media. Meanwhile, I was watching in simultaneous horror and recognition, knowing that this was *exactly* the God of evangelical Christianity.

This was the God I had left, and as that day wore on, I found myself trying to explain him—and his followers' dog whistles—to people who did not speak this language, who do not know the history of the enmeshment of white supremacy and the American church and state, who do not understand how contemporary evangelicals have so profoundly missed the mark on the commandment to love their neighbor.

☩

I'm not the only one who watched the insurrection and wished I didn't understand exactly why and how it was happening. Millions of millennials who grew up in the evangelical church have left it, as the extraordinary levels of cognitive dissonance demanded by American evangelicalism have proved too great for many of us to maintain. Many of us left because we were queer, because we came out and found the truth of ourselves to be absolutely irreconcilable with a religion that teaches that *God doesn't make mistakes.*

Religious trauma is something that many people in this country are walking around with, without having a label for it. Compounded by the fact that religion is often dismissed in liberal, academic, queer, secular, and, depending on the geography, urban communities as foolish, as something only *Hillbilly Elegy*-type uneducated rural poor people would be ignorant enough to believe in, there is a silencing of the grief before it can be addressed. In my experience, what drives belief is often not ignorance, but hope.

Religious trauma studies is a relatively new field that has sprung up around the generational exodus from evangelical Christianity here in the United States. Religious trauma syndrome, first proposed by psychologist Marlene Winell in 2011, is not in psychology's treasured *DSM*; it's new and, depending on who you talk to, controversial. People who fit the bill can experience a wide-ranging assortment of symptoms that look remarkably like those of folks who experience PTSD.

I would say I have religious trauma. I wouldn't go so far as to call it a syndrome, but as someone who has had to explain to more than one previous therapist what the Gospels are and how purity culture affected my repression of my sexuality, I'm all for academic interventions that introduce more religious literacy into the mainstream and normalize an understanding of organized religion's potential for institutional harm. I am interested in treating the experience of those who have been hurt by everyday religious extremism with more nuance, in ways that move beyond the sensationalist and voyeuristic on the one hand, and the dismissive, neoliberal idea that anyone who has ever remotely been involved in religion is somehow less intelligent or is deserving of what they got, on the other.

My girlfriend is also ex-evangelical, the daughter of church planters and granddaughter of ministers. It's one of the things we first bonded over when we met years ago. We were fast friends, in part because we shared a language: we understood each other's obscure biblical references and humor, a rarity among a certain breed of queers in New York.

*Do you miss it?* she sometimes asks.

I tell her what I always tell her while she cooks me dinner in my Brooklyn apartment. That I miss having people who come together for a common belief. That the multiple experiences of shunning still sting, years later. That, as grateful as I am for disparate individual connections with highly spiritual, even witch-identified, individuals, I miss the collective experience of calling in the divine. That I miss—that I *crave*—worship.

Religion is meaning-making: something that offers a world-view, a culture, a community. Religion has withstood, adapted, and grown alongside the development and spread of philosophy and reason, of scientific advancement. For many Christians, and especially conservative, "Bible-believing" *evangelical* Christians, to walk away from the faith is to lose, or risk losing, just about everything and everyone they have ever known. The loss of community and identity can be totalizing, and we are only beginning to create the language and space for it in contemporary society.

But I do not miss the authoritarian, rigidly patriarchal spaces where only men are onstage and in charge, where whiteness is the default. I do not miss preachers who wield scripture against me, who tell me that my obedience is the only valid expression of my spirituality. I do not miss the scriptural and hymnal insistence on humanity's depravity and worthlessness. I do not miss being in spaces that diminish and demean women, that outright deny the validity and existence of queer and trans people, that would insist on established torture practices like conversion therapy to suppress us. I do not miss the people who tell me that they love me but hate my sin, and I do not miss—and still struggle with shame for—the version of myself who used to say that.

"There are recovery programs for people grieving the loss of a parent, sibling, or spouse," the late Rachel Held Evans wrote in *Searching for Sunday*. "You can buy books on how to cope with the death of a beloved pet or work through the anguish of a miscarriage. We speak openly with one another about the bereavement that can accompany a layoff, a move, a diagnosis, or a dream deferred. But no one really teaches you how to grieve the loss of your faith. You're on your own for that."*

✜

It's been almost a decade since I walked into that courthouse—since I left my husband, came out, and left the church. I've lived what's felt like several lives since then.

I know this for sure: that I do not want to return to that faith, to a rigid way of organizing life and the people in it, to a way of believing and being in the world that is predicated on my own sin and worthlessness and that of everyone I loved. "Better to reign in hell, than serve in heaven."†

But I also know this: that there is something to the sacred, something special that happens when people gather communally, intentionally, and call on something greater than themselves. That community matters, that ritual matters, and that religion is one of the few bastions in an increasingly digital, disconnected world where we unlock the power of those things. But when we walk away from the harm of some organized religions, how do we recover the communal sacred for ourselves?

---

* Rachel Held Evans, *Searching for Sunday: Loving, Leaving, and Finding the Church* (Nashville, TN: Thomas Nelson, 2015), 48–49.

† Milton, *Paradise Lost*, 1.263.

"I think it is healing behavior, to look at something so broken and see the possibility and wholeness in it," adrienne maree brown writes in *Emergent Strategy*.* I have never been able to ignore the possibility of the spiritual altogether; my brushes with synchronicities, with the divine, with the unnamable, have been too numerous and too real for me to dismiss whatever else is out there.

So here I am, in a liminal space. Not a Christian anymore, let alone an evangelical, but also too invested in nourishing my soul to be truly agnostic. Someone who listens to hymns, whose language is peppered with references to Bible stories, but who celebrates Yule, not Christmas, and certainly not Easter. Someone who is attuned to every dog whistle of evangelical politics that many of my peers in academic, literary, and media circles simply do not have the background to hear, let alone acknowledge or take seriously; someone who was not surprised by Trump's election or the Capital insurrection, but who feels appalled at the number of my peers who hate Republican politicians but love cultural evangelical celebrities like Chip and Joanna Gaines or Justin and Hailey Bieber. Someone who has relinquished, and is working on coming to terms with, the beauty of not knowing, of not having the kinds of answers that Christianity so readily provides.

This book is about the loss of faith, about the profound grief that our society is still working out language and narrative for. But it's also about the journey to the other side: the work it takes to get there, and the healing that is possible. I once was blind, but now I see.

---

* adrienne maree brown, *Emergent Strategy: Shaping Change, Changing Worlds* (Chico, CA: AK Press, 2017), 19.

# 2. A WALL TO WORK UPON

**A**RE *WE READY, GIRLS?* MOM ASKS.

There is a routine to the church parking lot on Sunday mornings, especially on mornings like this, when we've all had a hard night. Not that we're going to talk about it right now, when a Point of Grace cassette was just blaring in the car. After a five-minute drive—the main attractions of which are cornfields and pastures of grazing cows and one llama farm—Mom pulls our red station wagon into her usual spot in the back of the lot. Who voluntarily parks at the back of a nearly empty lot? We have a ways to walk toward the old brick church, so we aren't immediately accosted by folks hugging and saying hello, because it's a small town and a small church and we all know each other here. I am annoyed at having to walk so far, but I know Mom prefers having the extra time to get her bearings.

*Jeanna, you are a reflection on the family. Best behavior in there,* Mom tells me as we get out of the car. Every week, the same admonishment. As if I'm ever anything less. I have all my Bible verses memorized for Sunday school.

I smooth the front of my clean, just-ironed hand-me-down dress. Mom unbuckles Jo from her car seat in the back. Jo takes off running ahead of us the minute her feet hit the pavement.

*Johanna Kadlec, slow down! There are cars!* To no avail, my sister is already on the church lawn with the other kids. Trying to contain my sister is as pointless as trying to domesticate the stray cats in our yard. I dutifully slip my hand into my mother's, and we walk together toward the church.

Mom has already refreshed her makeup from any residual tears after we parked. Her long sleeves are prim and tucked and don't reveal anything that might raise questions. Iowa summers are awfully humid; she must have been so hot.

*You look so pretty, Mommy,* I say. She smiles. I watch her say *Thank you,* but her eyes don't believe me.

✣

Having grown up in the rural Midwest, and even after living in Minneapolis for a year, moving to Boston for graduate school was culture shock. The Midwest is a vast, sprawling landscape built on colonial conquest, on American individualism and Christianity, littered with now-dilapidated one-room prairie churches. So many towns are named after Indigenous peoples who have long since been forced off their lands. The region is now inhabited by the descendants of white folks too poor or otherwise stuck to "make it" out east, who headed out to colonize the West, believing themselves blessed with manifest destiny by God himself; by Black folks who were refugees from their own homes in the oppressive Jim Crow

South; by immigrants from all over the world who came through Ellis Island, San Francisco, and the Southwest and just kept going. The Rust Belt, Great Lakes states, and Prairie states have distinct cultures, but they're loosely held together by an undercurrent of libertarian self-reliance and an ironic mistrust in outsiders' authority, blended with an awestruck, sometimes awful reverence for the divine that can level an entire city with an F5 tornado with no warning at any time.

New England, on the other hand, is marked by physical monuments to the kind of mythological American history that the Midwest doesn't have—in Boston, you could turn your head on the sidewalk and be eye to eye with Samuel Adams's grave, take a few more steps and see the steeple of the Old North Church off in the distance, reaching toward the sky. All that history just *standing there* on Tremont Street, mixed in with modern architecture and chain stores as you walk by on your errands—you can leave a penny at Paul Revere's grave and then go pick up lunch at McDonald's across the way. My twenty-three-year-old self, who had uncritically gobbled up so much of the propaganda from my US history class, couldn't get enough of the centuries that confronted me on every corner.

The push into what was once called the "Old Northwest," now known as the Midwest, was a violent extension of empire that was predicated on genocide and the idea that religion could "civilize" what was seen as a wilderness.* The region was initially settled by white men who became the target audience of early Methodist and Baptist traveling preachers, or circuit riders, who were essentially in

---

* It's been noted that the colonization of the Midwest resembles that of Australia.

a "land grab" for souls.* In *An American Colony: Regionalism and Roots of Midwestern Culture*, Edward Watts calls the Midwest the first "colony" of the United States itself, pointing out that the resentful relationship between the Midwest and the East Coast is one that can be compared to how the East Coast views Europe, "its own erstwhile colonial parent."† Watts, a born-and-bred Midwesterner, writes that his "ignorance of the East was a source of ridicule" while his "eastern friends' provincial ignorance of the Midwest was, if anything, a badge of sophistication."

I could relate.

In my doctoral program, my peers weren't just surprised that I was married. They were surprised that I was a Christian. To them, religion and intelligence simply did not go together. Some of them had spent their entire lives assuming that people who earnestly believe in Jesus are brainwashed and entirely without critical thinking skills, uninterested in higher education. And yet, there I was, sharing space in the same humanities doctoral program.

*Do you believe in science?* someone asked me while we were sitting in the graduate student lounge on cheap thrifted couches with our packed lunches and vending machine seltzers. *Of course,* I said, *although I'm not sure that scientific reality is something you get to "believe" in. Things like gravity and rising ocean temperatures aren't exactly up for debate.* My coastal peer seemed shocked by this answer from a religious Midwestern person who wasn't, as the media had led them to believe, a climate change denier.

---

* As were Catholic priests determined to make headway in a distinctly Protestant nation.

† Edward Watts, *An American Colony: Regionalism and Roots of Midwestern Culture* (Ohio University Press, 2002), xvii.

The plan had always been simple: get an education and use it to get the *hell* out of the small, nowhere Midwestern towns I had grown up in.

My fanatical focus on college began in elementary school. *Out out out* was all I could think. Away from my parents, away from our terrible house, but also away from structures I had yet to identify— away from the observational specter of rural life, away from the expectations of marriage and children. I wanted to write books. I wanted to live in a city. But when I would say these things early in elementary school, my parents would laugh, amused, and ask, *And what's your* real *job gonna be?* I knew no one who was a creative professional, and neither did my parents or anyone in my extended family. Novelists existed only in movies like *Little Women* and *Finding Forrester*. The possibility of making a living doing anything but working for other people was not something any adults around me knew how to conceptualize.

Like so many of us who ended up in an English PhD program, I was obsessed with language and books from an early age. My mother encouraged me by reading to me, and I mimicked her habit of keeping a journal. She fostered my eagerness to learn as well as my faith. My dad was also delighted by this; I wasn't the left-handed pitcher he so often said he'd wanted, but I was a good student, and that counted for something. Also helpful was that my dad's conservative understanding of gender roles was more casually traditional than the assertive suppression in the name of "God's will" I often saw enacted by my friends' parents at church. He was far too great a fan of Rush Limbaugh even then for my mother's liking, but when it came to his *own* daughters, he wanted us to succeed. The not uncommon double standard of Republican men.

"God gave me this big mouth, so I think it can be no sin to use it," says the titular character in Karen Cushman's 1994 middle-grade classic *Catherine, Called Birdy*, something I, as a seven-year-old, desperately needed to read and promptly internalized.* From an early age, I had been, problematically, the only girl placed in our rural elementary school's fledgling "Talented and Gifted" program, won poetry competitions at the public library with my simple A-B-A-B rhyme schemes, and was perpetually a teacher's pet. Like Birdy, I felt that my smarts and big mouth were God-given talent. My teachers and the media reflected back to me that if you put in the effort, people with few resources could compete with people who had everything and still come out on top. In such a worldview, God-given talent was, theoretically, enough.

My parents were pleased with my academic achievement and goal of making it to college because, when I was growing up, neither of them had a college degree. The first time I published an essay stating this, and calling our family working class, I got an email from my mom, who was hurt and wanted to correct the narrative. She had gone back to college to finish her degree when I was in high school, she reminded me. She and I had graduated together in the same year: me from high school, she with her bachelor's. Didn't I remember?

Of course I did. I was, and am, so proud of her for doing something so difficult, particularly given that she had two daughters still in school and a demanding job. But my mom finishing her degree when I was eighteen years old did not change the fact that her earning potential—and my dad's, who had signed up for four years in the navy upon graduating from high school—was deeply influenced by the fact that there was no degree on her résumé for the entirety

---

* Karen Cushman, *Catherine, Called Birdy* (New York: Houghton Mifflin Harcourt, 1994), 173.

of my years under her roof. The fact that neither of my parents had a college degree before I turned eighteen significantly affected their income cap, and their ability to provide my sister and me with the tools to climb the class ladder.

✛

My dad barely graduated from high school, but he has a sharp, articulate, deceptive charisma that can—and almost always does—pull people in before he pulls the rug out from under them with the ferocity of his bullheadedness. During the 1996 presidential election, his forceful line of questioning at a precaucus event ended up putting him on a nationally televised panel of Iowa voters with Dan Rather and a CBS crew in our house, who took hours' worth of footage of our family for a five-second intro clip.

In a more everyday way, I often witnessed him make friends easily, such as with the DJs at KCRR, the classic rock radio station located on the same floor in his office building, where he landed a regular Monday-morning guest spot as "The Guy from Down the Hall" to analyze and dissect the Sunday sports events with the hosts. He'd occasionally bring Jo and me into his office with him, in the summers or on snow days, and we'd get to visit the radio station too, promising to be very, very quiet in order to stay in the booth while he was on air, getting to scream *HI MOM!* as loudly as we could on cue, even selling Girl Scout cookies to folks who called in.

It was whiplash, to get to say a loving hello to your mom with your dad from the radio station, and then watch him scream at her once you're home for dinner.

✛

The Midwest is often called the heartland, a term associated with "mainstream" or "traditional" white values. The heartland is different from the Bible Belt, but there's some overlap. Notably, the heartland and Bible Belt are two terms used to denote unofficial regions of the country that didn't enter the American lexicon until the twentieth century, when the regional relationships with morality, religion, and political conservatism emerged in the wake of Prohibition, white women's suffrage, and the midcentury civil rights movement.* As historian Kristin L. Hoganson puts it, "National mythologies have dumped an overwhelming load of baggage on the heartland's shoulders."†

The US Census Bureau defines the Midwest as consisting of twelve states—Illinois, Indiana, Iowa, Kansas, Michigan, Minnesota, Missouri, Nebraska, North Dakota, Ohio, South Dakota, and Wisconsin. Any way you slice it, the Midwest is the center of the country—Lebanon, Kansas, is the geographic center of the lower forty-eight; Butte County, South Dakota, the center when including Hawaii and Alaska.

One of the most common assumptions about Midwest states is that they're thoroughly red, part of that mass of blood in the middle of the map that dominates screens on election night. Never mind that these twelve states are more often than not voter-suppressed states, that Iowa was the third state to legalize gay marriage, that

---

* The term "Bible Belt" was coined by H. L. Mencken in the 1920s. (See Joseph L. Locke, *Making the Bible Belt: Texas Prohibitionists and the Politicization of Southern Religion* [New York: Oxford University Press, 2017].) "Heartland" was coined by a British geographer, Halford Mackinder, in 1904, to refer to the geographical center of Eurasia; the word wasn't applied to the American Midwest until later in the twentieth century.

† Kristin L. Hoganson, *The Heartland: An American History* (New York: Penguin Random House, 2020), xxii.

Michigan and Minnesota elected Rashida Tlaib and Ilhan Omar, and that activists in Kansas have been slowly turning the tide in the state legislature there for years. But the media's "red state" shorthand makes easy assumptions that equate rural with uneducated, religious with uneducated, "family values" with rural with uneducated with Republican. If you know better, it's implied, you're supposed to want to move to a city. To a coast. Away from all that empty space in the middle that the smart people fly over.

I grew up wanting to move away, of course. And I did. But it wasn't because I thought that a city, or a coast, was the only place I could write, or be successful. I just wanted to get away from my family, from everyone I knew, from everything I grew up with. As soon as it was financially viable for me to do so, I ran a thousand miles away, stopped only by waves crashing against a rocky Massachusetts coast.

Thing is, I moved away only to find that there is a kind of condescending idealization of the pastoral by coastal and metropolitan city folk, the assumption that there is a simplicity to a life that revolves around faith and family. That a place not known for its movie studios or financial centers must, then, inevitably collect the unambitious whose capacity for production (of labor, of children) does not require skill or strategy. As Texas-born Iowa resident Lyz Lenz observes in *God Land: A Story of Faith, Loss, and Renewal in Middle America*,

Whenever people ask me if I'm going to move, and I say "no," they quickly note that the Midwest "is a great place to raise a kid." Everyone says that—liberal, conservative, Christian, or atheist. There is a consensus that whatever is here is good; whatever is here is pure, because here we raise food and children. Because here, even in cities, we are close to nature. Proximity to nature is supposed to mean some sort of purity of heart and mind.*

A great place to raise a kid. As if simply *being* in the Midwest guarantees raising children well.

✛

When it's just Daddy and me and Jo, it's like we forget all the tension in our house. We climb on Dad like he's a jungle gym. We dance around the living room, yelling and screaming to classic rock and newer stuff like "Sweet Child o' Mine" while Mom cooks dinner, and he picks me up and swings me around and invents new lyrics to his favorite Ted Nugent and Melissa Etheridge and Rolling Stones songs, and it is as if, in that moment, playtime will never end. It's as if our dad is the best dad in the world.

At six or seven, I stood barely at my dad's hip. My dad was called the runt of his brothers at six two; he was the youngest son in a big Catholic family, and, even at his height, the shortest. To me, he was the definition of big and tall—boxy and muscular from years of manual labor, with calloused hands and feet and a beer belly from his favored coping mechanism. Then there were my mom's favorite features—his black hair that started curling if he went a day too long without a cut, and the kind of piercing turquoise-blue eyes I only ever saw on movie stars, complete with the Santa-like twinkle. *When we met, your dad was the best-looking guy in all of Cedar Rapids, and he dated half of Cedar Rapids before going out with me*, my mom used to say.

---

* Lyz Lenz, *God Land: A Story of Faith, Loss, and Renewal in Middle America* (Bloomington, IN: Indiana University Press, 2019), 32.

We stop dancing and come in to sit down for dinner, still laughing. Mom asks me to pray for our meal, which is probably Hamburger Helper or a potato chip casserole. I mimic her prayer, asking God *to bless the food to nourish our bodies so that we may love and serve you better, in Jesus' name, Amen.*

Daddy pounds beer after beer. The mood at the table shifts, starting with something small, something inconsequential. Dinner is cooked wrong, or her tone of voice isn't what he wants to hear. Jo's and my room wasn't cleaned properly. Anything; nothing. Mom would try to defend herself against the inevitable, seeking to prolong a stasis that had been days or weeks or merely hours; but inevitably, an explosion. Heightened volume, the kind of internal disruption that leaves bruises on another person the next morning.

My sister and I are eating our dinner when he erupts, voice raised, fists slamming the table. He rises to stand over her, and we crouch in our seats, crying. Mom rises to meet him; she fights back, she always fights back.

I scream at my dad to stop.

*Shut up, Jeanna,* he says, *this is between your mother and I.* He never lashes out at my sister and me, but then, he doesn't seem to care that we can see him going after her, either.

*Go upstairs,* Mom says, her voice shaky, and I grab Jo's hand, reluctantly pulling her away from the table. If I am there, maybe the worst things that my mom tells me about later won't happen, but I am also afraid of my dad when he's this mad, when he's this drunk. Sometimes, Mom shoves him back, right before Jo and I are up the stairs; I always root for her, hoping that one of these days she lands a blow that makes him stagger back and crack his head open. I am that child who regularly yo-yos between dancing happily in her daddy's arms before dinner and actively wishing for his death in the hopes that it means her mom will be safe.

I take JoJo upstairs. When they're fighting too loud, too fast, too furious, when Dad is too wrathful for Mom to get a word in edgewise, Jo and I go upstairs to our shared bedroom. I put on music loudly, hoping it will drown them out (it doesn't; my dad is so loud and this boom box is so cheap). I shut the door and pull out our Barbies, or, if it's past Jo's bedtime, I turn the lights down and try to get her into bed. If she won't go to bed (which is usually the case), I try reading her a book, which turns into two books, then many books. As many books as JoJo, who is three, four, then five years old, wants. As many books until the noise dies down.

As many books until Mom comes up to tuck us in, having put herself back together, a feeling I do not then know is relief washing over my six-, seven-, eight-year-old self when she walks through our bedroom door alive.

All that space in the country and how my mama's screams could fill it, my prayers unanswered.

✛

Growing up on a whole acre of land in the country, I also knew quiet: the kind where the earth gets so still that you can practically hear every blade of grass rustle when you're lying on your back under a shady oak tree in the middle of the summer, looking up through the leaves at the clouds passing by overhead. The kind that's only accessible in deeply rural places, in the heart of the country.

There was a lot of yelling in my home, and there was a lot of yelling in church. But Mom wasn't scared at church, so I wasn't scared at church. Daddy wasn't at church, which made church special, and safe.

When we got home from church on Sunday morning, Jo and I

running into the house, we were greeted by the sound of NASCAR on the television, the commentary so evocative you could practically smell the rubbery tires getting eaten up by the racetrack; by the heady scent of fried chicken Daddy was cooking. *Careful!* he'd warn me if I tried to hug him, eye level as I was with the cheap splatter screen that was supposed to catch the sizzling grease.

Quick change out of our hand-me-down Sunday best and into garage sale playclothes that could get chicken grease on them, that could withstand the rough-and-tumble of the sandbox or the aluminum swing set, of the Grundy County dirt.

To me, as a young child, the quiet sounded like God.

✢

There was a big wicker chair on our west-facing screened-in front porch that looked out over our expansive yard, across the two-lane highway to Randy's farm and all the fields beyond. In the summer, a perfect day meant spending the whole afternoon curled up in that chair with a library book, ignoring my parents' exhortations to go outside and play, and with the occasional glance up to watch the cows across the street or various birds, squirrels, and stray cats that occupied our yard.

If I timed it right, I could be on the porch with a popsicle after dinner to watch the sunset dip below the horizon in those far-off fields. If it was a summer when the fields were planted with soybeans, I could hike up my sundress and bolt out the front door, charging across the fields through the tidy rows of short plants, chasing the seam where the sun met the earth, seeking escape.

My childhood journals are full of entries—details about playing Barbies with my sister, lists of books I was reading, complete with a five-star ranking system. My favorite things I was learning in Sunday school or at VBS about the Bible. Nowhere is there any mention of my dad's drinking, or all the times my mom took me into her confidence. About the thick swell of uncertainty—all consuming and inescapable, like a sticky summer day—that filled our home.

As it was, I would stay like a good girl on the porch steps, my ankles crossed, a napkin on my lap for the popsicle, reminding Jo to wipe her face and not throw trash on the ground, keeping any stray thoughts about leaving home and chasing bigger horizons to myself.

✢

Iowa sunsets in the summer heat look like a spilled tray of watercolors spiraling out for miles in every direction, unobstructed by any building, rippling over the sweet corn and soybean fields, sky bursting with the kinds of vibrant pinks and purples and reds and oranges New Yorkers keep bound up in nicely printed coffee table books.

I took them for granted, then.

✢

Growing up, I called my dad a "field engineer" but it would be years before I understood that my dad was not an engineer in the same way that one of my uncles, for example, was an engineer at Rockwell Collins, designing airplane parts. My dad was the kind of field engineer who had gotten his start in telecom digging ditches—a game my sister and I played while crammed into the truck seat, driving on the highway between Waterloo and our hometown growing up, was counting how many of the orange "call before you dig" signs our daddy had installed while we had daddy-daughter sing-alongs to the Counting Crows or Alanis Morissette.

My parents insisted that we were middle class because, as Sarah Smarsh writes in *Heartland*, "We were so unaware of our own station that, in the rare instance that the concept of class arose, we thought we were middle class . . . we recognized it to mean 'not poor, but not rich.' Since we had enough to eat, that's how we thought of ourselves."* Our family also consistently had a roof over our head—my dad was always gamely employed, as he put it, and paid the bills on time. We had Christmas gifts, however modest.

There's also a morality to calling yourself middle class; it's not a simple question of lifestyle. Numerous studies have been done on Americans' proclivity, in particular, for calling themselves middle class even when they are obscenely rich or obviously poor. A 2015 Pew Research survey revealed that almost 50 percent of Americans consider themselves to be middle class, with the number increasing if you take into account the qualifying descriptors of upper or lower middle class.† It goes back to the Protestant work ethic: to be middle class is to be moderate and hardworking. When presidents need to stoke morale around economic policy, they talk about having a "strong middle class." After all, to be rich is to have a difficult time getting to heaven (as Jesus said, "It is easier for a camel to go through the eye of a needle, than for a rich man to enter into the kingdom of God"‡). To be poor is to be associated with an often racialized, "un-American" lack of discipline. Middle class is the marketing slogan.

---

* Sarah Smarsh, *Heartland: A Memoir of Working Hard and Being Broke in the Richest Country on Earth* (New York: Scribner, 2019), 28.

† Danielle Kurtzleben, "Why Do So Many Rich People Consider Themselves 'Middle Class?,'" *Vox*, March 12, 2015, https://www.vox.com/2015/3/12/8193113/middle-class -rich-poor.

‡ Matthew 19:24 (NIV).

For my parents, it was aspirational to affirm that we were comfortably middle class. My sister and I certainly grew up with more stability than my poverty-raised mother, but this is where the cracks in a lack of class consciousness show: anything that is remotely better than the instability of impoverishment becomes "middle class," even when it's objectively not. Given that we had some relatives who were themselves actually middle class, and one who was full-on millionaire rich, I remain surprised that my parents maintained this belief. We were toward the bottom of the economic barrel on both sides of the family; my folks both have a *lot* of siblings, most of whom had finished college and otherwise gotten better-paying jobs than them. One example: the rest of my mom's large family—grandparents, aunts, uncles, cousins—once took a cruise vacation together, and we were the only ones who didn't go. (Our family didn't go on vacation, *period*. To this day, I've never been on a plane with my parents.) That kind of thing makes it pretty obvious who has disposable income and who doesn't. *God will provide*, the pastors and my mother said, but based on my limited sample, it sure didn't seem like he provided equally.

There's only so far up you can go when you literally start in the ditch, no matter how hard you work.

✛

The best time with my daddy would be after his return from stalking off in a nearby field to kill squirrel or some other small game for our dinner, some bleeding dead carcass in his hands.

*Downstairs!* my mom would screech. *Not in the house!*

*Jeanna, want to come with?* he'd ask, and I would scramble to put shoes on so I could run out the kitchen side door, following my dad to the back entrance to our unfinished, cement-floored basement that flooded most every spring, where he had built a raised workbench he used to clean game.

My sister was too young and chaotic to be trusted around a dead animal, and my mom found the cleaning process repulsive, but I loved watching my dad clean a fresh kill. I was so proud of him, that he could hunt and provide for us. I absorbed significant, decidedly normative ideals about masculinity while standing next to my dad at that workbench.

Dad used my fascination to make what could be an otherwise mundane task a teachable moment. He explained what he was doing, and made sure to quiz me on different parts of the animal.

*Do you want to touch the heart?* he always asked me, a mischievous grin on his face. *If you're careful, you can hold it.* The heart, which looked so small between Dad's fingers, seemed to enlarge when he placed it in my palm. I held so still, staring at that squirrel's heart as it cooled, blood dripping in my hand. It was like a magical talisman from a fairy tale, the last bit of a potion a wicked witch may need.

Long before *The Lion King* came out, Dad was giving me less eloquent versions of its "circle of life" message, speeches about survival and how you shouldn't hunt more than you can eat, how you should probably hunt only if you are going to eat what you kill. He despised rich men who shot endangered game for the trophies and ranted about the guys he knew in town who hunted for sport out of season.

He liked to go pheasant hunting with his buddies, bringing the best feathers back for my sister and me. But back then, he would regularly go out and shoot small game in the fields when our family needed meat we couldn't otherwise afford.

*We're on a tight budget* was something I heard him and Mom say constantly during those early years in Iowa, and my dad's ability to provide for dinner when food was so expensive must have made things easier. He would also barter his physical labor with a neighboring farmer in exchange for a hog here, a freezer full of cow there. Dad kept an always-thriving vegetable garden for produce that we froze or traded; Mom tended the flowers. We'd pull over on the highway to buy cheap, fresh-picked sweet corn off the back of a pickup truck. Eventually, Dad bought two rabbits, a buck and a doe, in order to breed them in our backyard shed for a steady supply of meat, the basis for much of our diet.

This was blue-collar country life, no safety net, just surviving with what God had given you and hoping it was enough.

A few years later, we moved to northern Wisconsin, where Jo and I thought we'd finally made it because we lived in a nice-enough house in town where we each had a proper bedroom with a door and could ride our bikes on paved roads to go see our friends.

Soon after we moved, *The West Wing* premiered, and it quickly became the show that Dad and I watched together in the living room on Wednesday nights—he in his comfy "big chair," me curled up under a blanket on the couch near our woodstove that heated the whole house. Politics and game cleaning: things that Mom wasn't interested in and that Jo was too young to appreciate. This was our show, our father-daughter bonding time, for me to fantasize about working in politics, for him to arbitrarily lecture me on the conservative side of the issues that the White House staffers on the show would argue about.

At the time, I was bored by Martin Sheen's professorial President Jed Bartlet, who oscillated between quoting scripture and economic theory. My eleven-year-old self was enamored instead with Allison Janney's brilliant, no-nonsense C. J. Cregg and then, in the second season, with Emily Procter's conservative Ainsley Hayes, a socially awkward but ambitious lawyer who excelled at eviscerating men on national television—characters who I personally considered to be career goals. *That's gonna be you someday*, Dad would tell me whenever Ainsley was on-screen, though what went unspoken was that neither of us had any idea as to how I could get there.

What I underestimated, at the time, was the impact of watching years' worth of network television in which the president was a readily acknowledged Nobel-winning genius who also happened to be an incredibly devout man of faith*—even one who, in moments of grief, argued with God in Latin and ground cigarettes into the floor of the basilica with his polished loafer. There was space for doubt in Bartlet's Catholicism; space for arguing over scriptural interpretation with his wife and his Jewish staffers. But the gravity and prominence of his faith were never in question, a rarity for television. His first line in the pilot as he enters the "Mural Room," in response to an evangelical blowhard preacher asking "Then what is the first commandment?" is to quote from scripture: "I am the Lord your God; thou shalt worship no other gods before me."

That you could be both faithful and smart was a lesson I absorbed watching *The West Wing* without realizing it. Dedicated to God *and* reason. I was too young to consider the privileges that, in the real world, would go into supporting both the faith and the

---

* My dad's family is Catholic, and we were very close to my grandparents, so I'd clocked more than enough hours attending mass to have been readily disabused at an early age of the popular evangelical idea that Catholics aren't Christians.

intellectual pursuits of a generationally wealthy white man like Jed Bartlet, but that didn't matter. I'd unconsciously found the template on which I'd build my future.

I didn't understand, then, that upward mobility usually has a ceiling, that the rags-to-riches exceptions who thank God in their Oscar and inaugural speeches are trotted out as examples that the American Dream works. But exceptionalism is a feature, not a bug, one designed to keep everyone else in their place. For religious Christians, the idea that what's happening to you is "God's will" is an essential part of this mythology.

*I've never worked for a poor man* is one of my dad's favorite sayings, and a common one among other conservatives invested in justifying tax breaks for the rich at the expense of policies like universal health care and other social safety nets that would benefit blue-collar workers like, say, my father. No matter that the earning cap for many of these voters is nowhere near that of the Republican representatives on the docket; "generational wealth" is an idea that I didn't learn until I was in college, it was so foreign.

Growing up, my sister and I were inculcated by my father with a profoundly naive commitment to and belief in the American Dream. There was also my mother's financial philosophy, summarized by country singer Brandy Clark as "pray to Jesus and play the lotto." But my parents didn't teach us financial literacy, how to do our taxes, how to save or invest—I'd have to figure that out on my own. *Work hard and get a job* was as far as the advice went. There were also the ever-present reminders from my mother to *trust God in all things*, that *God will take care of us*, that, as the children's song goes, "he's got the whole world in his hands." That, to paraphrase Luke 12:7, *he knows every hair on my head*, which translated to his supposedly knowing every dollar in our bank account.

The American Dream is a classic case of what the late theorist Lauren Berlant called "cruel optimism"; which is to say, optimism is cruel when it does not—and, in fact, will not—measure up to what it has promised. For Berlant, this promise of the possible is especially cruel when the attachment to the promise, or optimism, continues to sustain even when what is sought is nonexistent. "Cruel optimism is the condition of maintaining an attachment to a significantly problematic object," Berlant says, such as the attachment to upward mobility. The fear that drives the maintenance of this condition is that "the loss of the promising object/scene itself will defeat the capacity to have any hope about anything."*

This was true for us: we had to have trust in next week's paycheck and my father's continued gainful employment, even in the face of a fridge full of Budweiser, because to consider the alternative was to plunge ourselves headlong into destitution. This belligerent hope in America's provision, in the American Dream, also dovetails with faith. We had to trust God would provide, even when there was evidence around us—in a drought year, for example—that he didn't. The cruel optimism of America is supported by the mythos of God's will in evangelical Christianity.

The myth of the American Dream also performs a kind of racial isolation and siloing, a keeping of one's own. Berlant says, "The American Dream does not allow a lot of time for people it is not convenient or productive to have curiosity about."†

---

* Lauren Berlant, *Cruel Optimism* (Durham, NC: Duke University Press, 2011), 24.

† Berlant, 30.

It's true that as white folks, we were in a better position than many; a 2018 report by the Samuel DuBois Cook Center on Social Equity at Duke University notes, "A white household living near the poverty line typically has about $18,000 in wealth, while black households in similar economic straits typically have a median wealth near zero. This means that many black families have a negative net worth."* As Lauren Michelle Jackson writes in *White Negroes*, "Nothing is as predictive of success in America as being born white."† Even white people born at the bottom of the class ladder are miles ahead, socioeconomically speaking, of people of color. A 2016 study that Jackson cites in her book from the Institute for Policy Studies "found that if current trends continue, the average black family won't reach the amount of wealth white families own today for another 228 years."‡ For so many Black Americans and other people of color, hard work is simply not enough to bridge that gap in this lifetime, and to pretend (and legislate) as if the reality is otherwise is profoundly harmful.

But for my white working-class family, hard work was an easy ideal to get behind. By virtue of our racial privilege, it could reasonably provide us with what my parents deemed a good-enough life. My parents' confident assertions that my sister and I would be fine, that we'd be able to find decent jobs here in the Midwest if we put in some effort, applied ourselves, and avoided getting into too much trouble, were founded.

---

* William Darity Jr. et al., *What We Get Wrong About Closing the Racial Wealth Gap* (Durham, NC: Samuel DuBois Cook Center on Social Equity/Insight Center for Community Economic Development, 2018).

† Lauren Michelle Jackson, *White Negroes: When Cornrows Were in Vogue... and Other Thoughts on Cultural Appropriation* (Boston: Beacon Press, 2019), 5.

‡ Chuck Collins et al., *The Ever-Growing Gap: Without Change, African-American and Latino Families Won't Match White Wealth for Centuries* (Washington, DC: Institute for Policy Studies, 2016).

There was a lot of talk at the dinner table about how America was the greatest country in the world, but my parents' idea of "good enough" was only ever at a baseline of not having to worry about losing their jobs and health care. We still lived paycheck to paycheck. "Good enough" was precarious, subject to the whims of capitalist policy interpreted as God's will. The Protestant work ethic, indeed.

The Protestant work ethic has helped shape and create the ideal American citizen, which is to say, American whiteness, and the justification of white supremacy. Even more insidious is its encoding of "hard work" and "discipline" as the fruits of a godly life. American evangelicalism can reasonably be called a civil folk religion because of rhetoric like this: these religious ideas that have so smoothly transposed Puritanical theology into the mainstream and shifted it into a kind of xenophobic patriotism, transforming instructions on "how to be a good Christian" into an instruction manual for how to be an "America first" citizen. This is how it became possible for anyone to vote in line with evangelicals—or to consider themself an evangelical—without ever stepping foot in a church in the first place.

This conflation of faith and politics has led to a collective forgetting of the foundational role of religion in white supremacy. This purposefully cultivated amnesia has occurred to the collective detriment of the United States, directly contributing to the rise of fascism.

✛

In the current media climate, even preceding the election of the forty-fifth president, being religious was associated with being uneducated. And when the media says "uneducated," what they actually mean is "bigoted." There is a linguistic gymnastics happening here, coded for liberal white people's comfort: if *we* are educated, if *we* are smart, therefore we cannot possibly be in that same group as those *other* white people, those *bad* white people who have those traditional and racist and sexist views, who save themselves for marriage and who value obedience to an invisible God and fall for Republicans like Trump.

I can't pinpoint precisely where or when I came to understand that this is how "liberals" and "coastal elites" thought of people like my family—God-fearing people who went to church and lived in rural places. I don't know whether it was through the debates about teaching evolution versus creationism in schools, which seemed to be everywhere; through listening to adults talk in coded language about the right to life at church; through all the Fox News my dad watched every night; through the conservative talk radio that was on every morning. It was in the air, a part of the "culture wars" I absorbed as a child.

By the time I went to graduate school, I was long since disillusioned with conservative politics and their media outlets. Yet I was to discover that Fox News' articulation of this one aspect of the beliefs of "coastal elites" was right. I was now surrounded by people who thought anyone who hadn't grown up in Boston or New York or California was inevitably, hopelessly "behind."

The idea often associated with leftist thinking that religion is for people who are weak, stupid, or otherwise incapable of fending or thinking for themselves is deeply harmful. It's colonialist, itself an idea embedded in white supremacist enlightenment, dismissive of animist traditions the world over and other Indigenous traditions. The same progressive thinking that wants to halt climate change in its tracks and favors turning over land management to Indigenous populations for their generational wisdom often fails to understand the ways in which that wisdom is itself grounded in animist traditions that treat the land with respect precisely because it is itself possessed of spirit.

The idea that education serves an inherently moralizing purpose is itself part of Americans' ideological inheritance from the Puritans (and Kant, but that's a different essay). Education, conceptually, is neutral, but institutions are not. Institutions have a goal. Schools were cited by theorist Louis Althusser as having replaced the church in America as the primary ideological state apparatus of the twentieth century; ideological in opposition to more visible repressive state apparatuses like the military. School is where we learn to relate to the world around us, where we are taught how to produce and then—if the state has its way—to reproduce our existing conditions. For most of us, school is where we learn to maintain the status quo.

News articles and social media outrage cycles are continually surprised by public school teachers who were Trump voters, who have "secret" white supremacist podcasts. But the enforced whiteness, and in many cases, the enforced evangelical religious values of sexual repression, are ingrained into public school spaces. Public school teachers are private citizens, and schools are run by people shaped by their community's values. This goes far beyond K-12 education. The regular horror when it surfaces that GOP politicians were educated in the Ivy League (G. W. Bush at Yale, Ted Cruz at Princeton; the list goes on) is indicative of the stranglehold that the "good education equals liberal morality" narrative has on the left. It belies the naive liberal mythology that intellect somehow correlates to a lack of bigotry. Critical thinking can be and is readily employed in the service of tradition, of conservatism, of fascism, of bigotry. How else does horrific injustice become codified law? How else do multinational corporations become multinational corporations? White liberals' commitment to the innate morality of a "good" education is embarrassingly spoon-fed, and is specifically designed to excuse them from examining their own psyches too closely, lest they not like what they find.

Bigotry is not indicative of an intellectual failing, but of an emotional one. Of a lack of capacity for empathy, compassion, and love.

Having grown up in conservative churches in the Midwest where the congregants ranged from people who had been previously incarcerated to doctors and professors, I have generally understood that "education," in and of itself, means approximately nothing when it comes to beliefs and is in no way an automatic indicator of politics or values. Bigotry, like faith, knows no regional, socioeconomic, educational, or institutional boundaries. But that's not how it's discussed in mainstream media—which itself is codified by institutional, cultural, regional, and economic commitments. Consider *The New Yorker*'s founding 1925 tagline: "Not for the old lady from Dubuque."*

Dubuque is, of course, in Iowa.

When I was younger, I thought college was my ticket out. Not just for success, mind. I thought it would be a guarantee I wouldn't end up like my mom: stuck in a nowhere town, financially trapped in

---

* See the Associated Press obituary of Mary Hayford, a Dubuque resident who took it as part of her life's work to counter *The New Yorker*'s prospectus: "Mary Hayford, 85, 'Little Old Lady' in Iowa," *New York Times*, June 14, 1989, https://www.nytimes.com /1989/06/14/obituaries/mary-hayford-85-little-old-lady-in-iowa.html.

a no-good marriage with a man who provided for you but didn't appreciate you.

An education would get me away from the country, away from small towns and small minds and the kind of God-ordained heteronormativity that chased women like me until it choked the life out of us.

I wouldn't find out until later that higher education is only another example of liberal America's and academia's own cruel optimism, where what is given financially, energetically, emotionally, and even physically, so overwhelmingly, and so often, exceeds the actuality of what is received.

# 3. YOU ARE (NOT) YOUR OWN

I ALWAYS KNEW I WOULD SAVE MYSELF FOR MARRIAGE. LIKE I KNEW THE SMELL of tornado weather, before the sky ever turned green; like I knew that you were supposed to alternate between planting corn and soybeans in the fields every year, since rotating your crops was healthier for the soil. It was a fact. The kind of knowledge that is so natural to you, and to your environment, that you simply don't question it.

In 1 Corinthians 6:19–20 (NIV), the Apostle Paul writes, "Do you not know that your bodies are temples of the Holy Spirit . . . You are not your own; you were bought at a price. Therefore honor God with your bodies." I didn't have to explicitly think of Bible verses to know what the Holy Spirit inside me wanted me to do: my body already knew. I was not my own; any human desires are unimportant, unworthy, and depraved. For young evangelical Christian girls, the best, and arguably only, way to be a good Christian is to be a virgin. The ease with which I accepted this fact—that my body was not my own—and subsequently dismissed romance was evidence of a fruit of the spirit, a sign of self-discipline. It was indicative of my strong faith.

✢

I was one of millions of American teenagers in the late 1990s and early 2000s who were part of a mass revival of purity culture. Beyond the effects ingrained into public education systems, there was an entire evangelical-driven cottage industry organized around the perpetuation of abstinence-only education, "True Love Waits," and sexual purity, an industry that started gaining momentum in the 1980s and reached its zenith at the turn of the millennium. Modesty in clothing and language, monitoring one's media intake, and not being alone with the opposite sex: all of these practices were essential components of the culture. Marketed and exported by evangelicals to other Christian denominations who shared these values, this powerful, targeted messaging was put into the hands of Catholics and mainstream Protestants, further normalizing a hypervisible emphasis on young girls' virginity as a symbol of faith.

When I was in middle and high school, conversations about "saving yourself for marriage" were rampant. Girls were slut-shamed in my high school whether they were religious or not; across the country, schools instituted dress codes to try to control the "revealing" spaghetti strap fashions of the late 1990s and early 2000s.

The history of these sexist practices, while widespread, isn't exclusive to any one organized religion. The idea of not having sex before marriage, even, is more of an inheritance from hetero-patriarchal economic structures than religious values. Women's virginity, particularly upper-class and noble-born women's virginity, is historically one of the most valuable global commodities. It was often women's only commodity, one that was bought, traded, and sold by the men who gave them away at the altar; in ancient Rome, marriage vows were traded between a bride's father and her husband-to-be. Understanding women's virginity as an economic good that, for most of history, was owned by men puts other aspects of women's sexual experiences into perspective. Historically, rape is a property crime; a rapist is ruining another man's property, not violating another person's actual agency. That person is not fully a person, because she does not have the right to decide what happens to her own body. In the Book of Genesis, which contains perhaps the most famous rape story in the Bible, Dinah's brothers Simeon and Levi are not enraged because she is personally violated, but rather, because her rape is interpreted as an insult to their family and their own honor.

All this context is erased in contemporary conversations around sexual purity in the church. What evangelicalism has done—in recent decades, especially—is to conflate a person's sexuality with the state of their soul. Though evangelicals tend to claim that saving oneself for marriage is a traditionally Christian virtue that signifies the strength of a person's individual faith, implying that this is the way things have always been, this particular interpretation of sexual purity is a recent development in church history. While Christianity, like most every major religion and state power, has historically commodified women's sexuality into a good that can be bought and sold, training women to commodify *themselves* is new. Put another way: it is an old cultural value with new religious marketing.

In order to understand the emergence and popularity of purity culture in the latter half of the twentieth century, it's essential to understand that it is, in part, a reactive movement against the slow but steady progressions in gender equality and sexual freedom, particularly in the United States. Saving oneself for marriage is often marketed as protection against the evils of abortion and feminism, which white evangelicals have been taught to fear as implicit threats to racial "purity." Remember, it was tax-exempt segregated Christian colleges and not *Roe v. Wade* that initially radicalized an evangelical "moral majority" in the 1960s and 1970s, in spite of the outsize focus today on abortion rights.

Evangelicals interpret women's sexuality, exercised without men's permission, as a direct threat to the faith; women assuming control and asserting their agency in any capacity is perceived as a sin against the God-ordained order of things in which white men are in charge of churches, marriages, and countries alike. Bearing this in mind, we should find it unsurprising to realize that the evangelical marketing push for purity culture emerged and consolidated itself specifically in response to the women's, civil rights, and gay liberation movements of the 1960s and 1970s. Collectively, these events were seen as an assault on white men and white women's inherent "God-given" gender roles, on women's role in the home, and on the absolute necessity of women's sexual purity. Controlling white women's bodies and reproductive capabilities is central to the project of white supremacy, but that developed as a secondary, more politically acceptable concern in the aftermath of evangelicals' initial obsession, segregation. Bible studies, women's ministries, publications, and conferences emerged to affirm and perpetuate evangelicals' rigid patriarchal practices around gender and sexuality—while simultaneously marketing the evangelical lifestyle as "countercultural" to the sinful, lustful ways of the world.

The marketing worked on people like my mom, women who

were hurt and looking for answers. My mom didn't grow up in the evangelical world—the daughter of devout Episcopalians, she and her twin sister were "born again" with dramatic midnight baptisms while they were in college. In her midtwenties, she was a newlywed and then a new mom with infants who was often attending church alone, a zealous convert. There, she found the rich and enduring support of other new moms, who are her friends to this day, but there was a steep price: the continuous judgment of her attending church without her husband.

Of all the evangelical narratives actively championed by my mother, this was dearest to her heart: that my sister and I would not repeat what she interpreted as her mistakes. She had lived with my dad for years before they got married. He got the milk for free, she said unironically. In her eyes, lust had made her willing to overlook their lack of shared faith, which she saw as the source of their unhappy marriage. If our daddy believed in God, she said, then he wouldn't hit her, wouldn't drink, wouldn't treat her so poorly. She believed she was setting us up for success by telling us this, by immersing us in her faith and hope that we would stay virgins until our wedding nights, marry godly men, and not repeat her story.

*Listen to me, Jeanna: You can't change men. You can only marry the right one. As long as he loves God more than he loves you, you'll be fine.* I was taught to fear my mother's self-described failures. Mostly, I wanted to make her happy.

Both my mother and my youth pastors taught me that the key to choosing the right man was not having sex with him before we said our vows. After all, if he was devout, he would understand, and he would have saved himself for me, too.

✢

It is, of course, a fool's errand to try to tell teenagers not to have sex, although my mom, the church, and the federal government thought otherwise. Evangelical voters and the politicians they elected are responsible for various legislative iterations of abstinence-only education packages, which means that if you were an American teenager during or after the 1990s, you have been directly affected by the Religious Right's burgeoning political power. Congress' Title V Abstinence-Only-Until-Marriage Program (also known as AOUM) was federally funded, theoretically part of a 1996 welfare reform package, but in reality, a conservative, reactionary response to the comprehensive sex education and HIV education programs that grew out of the feminist and gay rights movements of the 1970s and 1980s. The US government spent more than $2 billion funding abstinence-only programs between 1982 and 2017, and more than $1.6 billion in foreign assistance promoting AOUM around the globe.* AOUM expired in 2009, but Congress has already replaced it several times over with the "Competitive Abstinence Program" and, most recently, "Sexual Risk Avoidance Education." Like a Hydra, abstinence-only indoctrination is the monster that Republicans will not let die.

The only reason lawmakers in the federal government care about telling teenagers not to have sex is because highly motivated evangelical voters care about teenagers not having sex, and harnessing the power of that voting bloc is essential to the GOP's survival.

---

* A stipulation for AOUM programs that receive funding is that they cannot instruct, promote, or otherwise give any statistical information about contraceptives or condoms, except to share their failure rates. California never accepted AOUM funding. By 2009, nearly half of US states had opted out of funding. See "Abstinence-only-until -marriage policies and programs: An updated position paper of the Society for Adolescent Health and Medicine," National Library of Medicine, July 9 2019, www.ncbi.nlm.nih.gov/pmc/articles/PMC6615479/.

The long-since-proven inefficacy of abstinence-only programs does not matter to evangelicals, driven by a commitment to seeing their beliefs enacted on earth, or to the Republicans, who use the evangelical belief system as a shield to accrue and maintain power.

As long as the rights of the church are protected, contemporary evangelicals do not see their support of policies that infringe on others' autonomy as anything but maintaining their rightful foothold in American politics. If people were guided by a strong belief in Jesus Christ, according to the Far Right, people wouldn't *want* to sin, wouldn't *want* the right to abortion or same-sex marriage. In the evangelical worldview, most Americans have been sinning on a mass scale *and* are advocating for those sins to be enshrined in public law—Christ's power on earth is in danger, and they must protect their secular neighbors from themselves through law if they can't reach them directly through faith.

But securing power starts at home. Lessons taught to me as a child seemed designed to deny, redirect, and obscure my instincts, to mold me and my sister and all our friends into rule followers who didn't challenge authority. "Children, obey your parents in the Lord; for this is right!" (*clap clap!*) went one such song (which is, in fact, a verse from Ephesians 6:1) from pre-K Sunday school that, even today, randomly comes to mind, an earworm I can't get rid of. Instilling obedience in churchgoing kids starts early, as this is a foundational building block for what's to come.

I learned in Sunday school and in evening prayers with my mom that God was always watching. The Holy Spirit, inside each of us, knows everything we do. One of my uncles, also an evangelical, used to tell us that when we got to heaven, an entire movie of our life would play in front of everyone else; as a child, the idea of my life being watched by anyone else filled me with terror and especially shame. For evangelical young people, weekly church attendance, the summer day camp that is Vacation Bible School, and youth group provide a soft, consistent reinforcement of the worldview you have absorbed since the earliest stories your mother read you and the songs you learned: that you are a sinner, and that no matter how much you try, you will never be good on your own. Scaring kids straight is a last-ditch intervention tactic; the long game is about entrenching children and young people so deeply in their own self-denial and shame that they never get in touch with their "sinful" desires in the first place.

For me, sexual purity didn't feel like an extreme demand. Rather, it offered a religiously sanctioned excuse for removing myself from the teenage anxieties of dating and sexual experimentation. I put on a boy-crazy show at the lunch table, but my heart wasn't in it. I preferred to funnel all my emotional turbulence toward an obsessive relationship with faith. There is a particular, peculiar romance to religion: "How infinitely passionate a thing religion at its highest flights can be," William James writes in *The Varieties of Religious Experience.*"* Or, as Heath Ledger's William recalls in a formative film of my adolescence, *A Knight's Tale*: "Don't you remember church as a boy? The fear, the passion!"

I craved love, belonging, and emotional intimacy among my three best friends, all girls. All I ever wanted was to be with them, whether we were spooning together on a pull-out couch at a sleepover or on a four-way landline call, racking up our parents' telephone bills on a school night. In the quiet hours of the night, boys held little appeal for me, which I chalked up to spiritual maturity. I wasn't going

---

* William James, *The Varieties of Religious Experience: A Study in Human Nature*, 48, https://www.gutenberg.org/files/621/621-pdf.pdf.

to act on any temporary crush, because I was a Christian and I was going to college and I wasn't getting married any time soon—so why would you date someone if you weren't going to marry him?

This self-abnegation is the foundation of purity culture and evangelicalism itself. Conditioned since birth, you may not even realize you're denying yourself, involved in a constant process of retraining yourself to want what you are told God wants for you. The unconscious mechanism of self-surveillance works seamlessly. A "sinful" thought crosses your mind, and you immediately identify it as *not God not God not God*. The thought may be innocuous, such as frustration with your parents, or it may feel more insidious, like noticing a woman who is attractive. No matter the sinful thought, the process of repentance is the same. You turn the thought over, release it, let it go, so that your mind is empty, a pure vessel for the Holy Spirit. You may confess it at youth group, or to your journal, or to your mom, or to your evangelical friends. You repent, knowing that real repentance means following through on a daily basis.

Churches call self-abnegation "conforming oneself in Christ's likeness." In *Discipline and Punish*, philosopher Michel Foucault frames the concept a little differently. Foucault writes that the creation of docile, obedient bodies is essential to a well-ordered society or, in this case, a functioning and effective church. But in order to create docile bodies, disciplinary institutions like churches must be able to constantly observe and record the bodies they control. Given that this is an impossible task in the real world, it becomes vital for institutions to then ensure that people have internalized the necessary beliefs to the point that they don't require direct surveillance in order to behave.

This is the endgame: Christianity builds a prison inside a person. The Holy Spirit is Foucault's ideal panopticon, the penitentiary where inmates never know if they are being watched, a system of surveillance that requires no external guards, instead running entirely on internal self-policing. The real-life result is an entire voting bloc of the citizenry more concerned with obeying an invisible sky god than engaging with systemic oppression or truly loving their neighbor.

As an evangelical teenager, I didn't trust my own mind, too afraid to sin. Straying too far away from the early Christian internet could lead to temptation, to lust, to anger, to doubt. Perpetually aware of my own failings and ever the budding perfectionist, I aspired to a nearly ascetic level of spiritual self-discipline, which was in fact self-denial. I believed that I had chosen my faith for myself, not realizing that I had been conditioned all my life to be the ideal, obedient subject.

☩

When I was twelve years old, I went to a hayride, a fun, invite-your-friends "outreach" event put on by my middle school youth group. It was at a church member's farm and was chaperoned by adult youth leaders and parents, tough Wisconsin men and women who blended together in an indiscernible mix of denim, flannel, and Carhartts. The same parents who wore suits and dresses on Sunday morning and cornered me in church hallways to tell me my sweaters were too tight.

The hayride was notoriously a gender war. There were two wagons, both pulled by tractors; there was a "safe" wagon, where the girls could sit if they didn't want to run around and get tackled, and the "fun" wagon, where you were at risk of getting pushed or yanked off by the boys who climbed on the moving vehicle like it was a jungle gym. All the teenage girls sat on the "fun" wagon, while the moms watched from afar on the "safe" wagon. That crisp night, so cold you could see your breath, was filled with adolescent shrieks and laughter as boys chased girls, tackling them and stuffing hay down their shirts. Somehow, this was acceptable to the chaperoning parents who preached sexual abstinence and rigorously policed mixed-gender interactions at church. The general attitude seemed to be that this was playful, all in good fun, a relatively innocent way to let off some hormonal steam. After all, with parents watching, nothing bad could happen.

I got caught up in the fun, in the way running warmed my body against the chilly night, in the thrill of being wanted. I didn't pay attention to my surroundings, didn't notice that I was being chased to the edge of the woods, away from the open field, until a gang of boys was on top of me, pinning me to the ground, hands everywhere. If you've ever watched a pack of lions hunt on the Discovery Channel, you know how this game ends.

This is the last memory before my mind short-circuits: I am lying on my back, pinned beneath at least six boys who are on top of me, screaming at them to stop. I can barely breathe, they are so heavy. So unwanted. So not caring about me or that I am the embodiment of the phrase "kicking and screaming." Can anybody hear me?

Then, nothing.

I don't know if I actually blacked out or if this is one of those moments in time that have buried themselves deep in a memory cave, guarded by one of my inner dragons, who will never again let it see the light of day. Either way, there is a missing piece. A blip in the tape. Honestly, I have little interest in recovering it.

This is where the tape picks up: I am lying on my back, alone. All I remember is the dampening field beneath me, soaking my jeans.

I rise in the middle of the dark night, and as the numbness wears off, it gives way to something else, something quiet and primal. I stumble over my feet at first, but quickly find my footing on the soft ground as I run as fast as I can. I sprint toward the first boy in my line of sight like I am hunting, like I am closing in for a kill. He could have been one of the boys who attacked me; it's equally plausible that he wasn't. I don't know, and I don't care. I take a swing at him; he punches back. Fair. His fist lands squarely on my nose, which promptly starts bleeding, and diminishes my adrenaline rush.

That night, I could not see what those boys did to me as their own sin, as a violation. But when I came to, I was full of wrath—that feeling, I knew, was sinful. My first instinct hadn't been to pray; it had been to fight.

After the hayride, the chaperones corralled us together into one of the barns, where we sat on hay bales around a fire while the youth pastor opened our worship service with a word of prayer. I sat in the back; I was a late straggler coming in, and I wanted to hide my bloody nose. After Pastor Josh finished praying, thanking God that we could all come together this evening, we opened our Bibles and had a Bible study.

I focused on the scripture in my lap and ignored the crusted blood drying on the work glove one of the dads driving the tractors had given me to stanch the bleeding. He hadn't asked how I'd gotten hurt. The adrenaline had faded by that point. The process of repentance had begun. My bloody nose and achy limbs were my own fault, collateral damage, a result of wandering off too far. I ignored the pain in my body and prayed. My choices were the only thing to blame. I'd lost sight of God, of the point of the youth group event. His teachings were so much more important than the "fun" I'd been focused on having. I'd wanted to be wanted, had focused on my body instead of the state of my soul, and I'd been duly punished.

In the years following, I would turn this story of trauma into a humorous anecdote of my first fistfight. Look at how tough I was, fighting boys at a middle school youth group event. I told this story for years before a friend gently pointed out to me—by then, in my midtwenties—that it wasn't really that funny, and that what happened to me at youth group kind of sounded like assault.

The framework of purity culture, so particularly insistent on women's virginity, teaches us, insidiously, that boys are allowed sexual transgressions in a way girls are not. "In the evangelical community, an 'impure' girl or woman isn't just seen as damaged; she's considered dangerous," Linda Kay Klein writes in *Pure*.* There is no framework of restorative justice for victims of sexual assault and rape within the cult of sexual purity, no real punishment for abusers, and certainly no chance for the recuperation of what we have dangerously been taught is our primary spiritual good. What's more, sexually abused, unmarried women and girls are implicitly interpreted as having "asked for it" anyway, our bodies an inherent source of temptation, "dangerous" to ourselves and to others. If you can make a man want you, you're responsible for what comes next. I'd made the choice to sit on the "fun" wagon, after all.

On November 20, 2017, Emily Joy, a Nashville-based poet and yoga instructor, tweeted her story of an emotionally abusive, manipulative relationship with her youth pastor when she was fifteen years old. She spoke of how he groomed her, but also of how her parents, upon discovering the relationship, made her apologize

---

* Linda Kay Klein, *Pure: Inside the Evangelical Movement that Shamed a Generation of Young Women and How I Broke Free* (New York: Simon & Schuster, 2018), 4.

for being a Jezebel, for her inherent promiscuity, for tempting him to sin.

Joy created the hashtag #ChurchToo, tapping into Tarana Burke's viral #MeToo hashtag chronicling stories of sexual assault. Abuse happens in churches, too, Joy said. Pastors protect their own. We have learned that churches will not hold themselves accountable, even when they know abuse is happening—when parents can see a group of boys chasing a girl to the edge of the woods.

In February 2019, a joint investigation by the *Houston Chronicle* and the *San Antonio Express-News* revealed that there had been well over seven hundred victims of sexual abuse from nearly four hundred Southern Baptist Convention church leaders, pastors, and volunteers over the last twenty years. The dam broke. The SBC is the largest, most conservative evangelical Protestant denomination in the United States, and it's the largest Baptist denomination in the world. Sexual abuse is its own kind of quiet plague within the church, a virus that has spread for years and years and years without any attempt at containment.

✢

In this singularly narrow, cisgendered, heterosexual religious worldview, in which obedient believers perfectly abide by the law of abstinence until marriage, there is no need to address consent, because there is no adultery, no rape, no sexual abuse of adults or minors. Because everyone who is able to engage in sexual activity is happily paired off. But this is a false image of the world, one predicated on the enforced denial and sublimation of individuality. Evangelicals' interpretation of gender and sexuality outright rejects the existence of queerness and gender expansiveness, of folks who do not want to marry or have children, of folks who are not monogamous. Purity culture then categorically lumps any nonheteronormative behavior together with sexual abuse as "sin."

But the broad strokes with which purity culture and evangelical churches seek to cover sexuality can't fully account for what even the most sheltered evangelical youth might absorb from pop culture—particularly those who have grown up with the internet. Parents and church leaders face a fundamental problem when preaching the importance of sexual purity: the Bible doesn't explicitly say not to have sex before marriage. The Apostle Paul's suggestion "it is better to marry than to burn"[*] is probably the closest we get, and even that is more of an exhortation to celibacy and the single life than anything else. There are verses that condemn "sexual immorality," which is rarely defined but is generally considered by theologians and biblical scholars to be a caution against engaging in ritual sex with sacred prostitutes[†] in the temples of other gods; the sin in question is idolatry. There are also verses condemning adultery, which is a sin American teenagers getting lectured about premarital sex haven't yet had the opportunity to commit. Which is to say: "no temple orgies" and "no cheating on your spouse" don't really apply to a fifteen-year-old whose sexual concerns are more likely to be around sending nudes.

There is a paradox, then, between purity culture and broader evangelical commitments. Evangelicals are all about biblical inerrancy (the idea that the Bible is never wrong) and biblical literalness

---

[*] 1 Corinthians 7:9 (NIV).

[†] Many academics utilize this term to distinguish sacred sex work from the so-called "profane prostitution" that happened outside of temples. However, I prefer a term used by occultist Gabriela Herstik: "erotic votaries." See Herstik's *Sacred Sex: The Magick and Path of the Divine Erotic* (New York: Penguin Random House, 2022), 115.

(the idea that you can read the text at face value). They also reject cultural relativism, insisting that they will not bend to secular pressure from outside the church (this is often trotted out when it comes to LGBTQ+ issues; for example, same-sex marriage and ordaining queer clergy). Simultaneously, they desire flexibility to ignore passages that don't serve them, as pastors readily dismiss verses that prohibit period sex,* instruct men to marry their brother's widow,† and demand that women's modesty in church extend so far as to prohibit jewelry and mandate head coverings.‡

This kind of inconsistency in practice raises uncomfortable questions for believers: Who decides how we interpret that scripture, and why? What gets to be "cultural context," and what mandates actually do apply to all believers for all time?

Because scripture itself doesn't say what evangelical leaders want it to say about sexual purity, they've created other sacred texts instead. The first purity icon to emerge was Elisabeth Elliot, whose *Passion and Purity*, published in 1984, during the Reagan years, was part autobiography, part instruction guide on how to find a godly man and engage in a pure, God-honoring romantic relationship prior to marriage. The book largely focuses on Elliot's relationship and marriage with her first husband, Jim Elliot, a missionary, which began in the 1940s and ended with his death in 1956.

Elliot's *Passion and Purity* resonated with me. I found my mother's copy from the 1980s on her bookshelf, and I kept it, dog-eared and well worn, on my nightstand. While Elliot had a lot to say about sex and marriage for Christian young people, she also affirmed

---

* Leviticus 18:19.

† Deuteronomy 25:5.

‡ 1 Timothy 2:9; 1 Peter 3:3; 1 Corinthians 11:2–16.

the radical notion that a woman could have a passionate, wholly satisfying relationship with God outside of any man—any pastor, any church, any father—which struck me. She framed her arguments around sexual purity not in terms of a relationship with an earthly husband, but with a heavenly one; for Elliot, the reason to stay pure was to focus on God. To a teenager who had grown up in an emotionally unstable home where my parents' divorce seemed ever on the horizon, where my dad might come home drunk and violent at any moment, and where I would then be responsible for picking up the pieces and helping reorient my mother's emotional stability—well, a reliable and constant relationship with God was fundamentally important to me.

*Passion and Purity*'s ideological descendent during the next decade was Joshua Harris's *I Kissed Dating Goodbye*, published in 1997, when I was ten years old. Harris, who cites the influence of *Passion and Purity* in his first chapter, was everything Elliot wasn't: a cishet man, but also young, unmarried, childless, and, despite the book's title, available (his sophomore book would be coauthored with his new wife). He was twenty-one, with no theological or seminary training, and no actual credentials for writing a book about love or sex, but he was handsome, Christian, and eager. The son of Gregg and Sono Harris, who were early pioneers of the Christian homeschooling movement, he was the perfect spokesman for the evangelical establishment's purity campaign. His book focused almost exclusively on sex, dating, and marriage for the Christian young person caught up in the late-nineties culture wars. Unlike Elliot, who had emphasized a Christ-centered approach to dating, and maintaining and pursuing one's individual faith through the process, Harris claimed wholesale that dating was a "training ground for divorce." Harris made other claims that suited conservatives as well, such as claiming that same-sex relationships and marriage were sinful, the devil's work. *I Kissed Dating Goodbye* was a wild success, selling more than one million copies, helping to drive purity culture practices such as rings and pledges into the mainstream.*

In the following decade, purity culture found messengers in the secular world, too. The most prominent poster child for purity culture at the turn of the millennium was a pop star who had music videos playing on MTV and whose face and bare midriff graced the covers of *GQ*, *Maxim*, *Rolling Stone*, *People*, *Teen Vogue*, and *Cosmo*: Jessica Simpson. Discovered by the head of a Christian music label as a teenager, Simpson reportedly had to quit touring in advance of her debut Christian album due to criticism of her body; evangelicals said she was inherently too sexual to be a Christian singer. She was only sixteen. "They said I was too pretty to be singing Christian music," Simpson later said. "I was in overalls and a ponytail, and they were telling me I couldn't go out there and sing because it would make boys lust."†

What made Simpson—a talented blond and brown-eyed Texan raised in the Baptist church—too much for the Christian music industry made her an ideal messenger for the secular world. Simpson was devout, a woman steeped in evangelical culture from infancy. Her father, Joe Simpson, was a Baptist youth minister, and she grew

---

* In 2018, Harris discontinued the publication of *I Kissed Dating Goodbye*, the same year he released a documentary entitled *I Survived I Kissed Dating Goodbye*, a film that was publicly criticized by ex-evangelicals who participated. Harris had stepped down from his position as lead pastor from his church a few years prior, in 2015. He divorced his wife and announced that he had left the church and was no longer a Christian in 2019.

† Adam McGill, "Jessica Simpson: Gospel Girl Gone Bad," *D Magazine*, March 1, 2002, https://www.dmagazine.com/publications/d-magazine/2002/march/jessica-simpson-gospel-girl-gone-bad/.

up singing in the church choir. Some of her first memories, as she has recounted to numerous interviewers, are of sitting in pews, listening to her father preach. She started wearing a purity ring when she was twelve years old.

So when Simpson made her virginity and her commitment to wait until marriage a cornerstone of her early career, we believed her. Britney Spears, Christina Aguilera, Mandy Moore, and Simpson had all been walking the same, impossibly unfair "virgin/whore teenybopper pop star" tightrope by this point—but Simpson had evangelical bona fides. This cohort of late-nineties pop stars had the same marching orders: Be sexy, but also the girl next door; virginal, but available; flirtatious, but not wanting it. Be a sexual object, but don't cultivate your own sexual agency. Simpson's faith gave her claims the ring of truth, making her seem like the most likely candidate to encourage her young fans to do the same.

While Simpson was busy promoting her second studio album, fully in the throes of pop stardom, Katy Perry burst onto the scene. Fresh off the failure of her debut gospel album, released in 2001 under her birth name, Katy Hudson, Perry pivoted to secular music. Similar to Simpson, Perry had grown up singing in her parents' evangelical Pentecostal church. But unlike Simpson, she didn't overtly identify as religious when launching her secular career. Her first single, the decidedly not evangelical-friendly "I Kissed a Girl," came out nearly ten years after Simpson's debut into a different social landscape in the United States. In 2008, gay marriage was already legal in Massachusetts, a year away from being legalized in Iowa. Barack Obama would be elected to his first term as president later that year; part of the pro-choice Democrat's platform was endorsing the repeal of the Defense of Marriage Act. This was a post–*Queer as Folk* world where the original *L Word* had been on the air for four years and *RuPaul's Drag Race* was about to debut. The evangelical anxiety about "losing" the culture wars had returned in full force, and Perry was held up as an example of how far one of the church's daughters could stray. Sexual agency didn't just mean having sex before marriage; now queerness was officially on the menu.

The Jonas Brothers, contemporaries of Perry, were the sons of an evangelical Assemblies of God minister, and were purportedly devout when their first album was released. They wore purity rings early in their career, but unlike Simpson, didn't seem to feel the need to talk about their faith and their decision to wait for marriage until an interviewer's threat to write that they were in a cult if they didn't disclose what their matching rings were. Except the Jonas Brothers didn't wait for marriage. Time passed, relationships came and went, the purity rings got taken off, and nobody made a fuss. Years later, they would laugh about "who took off their ring first" with James Corden in a carpool karaoke ride.

Men's obedience functions differently in evangelicalism. Even though the Jonas Brothers, and other young men like them, received the same messages of sexual purity and self-abnegation that Katy Perry, Jessica Simpson, and other young evangelical women did, there is one vital difference: boys consistently receive the simultaneous message that they are going to assume power in their adulthood. Men are told that they are God's chosen ones. It will be their job to lead a household, a church, a country—this is what they grow up seeing modeled in both their faith communities and the secular United States. For women of faith, there is no such promise of agency or power tempering the message of total surrender and obedience, only the constant reminder that a complete denial of self is what makes you faithful.

Pastors' daughters turned pop stars, under a spotlight whether they are in a sanctuary or a stadium arena, were subject to the kinds of standards that played out every day in churches around the country. In her memoir, *Open Book*, Simpson says that she was a virgin on her wedding night, that her faith was and continues to be the guiding force of her life. But she was doubted back then, and she is doubted today, her own testimony of her own experience dismissed as insufficient.

Simpson's experience speaks to a broader trend that extends beyond the intersection of celebrity and the church. No matter the power she may accrue in the secular world, even if devout or in the service of proselytizing, a woman is beholden and subject to evangelical standards—and in the church, a woman's job is to surrender. There should be a father, husband, or pastor to step in and speak for her. In evangelical Christianity, the strength of a woman's personal relationship with God is not based on her own testimony, but on how visible that testimony is to others; which is to say, how well she performs the right kind of Christianity. Ultimately, your purity isn't just between you and God. It's between God and the patriarchy.

✛

The summer before my senior year of high school, I took the last youth group camping trip I would ever take, though I didn't know it at the time. We went up to a small campsite on Lake Superior in "the Porkies," the Porcupine Mountains Wilderness State Park on Michigan's Upper Peninsula, where it could dip to the low fifties overnight in the middle of July.

We hiked at least an hour into the campsite, packs on our backs in a single-file line, about a dozen or so of us youths and the two married couples who were our youth leaders. I've never been particularly fond of camping, even less so of hiking, but we did both activities often in that youth group, where the money for "fun" experiences was nonexistent but the northwoods of Wisconsin were plentiful with their abundance. After all, this was God's country: the woods we camped in, the animals we saw and ate, the rivers and lakes we canoed and swam and fished. What could be more wholesome than a group of teenagers and adults going out into the woods for a few days for some scripture reading and outdoors adventure?

Upon our arrival at the campsite, where my seventeen-year-old self was already annoyed at having had to walk an hour with a heavy pack, it was evident that the hike had been worth it. The boys' and girls' cabins were on opposite sides of a babbling brook in a dense forest of sugar maple, white pine, yellow birch, and old, old hemlock, connected by a quaint, fairy-tale bridge. The brook fed directly out into Lake Superior, which went on for miles and miles, as far as I could see. We had the shoreline right there, all ours and also not ours at all. Lake Superior—as vast as any ocean to the human eye—disappeared into the horizon.

On our second day in the Porkies, the two youth leaders' wives asked me to come with them, privately, away from the group. They had taken me aside a few hours earlier and instructed me to wear a tank top and shorts over my swimsuit, which was already a one-piece. *So you don't tempt your brothers*, Linda, the elder, said. "Brothers," in this case, was a figure of speech for my "brothers in Christ," since I wasn't actually related to any boys there. I wasn't sure what else they could possibly want to speak to me about this time around.

After a long walk, we found a spot where we could sit by the creek undisturbed. The sunlight shone through the leaves, dappling the ground below in golden light. There, these women pulled out their Bibles and told me, a seventeen-year-old girl, all the ways my body was wrong. They reiterated how inappropriate my clothing was. They told me I was tempting my brothers to sin, that I was too loud, too flirtatious, and that I shouldn't laugh at boys' jokes, as it encouraged them. The implication was that I was too much, that this muchness threatened the sanctity of both my faith and all the men around me. They delicately questioned how serious I could possibly be about God if my body was as curvy as it was.

The problem was that, by the time I was seventeen, I had data on purity culture. These women, and women like them, had been pulling me aside telling me that my clothing was inappropriate for years. The primary way I learned my body was shameful was from church ladies telling me so. I knew that these disciplinary conversations were as likely to happen when I was wearing a swimsuit as they were when I was wearing a sundress, an ankle-length skirt, or a chunky knit turtleneck with jeans in the middle of a frigid Wisconsin winter. I knew that the problem was not my clothing, but my curves, and there was nothing I could do about those except cover up, apparently to no one's satisfaction.

I was upset at the insinuation that I was consciously trying to cause others to sin. I wasn't dating any guys in the youth group, but I was friends with them. I laughed at their jokes because I thought they were funny, and while I was already in the twilight years of thinking that boys' jokes were funny, telling me to not laugh at someone's good-natured humor struck me as profoundly absurd.

And questioning the seriousness of my faith. Well. That, I really took offense to.

But I said nothing. I probably *hmm*'d along in agreement. I sat there, as these two women with Bibles open on their respective laps prayed over me for my modesty and that I would be a more

God-fearing woman. I stewed as a furious, white-hot righteousness boiled up inside me. Correcting a younger woman in the spirit of Christlikeness, trying to train her on the right path, was an everyday act for congregants and church leaders. But it did not feel normal to me anymore. Something in me broke that afternoon, sitting there by the creek. Not the kind of full, world-shattering break I would experience years later, but the kind of fissure that runs through the earth of you and leaves a scar at the splitting, finally releasing some pressure.

My anger had settled to a simmer by the time we returned to the campsite, but it was still there. My thoughts, so trained by years of indoctrination, whispered, *But what if this is my fault?* The only way to figure out the truth, I decided, was to go to the source. So, I confronted the three boys whom my youth leaders had accused me of "tempting." I approached them all separately over the course of that afternoon, told them what had happened, and asked what they thought. In hindsight, they rolled with the punches as best as they could have. They reacted as you might have expected teenage boys to react: with wild confusion and stuttered, stumbled variations of "no," which was all I needed to feel justified in my anger.

In spite of my inner knowledge that something about this was all wrong, I looked to the patriarchy, not to myself, to understand whether or not I was sinning. External confirmation was necessary, since I had been trained since birth to believe that I was an unreliable narrator of my own life. But what would I have done if they had said, *Yes, you are the temptation, you are the problem,* even as another inner voice, barely an ember of flame, told me otherwise? How much further into myself and my shame would I have retreated?

It's not just that evangelical churches, like so many male-led institutions, rely on a culture of silence and suppression. It's that evangelicalism as a whole, as an entire religious sect, trains its believers, and in particular its women, from childhood to doubt themselves and to actively disconnect from their bodies and desires. *Your body is not your own.* The gaslighting is constant, a reinforcement of the institution's viewpoints as normative and reliable. Purity culture is about normalizing rape culture and calling it good citizenship. The god who insists on sexual purity is the same god who has exceptionally blessed America above all other nations—who has put white men in charge, whose will, according to the Republican Party, is that women not receive the reproductive health care we so desperately need, not have any agency whatsoever over what happens to our bodies, let alone any recourse for justice.

# 4. LIVE LAUGH LOVE

And the Lord God said unto the woman, What is this that thou hast done? And the woman said, The serpent beguiled me, and I did eat. . . . Unto the woman [God] said, I will greatly multiply thy sorrow and thy conception; in sorrow thou shalt bring forth children; and thy desire shall be to thy husband, and he shall rule over thee.

—Genesis 3:13, 16 (KJV)

I DIDN'T WANT TO GET MARRIED, NOT UNTIL I MET HIM.

I went to college sure that I wanted a career, but I was skeptical about marriage. I had long understood that marriage, defined by the confines of evangelicalism, would challenge my autonomy. One of my first college classes, long before I met Kyle, was on feminist performance art of the 1960s and 1970s. The class was made up entirely of women and queers. We studied Carolee Schneemann's *Interior Scroll*, first performed in 1975, in which Schneemann, then thirty-six, pulled a scroll from her vagina and read it aloud for the audience (the text was taken from her short film *Kitch's Last Meal*). Gina Pane climbed a ladder studded with sharp metal, barefoot, in *Unanaestheticized Climb* (1971). In Marina Abramović and Ulay's *Rest Energy* (1980), they mutually hold a strung bow and arrow, pointed at her chest.

In class we considered the politics of the bodies in question: of what it meant to exist in public—to have the *agency* to exist in public—and of how gender, sexuality, race, class, disability, and a variety of other intersections affected public perception and reception of your body itself. I was particularly fixated on the nudity that pervaded so many of these pieces, on how the presence of a woman's perceived immodesty could polarize an audience into fetish or hostility—or both. Purity culture, it seemed, was everywhere.

Carolee Schneemann's work in particular broke my eighteen-year-old mind open. Schneemann was a Jewish white woman who had been kicked out of Bard in the 1950s for drawing a nude self-portrait; she used her own often-unclothed body as a primary canvas throughout her career, for which establishment artists and critics labeled her pornographic. The criticism was obviously sexist, even to me, an evangelical freshman: Here was a woman claiming her body could engage in artistic expression, which was itself intrinsically linked to her subjectivity as an artist, a performer, a person. Her early critics didn't get it, too invested in the belief that a woman's nakedness rendered her desirous, that a woman's sexuality—or the mere hint of sexuality—was enough to taint the entire project, to label it artless and amateur. "A woman exploring lived experience occupies an area that men want to denigrate as domestic, to encapsulate as erotic, arousing, or supporting their own position," Schneeman later said.*

My own father sympathized with her critics. *This is what all my money is going towards?* my dad asked, incredulous. *You're learning about women who take their clothes off and call it art?* He sounded like all the men I'd read about who said that a woman's body wasn't worth studying, that anything that could be read as feminine was less than.

I also bristled at my father's implication that he was paying for my education. He was contributing, yes, but our family's situation wasn't like that of my wealthy peers, whose parents paid for their tuition with a single check and handed them credit cards to use for whatever expenses they needed. *My academic and theater scholarships are paying for most of my tuition,* I reminded him. He grunted.

*When are you going to get off your woman kick?* he asked, ignoring me.

*Probably never.*

For a certain kind of conservative adult Christian woman, piety looks like being a modest, submissive wife and doting mom who would rather stay at home than work. In the contemporary church, the shorthand for this particular set of life choices is called "biblical womanhood." I can't remember a time when I didn't know in my bones what the concept meant. When I didn't know that, by virtue of my desire to get out of my small town and have a career, I was already automatically failing at becoming a "biblical woman."

---

* Carolee Schneemann, *Imaging Her Erotics: Essays, Interviews, Projects* (Cambridge, MA: MIT Press, 2002), 32.

Here in the United States, there are entire religious and political industries set up to tell evangelicals that this so-called biblical way of performing gender and sexuality is God's design for the world, and that to do otherwise is to fall into the gravest of sins. Biblical womanhood is most often defended by verses lumped together as the "household codes," the most famous of which is Ephesians 5:22–24 (NIV), "Wives, submit yourselves to your own husbands as you do to the Lord. For the husband is the head of the wife as Christ is the head of the church, his body, of which he is the Savior. Now as the church submits to Christ, so also wives should submit to their husbands in everything." In this passage, which is as often a subject of Sunday sermons as it is emblazoned on merchandise, wifely submission is theoretically justified because wives' service to husbands parallels the church's service to Christ.

Other household codes,* such as 1 Timothy 2:12 (KJV)—"But I suffer not a woman to teach, nor to usurp authority over the man, but to be in silence"—offer similar exhortations to wifely and womanly modesty, although they also mandate children's obedience and were predictably used to defend the human rights abuses of slavery in the United States and elsewhere. In modern evangelical settings, the verses are most often used to bludgeon women across race and class demographics to be silent in church and to submit to their husbands and to church authority. These verses are so predictably cited in weddings that they have even become secular punch lines, as in 2005's *Wedding Crashers*, when the titular, clearly nondevout characters make a bet on which Bible verses will be read at a wedding: "Double or nothing, Colossians 3:12."

---

* See also Colossians 3:18–4:1; 1 Timothy 3:11 and 6:1–2; Titus 2:1–10; and 1 Peter 2:13–3:7.

"Biblical womanhood" isn't a phrase used in the Bible—or in church history, for that matter. It was coined in 1987, the year I was born, by evangelical heavyweights Wayne Grudem and John Piper, the creators of the Council on Biblical Manhood and Womanhood. Grudem was also on the translation committee for the unfortunately popular English Standard Version (ESV) Bible, a translation that came out in 2001 and arose from the concern that other contemporary Bible translations were too liberal, particularly in regard to how they treated gender.[*]

Biblical womanhood rests on the idea of complementarianism, or the idea that men and women are essentially created "separate but equal" by God. The second affirmation of Grudem and Piper's Danvers Statement, which was issued by their council, reads, "Distinctions in masculine and feminine roles are ordained by God as part of the created order."[†] These ideas articulate the basis for conservative Christian opposition to women in the workforce and the military and, of course, form the lynchpin of the faithful Republican's agenda: opposition to abortion.

But as with purity culture, biblical womanhood has required the creation of extrascriptural sacred texts to make a case for a coherent doctrine of women's subjugation in marriage and its extension to the public sphere. The Bible's own inconsistencies and the vital historical context surrounding those "household codes" have been addressed by thinkers like Rachel Held Evans, an award-winning author who famously left evangelicalism for Episcopalianism before her death. In her cult classic *A Year of Biblical Womanhood*,

---

* Beth Allison Barr, *The Making of Biblical Womanhood: How the Subjugation of Women Became Gospel Truth* (Grand Rapids, MI: Brazos Press, 2021), 132–33.

† "The Danvers Statement," The Council on Biblical Manhood and Womanhood, https://cbmw.org/about/danvers-statement/ https://cbmw.org/about/danvers-statement/.

she endeavored to take the Bible's admonitions to wives as seriously and consistently as possible, doing things like literally sitting on her roof as "contrition" for "verbal misdeeds" against her husband and keeping a swear jar that she had to add to whenever she didn't demonstrate a "gentle spirit" (Evans said this was especially difficult when watching football).* Evans, and others like her, have written in great detail about all the ways in which the examples of the *actual* women of scripture (like Deborah, Judith, Dorcas, and even the Virgin Mary) often directly contradict contemporary conservative ideals of how women should behave.

But evangelicals obsessed with reinforcing patriarchal gender roles within the home and state are not particularly concerned about women in the Bible who were prophets or who served as first-century deacons in the church (or who were pregnant, unmarried teenagers). They have weaponized patriarchy via religion and rebranded women's subservience as "biblical" in an effort to keep us in line and to justify right-wing policies that disenfranchise our rights over our own bodies—adult evangelical women are not deemed safe or trustworthy within their communities unless they are governed by a husband.

These are the "culture wars," and biblical womanhood is the quiet, deadly ringer.

✛

In college, I often felt pulled in two, as if my body were an ever-widening valley being stretched between Christianity and feminism.

---

* Rachel Held Evans, *A Year of Biblical Womanhood: How a Liberated Woman Found Herself Sitting on Her Roof, Covering Her Head, and Calling Her Husband "Master"* (Nashville: Thomas Nelson, 2012), 17.

I majored in women's studies while leading the women's Bible study. Feminist theory became a second language for me to use in understanding the world, and I desperately tried to merge it with that of my faith. I was determined to blend the two in academia, through a PhD, regardless of the constant tension I felt between my fellow feminists rejecting Jesus and my fellow Christians rejecting feminists.

Some women who have grown up in the church, disenchanted with evangelicalism's sexist double standards and belligerent insistence on "pro-life or bust," leave altogether as adults. But I loved Jesus, and I considered my intelligence to be evidence of his calling on my life, proof that there was more for me than marriage and motherhood back home, unlike so many other women at church and in my family. My critical readings of the Bible as a young person gave me the material I needed to justify this deviation from the direct path toward biblical womanhood: the Jesus I knew loved women and spent time with them, caring more about people than religious rules. Mary Magdalene was the apostle to the apostles, after all, the first person to whom Jesus appeared after his resurrection. In a time when a woman's word meant nothing, when women could not serve as witnesses in criminal trials, Jesus trusted them as the sole witnesses to his awakening from the tomb, a detail in all four gospels that—regardless of its veracity—moves me to this day. I took comfort in Christ's example. Why could a love and respect for women not be better integrated into the church? If we evangelical churchgoers were expected to be doing work in Christ's image, it seemed patently obvious to me, from the abuse and oppression of women I'd witnessed by men in the name of religion, that we weren't doing a very good job.

✛

I didn't date in college at all until Kyle, an asceticism beyond high school, even, where I had dated sparingly. I poured all my energy into academics, so determined to succeed that there was little left for other pursuits. Easy enough to do at a school on the "block plan," also called OCAAT (one course at a time), where students take one course a month, cramming a semester's worth of material into three and a half weeks. The schedule was intense, and I was triple majoring, and I didn't make time for romance.

I *did* have time for extracurriculars and friends. I was president of my freshman dorm's hall council and volunteered with the literary magazine; was involved with evangelical groups on campus and also the swing dancing club, the memberships of which were so similar and so white that you'd have been hard pressed to tell them apart.

When Kyle arrived for his first year on campus and talked a big game at our student-led Sunday-night services about how we were going to convert more of our fellow students, I was turned off, and not only because I was a sophomore who had been around ever-so-slightly longer than he had. He was a tall, blond-haired, and blue-eyed pastor's son with a classic runner's build who looked like he should have had the charm of a *Friday Night Lights* cast member, but whose delivery tended toward that of a televangelist.

It wasn't just that it seemed like he thought he was smarter than me that initially made me dislike him. If a nonbeliever wanted to debate him, he had no problem telling that person they were going to hell right there in the cafeteria during lunchtime. He took philosophy courses earnestly believing that he could convert the middle-aged professor teaching them.

And I fell for him—or at least the idea of him. How, you may well be asking? Well, we got to be friends, ever so slowly, after he calmed down about needing to prove his intelligence (an insecurity I could certainly relate to). We also quickly realized that we were two of the only people in our overlapping friend groups who *liked* to debate for fun, who were interested in the intersection where faith met intellect.

He chased me until he wore me down. I'd spent a lifetime being told that I was supposed to be pursued by a man who wanted to serve God more than he wanted to love me, but who also *really* wanted to love me—who was I to say no? Such a situation was clearly God's plan. Everything my mother had ever wanted had fallen into my lap, the fruits of my own strong faith. I was hesitant, but he was certain, and for some of us, certainty is an aphrodisiac.

Kyle had made it plain that he was dating me with the intention to marry me. As time went on, and we got more serious and the people around us got married, it just seemed like the thing to do after graduation. He became a rock, a physical reminder of my faith, enduring in the face of my crashing waves of skepticism. *I love you,* he said. *I want you,* he said. *I'm not going anywhere,* he said.

Being with him also took the bite out of my fear of marriage. We liked debating for fun, but if I actually got hurt, his demeanor would shift—he was a gentle person who had been raised by parents who had a deep love and respect for each other. I put a lot of stock in the fact that *his* model for marriage, however traditional, was more solid than mine. If I stood in front of him yelling or got otherwise activated in ways that hadn't yet been dealt with by therapy, he would sit on the couch in his dorm room quietly, waiting me out until I finished, and then ask, in the most loving tone imaginable, *Are you done? Do you want a hug?*

One thing he and I didn't really talk about was marital submission. When I said that I wasn't going to be like his mom, a traditional, conservative, stay-at-home pastor's wife, he said that he wanted someone who was different from her, that I was everything he had ever hoped for. He said he liked that I was smart. Liked that

I wanted to be a professor, like him. He had a vision of us serving God together in academia that I felt compelled by, included by. That's really all I had ever wanted: to be affirmed that I *could* use my mind for God.

Kyle knew that I kicked against the constraints of biblical womanhood, but he seemed to like it. Was amused by it, at least. *Of course you don't have to say "obey" in our wedding vows,* he said, chuckling. Well, here was a man I could marry. We were friends, and he respected me. My sister couldn't stand him—thought he was a prick, completely full of himself, and told me as much— but my mother adored him, repeatedly told me that this was the kind of man she had always prayed would come into my life. I was skeptical about male headship as a concept, but this one man, I trusted.

✛

The last Bible study I led while in college was on the subject of marital submission. Unbeknownst to me, Kyle (who was leading the men's Bible study) was only a few months away from proposing.

I was nervous as my friends filed into the formal lounge of the all-girls' dormitory where the women's Bible study met every Tuesday night. We dragged the chairs and couches into a circle in the middle of the room, as always. There was tea and coffee and cookies and girls in pajamas, huddled under blankets they'd brought down from their rooms, and girls in work clothes, coming to Bible study straight from their jobs. Bibles and notebooks were strewn across laps; the mood was ever one of quiet earnestness.

After asking a friend to open us up in prayer, I asked everyone to open her Bible to Ephesians 5. *We don't have to submit,* I said to the room full of twenty or so college-age women. *Marriage can be a partnership of equals.*

Instant uproar. Voices were raised, women were interrupting each other, blankets ended up on the floor as people anxiously sat up straighter in their seats to make a point. Lots of women in that room (myself included) would have had to put some money in Rachel Held Evans's "swear jar" for not possessing a gentle spirit as we virulently debated scripture.

What I was making a case for that night is called "egalitarianism" in evangelical circles: an argument that husbands and wives should submit to each other. The secular world might simply call it a partnership of equals.

Anyone who has ever suggested that education is the key to "breaking out" of conservatism would have been shocked to observe so many of the women, who were being educated at a well-respected, decidedly secular liberal arts college, loudly leap to the defense of patriarchy and biblical womanhood. *Male headship is God's will,* they repeated. Women who were my friends. Women who were intelligent. Women who said they wanted to work, but who also fervently believed that submitting to their future husbands would honor God more than pursuing a career.

*God's will,* they repeated. *God's will,* that men had dominance over us.

Always God's will, that we should bend and break for a man's whims.

✝

Kyle proposed in the religion section at the Borders bookstore I grew up going to. The religion section was right across from the women's studies section, which I had spent hours and hours sitting in, which was situated right next to the LGBTQ+ section, which I actively avoided; I was keenly aware of where the women's studies ended and the sinful, queer stuff began. All my books were right there, the ones I'd spent so many hours reading: *Backlash* and *Manifesta* and *Bitch*. Watching him as he knelt.

So what if I automatically started backing away when he got down on one knee? So what if he had to reach out and grab my hand to stop me from fleeing, so that he could put the small, ruby engagement ring on my finger? So what that I cannot actually remember saying an affirmative *yes* to one of the questions that would most define my life? Surely I said yes. Every woman says yes. Didn't I?

I did not cry, or shriek, or faint, or even kiss him, that most traditional of responses to such a moment. Instead, I fell against the bookcases laughing—hysterical. I doubled over, splitting my own sides, the unidentifiable emotions so strong in me I could not stand up straight. Couldn't think straight. The *yes* was clearly assumed, even by me.

Engaged to the son of a preacher man.

Was he scared, frightened, surprised by my reaction? I don't know how Kyle felt watching me in that moment. We never discussed it. But he didn't move to hold me, either, this maniacal woman laughing so hard she couldn't breathe, a shiny new ruby on her finger, a fire-hot brand of a thing. He didn't try to touch me; he just stood there.

*Do you want coffee?* he eventually asked, knowing me well enough to assess that the offer of my favorite beverage would snap me out of whatever meltdown his proposal had inspired and help ground me in the moment. As we were walking out, steaming cups of Borders Cafe coffee in hand, I realized we hadn't kissed. I froze right there in the parking lot, halfway to the car, like a Wisconsin ice storm had bolted me in place.

*Oh my* God, *we didn't kiss*, I said out loud, horrified, convinced this meant something terrible and foreboding. What couple gets engaged without sealing the moment?

He laughed and took my hand to jostle me along. *It's fine, Dove*, he said. *I'm not worried about it.*

Afterward, I became consumed with analyzing the scene of our engagement, even as I played the part of the joyful fiancée to my family and on social media. You weren't supposed to laugh when you got engaged. You were supposed to cry, embrace your beloved, be overwhelmed with joy.

In the days after, I could not shake the feeling that something was terribly wrong, but for the life of me, I could not identify what it was. Since Kyle had done what was expected, and was doting as ever, I had no reason to doubt that this was right, that it was God's plan. Therefore, my feelings of doubt themselves must be the sin. Practiced in the ways of the panoptical Holy Spirit, I prayed and tried to turn over my doubt to God. Tried to submit and cleanse. Tried to be the good Christian woman I was so dedicated to becoming.

✞

There is a key phrase in the Danvers Statement, at the very end: "We are convinced that a denial or neglect of these principles will lead to increasingly destructive consequences in our families, our churches, and the culture at large."

*The culture at large.*

This is a call to action, the affirmation that Christians *must* be concerned with the institution of biblical womanhood and women's submission and men's headship in the home and the church—else the "destructive consequences" spread. As Pat Robertson, the

wildly rich founder of the Christian Broadcasting Network, famously, unironically wrote in a fundraising letter for the Christian
Coalition (which he also founded) in 1992, "The feminist agenda is
not about equal rights for women. It is about a socialist, anti-family
political movement that encourages women to leave their husbands,
kill their children, practice witchcraft, destroy capitalism and become lesbians."* It may sound overblown, but this language is what
I grew up hearing about feminists and liberals in church, at the dinner table, at family gatherings. This has always been the messaging of evangelicals and of the Far Right, behind closed doors; these
days, it's just more out in the open.

But there is a delicious irony that in order to promote biblical
womanhood, you have to anoint and appoint certain women to promote its values in the public sphere. These women must be married and must be mothers: this is nonnegotiable. These women can
be professionals in the domestic space (like Joanna Gaines of *Fixer
Upper* and Magnolia fame) or elected politicians whose ultracon-
servative, decidedly pro-life platforms are dedicated to preserving
"family values" (like former Minnesota congresswoman and early
Tea Party champion Michele Bachmann, former Alaska governor
and vice presidential nominee Sarah Palin, Georgia congresswoman Marjorie Taylor Green, and Iowa governor Kim Reynolds,
to name a few). The most fraught position, perhaps, is occupied by
women who do assume some kind of spiritual authority, such as
the extremely Christian-famous "Bible teachers" Joyce Meyer and
Trump critic Beth Moore, women who must absolutely not, under
any circumstances, *ever* call themselves preachers—though that is

---

* The Associated Press, "Robertson Letter Attacks Feminists," *New York Times*,
August 26, 1992, https://www.nytimes.com/1992/08/26/us/robertson-letter-attacks
-feminists.html.

exactly what they are. All these women must be invested in export-ing evangelical values, and are given the trust to do so after having fulfilled all the requirements that biblical womanhood confers on them.

Even if you have a supportive husband, there is a danger in try-ing to exercise your career aspirations too soon. Rachel Held Ev-ans was initially told by a Christian publisher she couldn't write a book about biblical womanhood because, at the time, she was not a mother—as if the act of giving birth were somehow essential to her intellectual and creative processes.[*]

This elevation of motherhood in addition to wifehood, specifi-cally, is a marked shift in women's spiritual authority from histori-cal church tradition. As Beth Allison Barr writes in *The Making of Biblical Womanhood*, the Protestant Reformation changed things: before it, women could gain spiritual authority by *rejecting* their sexuality, by becoming nuns and taking religious vows. But after the Reformation, the opposite proved true for Protestants. "The more closely they identified with being wives and mothers," Barr writes, "the godlier they became."[†]

Catholic or Protestant, women in the church are fucked either way: reject any public expression of your sexuality, or funnel it into a heteronormative marriage. In a religion where even purportedly liberal Protestant denominations have been horrendously slow to ordain women clergy and even slower to ordain folks who are trans and queer, the options when it comes to seeking recognition of spir-itual authority or equality are grim.

---

[*] Kate Bowler, *The Preacher's Wife: The Precarious Power of Evangelical Women Celebrities* (Princeton, NJ: Princeton University Press, 2019), 243.

[†] Beth Allison Barr, *The Making of Biblical Womanhood: How the Subjugation of Women Became Gospel Truth* (Grand Rapids, MI: Brazos Press, 2021), 103.

✣

In the year of our engagement, the question arose of whether I was going to take Kyle's name. Everyone assumed I would. I hated the idea. Not only did I not care for his surname aesthetically (an opinion I kept to myself), I loved mine. *Kadlec* means "weaver" in its native Czech. As a writer, I connected to this idea of working with my hands as my ancestors had once worked at their looms, weaving words into sentences into stories.

*My husband's name or my father's—at least I had a choice with my husband,* one evangelical friend said, trying to reason with me. We are always taking men's names, one way or the other.

But I didn't think of Kadlec as my father's name. Intellectually, I understood patrilineal lineage, but somewhere along the way, Kadlec had stopped being my father's name and had become mine. Battles over pronunciation in the classroom, those were mine. Advice over how to handle boys who teased me by mispronouncing it as "Cadillac," that came to me from my paternal grandmother. *That's an old one,* she said. *Tell them you're an expensive car—too expensive for them.* My name is distinctive, easily Googleable, which is forever a blessing and a curse.

But it would be un-Christian, I was told, to not take his name. Disrespectful. Unsubmissive.

There is no biblical passage explicitly addressing this modern problem of surnames, merely a verse dictating that a man (and wife, presumably) shall leave their parents and cleave to each other.[*] More commonly quoted is the verse about wifely submission to her husband; these days, it's inferred that rendering one's name is part of the deal.

---

* Genesis 2:24.

But in trying to make my case, I found evidence of contemporary Christians in other cultures where wives do not necessarily take their husband's name. In France, women have maintained their maiden name by law since 1789; in Malaysia, South Korea, and many Spanish-speaking countries such as Spain and Chile, it is the custom for women to keep their maiden names. While I appreciated that some practices were coming from different cultural traditions, to me, the point was that Christians all over the globe could interpret the Bible differently as it applied to their lives and still be God-honoring.

I emailed Kyle these examples, essentially trying to get his permission to keep my name. I had graduated a year ahead of him, so he was finishing up his senior year at college while I worked in Minneapolis as a nanny, saving money for the wedding. The emails piled up, one on top of another, but he never offered his opinion in return. It seemed like he was giving me the space to work out the issue for myself. Instead, his one-sentence responses to my pages-long research emails—*That sounds fascinating, Dove*—cut me. I thought he respected me intellectually, that he wanted to read my research, but his short replies felt placating, at best. What I wanted was explicit validation, but I interpreted his silence like the church had trained me to.

I'd triple majored in English, politics, and women's studies; what would my professors say if they could see me now?

My conscious acquiescence was matched by the subconscious power of a lifetime spent imbibing the messages of how to be a woman in a way that God wanted me to be. The evangelical culture I had grown up in, and that continues today, is strong: strong enough to raise up a Religious Right in the 1980s and 1990s, strong enough to make abortion the single issue evangelicals voted on—erasing (for a time) mainstream memory of their opposition to desegregation. Strong enough to push abstinence-only education through public schools, strong enough to launch the Tea Party into existence, strong enough to eventually elect Donald Trump. And baked into every part of evangelical culture, every message about family values and service to the church and how God calls people equally but differently, is the message of male headship and wifely submission.

The success of my relationship was intrinsically tied to my success in faith. If I wasn't willing to give up my name, what did it say about the state of my heart? God doesn't put men like this in your path if you aren't supposed to marry them, take their name, and have their children.

One day in the springtime, mere months before our wedding, after I had prayed and prayed for months on end, once I had filled myself with shame and doubt and apologized to Kyle for my uncertainty—apologies he accepted—I was journaling, and it was as if I heard the voice of God. That he had brought me low in order to raise me up. I cried onto the pages as I came to the realization that the willingness to give up my name was enough: this process had been about cultivating the *spirit* of a faithful, submissive servant. I could keep my name and add Kyle's last name to mine. Two surnames was the compromise.

After the whole ordeal, I didn't feel a sense of victory, or accomplishment, or even relief. Maybe my friend was right. Father or husband. Father *and* husband. They were all men's names, in the end.

Hindsight reveals the truth: that my unspoken desire had been to not take my husband's name at all. I hadn't wanted to submit, but I had internally, automatically cut myself off from the choices that felt truest to me, since they ran contrary to the church. If that isn't submissive, I'm not sure what is.

✝

I want to be Carolee Schneemann, but I am not brave enough to walk away. Instead, I am Eve, I am the Virgin Mary, I am my mother and my grandmother and every other woman in my family who started saying yes and didn't know how to stop. I'm Mary Magdalene, faithfully praying at the foot of a wooden cross while a dead man hangs on it. Get up and leave, bitch. He can't do anything for you.

✝

In the months leading up to my wedding, I became obsessed with banshees. A figure of Celtic mythology, the banshee—*bean sídhe*, or "woman of the fairy mound"—is a feminine spirit whose shriek is said to hail the imminent death of a family member.

Banshees vary wildly depending on the source. Some are red-headed young virgins; others, weathered crones with silver, gray, or white hair. They are, unsurprisingly, either astonishingly beautiful or dreadfully ugly, with eyes bright as the clear-blue sky or blood streaked. They can be headless, naked, or shrouded in their funeral vestments. Some banshees are purportedly good-natured protectors of their bloodline, while it is said that others are harbingers of great evil. The unifying factor is that the banshee is always, *always* a woman whose mournful keen of warning can be heard from beyond her lifetime.

Once you're dead, they have to pay attention to you.

I did not hear a banshee's wail in those hot, humid months leading up to my August nuptials. I never saw the washer at the ford. There was no ghostly visitation, no haunting dream, no scream that followed me on my near-daily walks along the headwaters of the

Mississippi—unless you count the silent keen of my own body, the pressured anxiety in my ribs that kept me up at night asking, *Why are you doing this? Is this the only way?*

✛

My mother and sister tell me I had a panic attack the night before my wedding, that they both massaged me with essential oils in our hotel room at the Westin, a dozen floors above the gardens where I would get married the next day: rubbed my back and tended to my feet in an effort to soothe my anxious nerves.

I have no memory of this, my body's last revolt.

✛

*Jeanna has a teachable spirit. A willingness to submit, to learn, to be taught by her husband, is such an important trait in a wife.*

Kyle's best man was giving his speech at our reception in the Year of Our Lord 2011 with a microphone that barely worked, thank God, because the singular trait he chose to focus on when speaking to our hundred or so guests was my submission. My chest tightened, the red blush of anger creeping up my neck. The one word I had fought to have struck from our marriage vows, the one word I had struggled with the most in our premarital counseling, and there it was, chasing me down at my own wedding reception. I plastered a smile on my face. All eyes were on me, the bride; all I had to do was get through it.

My sister, Jo, made absolutely no secret of looking down the head table at me, completely aghast. *What the fuck?* she mouthed, not caring if anyone saw her swearing in a bridesmaid's dress. She wasn't the only one. A few seats down, another bridesmaid, a friend from high school, was also seeking eye contact, her expression one of total disgust—a *Can you believe this guy?* Amy, my maid of honor and best friend from college, seated right next to me, kept facing forward and smiling, but tightly squeezed my hand under the table.

They all knew how I had struggled with the fact that we were getting married so young, with the expectation of being an obedient Christian wife, even though Kyle said he wanted me to be myself. He wouldn't be marrying me if he expected a woman like his mother, the pastor's wife. He knew I was ambitious and headstrong, and when he assured me that he loved those things about me, I believed him.

I took deep breaths, trying to calm the anxiety that had risen during the best man's speech. I clutched Amy's hand—Amy, my emotional support, my first line of defense, my person. She put her other hand over mine, reassuring.

Kyle, who was seated on my other side, didn't seem to notice.

The words—"teachable," "submissive"—lingered in the air after the speech was over. I deliberately suppressed my discomfort at how trapped I felt. This was my new role: I was his wife now. I couldn't express my displeasure; I had to be nice to his friends, no matter what they said about me.

I walked over to the best man and hugged him. *Thank you, that was wonderful,* I said, doing my best to deliver a convincing lie. I glanced over at Kyle as Amy took the mic and started her maid of honor speech. My new husband was totally oblivious to my emotions. It was as if we were attending two separate wedding receptions. Was he not as bothered by the word, knowing how I personally felt about it?

I definitely looked the part of a dutiful Christian bride: a 1950s tea-length white dress with cap sleeves, a lace boatneck, and a V-cut back that was deep enough to be modern but not offensive to my new in-laws. The pearls in my hair, framing the drop pearl earrings. Pink and pale and neutral. Placid. Unthreatening. Virginal.

I looked how I had *planned* to look. And I could barely breathe.

✛

When we got back to our honeymoon suite after the wedding reception, I knew he wanted to have sex right away, simply because we could now. I didn't feel the same urgency. We were leaving the next day for our honeymoon in Provincetown; we were moving to Boston immediately after so that I could start my English PhD program. We had things to do: namely, going through wedding gifts to assess the cash situation. Our money had to be in order, and I had to be the one to organize it—as I had been the one to plan the wedding, plan our honeymoon, and find our new apartment in Somerville. I was in charge of our life. I was the one with the long-term vision. I knew that he was waiting, pining for sex, but we had far more important things to take care of first.

Toward the end of the card sorting and pizza eating, he asked if he could help me take my hair out. One of my bridesmaids had woven a necklace—a truly spectacular string of pearls—through my hair, which I inexplicably had chosen to wear in an updo.

*Be gentle*, I said, both because my coarse, curly hair tugged at the jewelry, and also because I wanted to preserve the necklace.

I don't know if his hands were shaking as he set about the task, but he tugged too hard, and the pearl necklace broke. Pearls flew out of my hair, scattering across the floor.

*Just let me do it*, I said, my heart falling as the pearls rolled away. I was frustrated with his lack of patience, with the fact that he didn't value an item that I had asked him to be careful with.

I couldn't stall forever. My dress came off; his hands were everywhere. He barely looked at my face, too fascinated by the rest of me. As if my face, and any reaction or emotion crossing it, were the least interesting thing in the room.

The first time we had sex that night, it was clear that something was wrong with me. It wasn't that it hurt; it was that I didn't feel much of anything. Based on what I'd heard from friends, from my mother, from my sister, from every song I'd ever listened to, every movie I'd ever watched, I should have felt *something*, even if that something was excruciating pain. It was just my inexperience, and his, I figured. But then, he wasn't having any problems. I was the one with a missing piece.

I tried to find it, or tried to ignore it, as I climbed on top of him, pulled him on top of me, tried and tried to dredge up something from deep within me that I had assumed would be there, but wasn't. It wasn't simply an orgasm that I was searching for; I didn't expect or need an orgasm.

Want. I was trying to find *want*.

He wanted to cuddle in bed after we were finished, but I didn't. I was tired, and we needed to be up early to leave for the airport for our honeymoon. But there was a flash of hurt in his eyes, and I bit my lip, guilty. Deep down, I knew that I didn't care about the romance nearly as much as he did: things like cuddling in bed or holding hands in public. When we had dated, he had always prioritized my needs, my desires. He had courted me, wooed me. But I was his wife now, and our hierarchy of needs had suddenly, intuitively rearranged, with his at the top. Intellectually, I had argued against wifely submission; instinctually, it was what I had spent a lifetime training for.

✛

Kyle was seasick on the whale-watching tour during our honeymoon. He didn't take Dramamine, because I didn't have any; I don't get seasick, and I didn't know he was prone to seasickness. We had never been on that kind of boat together. *How do you not have any?* he asked me, his voice slow from the nausea. *My mom always has it.* I had no response to that.

He wanted me to stay with him below deck, comforting him even though there was little I could do, but said it was fine if I went above deck for a few minutes. I was concerned for him, but I also wanted to see whales, which were new to my rural midwestern self, so when he released me from my caretaking duties, I practically ran.

When I reached the deck, a magnificent humpback whale breached six, seven, eight times right in front of the boat. *She's performing for us!* the guides said.

I leaned over the rail, watching the whale leap in and out of the Atlantic, which stretched out as far as the eye could see. The vast expanse felt endless, breathless, like if I closed my eyes, it would carry me away.

The breeze rucked my dress up around me, threatening a Marilyn moment, but for the first time in my life, I could have cared less. I was in my body, present, unselfconscious, in a new way. In a way that was foreign to me, and finally comfortable. I didn't have to be on guard about being overly modest; I didn't have to be on guard about men and their desires. I had a husband; I was claimed, I was married, I was safe. I could be at rest in my body, from the energy exerted in surveilling it as a single woman who might at any moment accidentally tempt a man to sin. As present and free as the whale, whose only delight was to jump out of the water and make a big splash upon reentry. Who had no idea how grand she looked doing so. To be that free of self-consciousness—this was entirely new to me.

✝

Is keeping a man's house for him and encouraging him to try to find a job all there is to a marriage? Asking him to pray with you? Wondering if he'll ask you how your day went? This is the big thing that pastors and parents alike cast a great shroud of mystery over?

I was journaling furiously, asking if this—me cleaning and setting up utilities and purchasing furniture, and him job hunting and eating on the couch and asking for sex—was all there was. Was this the idyllic Christian marriage of my mother's dreams? Was this what all the fuss was about?

*Is this it?* The entry in which I ask that question is dated August 30, 2011. We had been married for twenty-three days.

There was already distance between Kyle and me. Where once there had been ease, and humor, and the camaraderie of friendship, now there was . . . nothing. Was silence nothing? Was it a sign of comfort, or a sign of something else? Something that was wrong?

After the honeymoon in Provincetown, we moved into our new apartment—which my father cosigned for—in Somerville, just outside Boston proper. It was a small, first-floor apartment—one bedroom, six hundred square feet, galley kitchen with shit ventilation. But I tried to make it as homey as I could. We had two large Target bookshelves where his books and mine collided (his: theology, philosophy, the hard sciences; mine: literature, poetry, women's and gender studies). We'd often sit on the couch at night, reading quietly. He would pull G. K. Chesterton or C. S. Lewis off the shelf, or some epic tome like *Systematic Theology*. I was getting ready for graduate school, reading Romantic poetry by famous men like William Blake and William Wordsworth and less famous women like Anna Laetitia Barbauld and Charlotte Smith.

I was also busy setting up house while he looked for work and began preparing materials for a second round of PhD applications. He rejected the assistance I offered on his applications, and declined to discuss his own process. I worked to make space, to try to be a supportive partner.

*Can I help at all? I work with folks developing and editing their application materials in the writing center,* I said over dinner one night.

*I'm just more comfortable talking with my guy friends about this,* he said.

*You mean you would rather talk to your friends at Moody who aren't in graduate school and who haven't successfully applied to any kind of graduate program than your wife, who helps people apply to grad school all the time?*

He looked down at his plate and didn't answer me.

I wasn't the person he wanted support from. As a wife, I had failed. Christian wives are supposed to support our husbands: to be the person they lean on. To be their helpmeet. I might have chafed at the idea of marital submission, but emotional support? Pragmatic career advice, like helping him brainstorm and then edit a statement of purpose—or simply being there to talk it through? This, I was willing and ready to do.

To be sure, I appreciated his desire for companionship with same-sex friends—my closest, most intimate friendships had always been with women—but I opened up to him. I was trying, damn it. I asked him for information about his feelings, his interests, how he was doing. He rejected my attempts, routinely and often.

Why marry me, then? For the sex? It increasingly felt that way, like this God-ordained marriage of ours existed solely for the purpose of him avoiding sexual sin. Anytime I offered a touch of emotional connection, he would decline to discuss, but immediately follow it up by asking for sex. *This is how you can support me*, he said, reaching for my waist. Not with my mind, not with my words, not with my heart. Put in one emotional token, get one orgasm. A vending machine wife.

*Your body is not your own.*

✝

I knew that my body as a single woman in the church had been constantly under a microscope. It was naive to think that my body as a married woman wouldn't be, too.

There's a reason that "Christian Girl Autumn"* is a meme that has taken off in recent years, identifiable by sorority-style pictures of white women with fresh blowouts and modest but tight-fitting clothing: pale crew neck shirts and loose sweaters tucked into bright blue jeans, or, alternatively, long-sleeved, high-necked tunic dresses, all paired with knee-high camel-colored boots. Add a chunky knit infinity scarf for flavor.

No black. No jewel tones. No short hair. No visible tattoos or piercings. Just *beige beige beige*, neutral leathers, and good ol' American denim, ad infinitum. And blond hair, unnaturally-bleached-to-within-an-inch-of-its-life blond hair.

This is a religious aesthetic defined by its warm, neutral Instagram filter. A Christianity tethered to and born from America's long-standing project of white supremacy. The contemporary aesthetics of Christian Girl Autumn can't be bothered to obscure its commitments to the propagation of whiteness. A Christianity that creates a kind of purportedly inoffensive conformity, with its rusts

---

* David Mack, "The Women In The 'Christian Girl Autumn' Meme Want You To Know Something," *Buzzfeed*, August 13, 2019, https://www.buzzfeednews.com/article/davidmack/christian-girl-autumn-meme-caitlin-convington-emily-gemma.

and camels and ecrus and "live laugh love," that, in the age of social media, can be easily sold and consumed as wellness, as minimalism, as an aspirational middle-class lifestyle.

A casual sampling of one day I spent on #tradwife ("traditional wife"), #christianwomanhood, and #biblicalwomanhood Instagram in fall of 2021, where numerous posts insist that "the future is *not* female—it's family"; lists of "my jobs" as "wife, mother, and homemaker," with the definition of wife being "to submit to and to respect one's husband"; statements like "yoga pants are killing femininity" and "find a man worth submitting to" in the same account; "women should be *feminine* not *feminist*"; "make america godly again"; and, in compilation posts underneath the title slide "Ways to Honor Your Husband," reminders to never disagree with him in front of your children, lest they take your disagreement as permission to disobey the man of the house. "Women who demand respect are showing signs of toxic masculinity," reads another post. "I'd rather have his adoration than respect!" is a common affirmation.

You have to be willing to look *and* talk the part.

✛

There is an inconspicuous journal entry from the early days of our marriage. Between my sermon notes from Sunday, September 4 (when Kyle and I attended service at Hope Fellowship on Beech Street in Cambridge), and our Tuesday-night Bible study at the church plant we would eventually join, there is a small, fragmented paragraph detailing a dream:

> The night before I started grad school, I had two nightmares that tormented me—about snakes. I had frequent nightmares about

snakes when I was a child. The snake, tempting Eve to knowledge—I am attacked, surrounded, consumed by them—snakes inside me, needing to be cut out.

✛

Sex continued to be tedious. All the fan fiction I had read over the years praised the importance of foreplay, which, when I read about it, sounded alluring, but, when my husband was touching me, felt unappealing. I wanted sex over with as quickly as possible. *No, I'm not like other women*, I told him when he asked about foreplay, clearly having been given the same warnings I had been. *I don't need foreplay.* I bought copious amounts of lube to make up for it. I didn't want to cuddle after. I wanted to put clothes on and go back to my computer at our dining table, where an endless amount of work for my graduate program awaited me.

*Stay in bed with me*, he'd continue to ask, and I'd shrug off his advances. I'd already established the rules for cuddling on our wedding night, when I'd moved to my side of the bed, right at the edge, as far away from him as possible, as if I were trying to escape.

We had sex once a day on our honeymoon, and that week he regularly expressed disappointment that we didn't have more. This set the tone for our early married life—that no amount of sex was enough for him. To go three or four days without sex was to watch the slow storm of his upset come in. He would tell me that he was going to sin, and that it would be my fault. In this instance, "sin" is evangelical code for "masturbate"; while this may sound ridiculous to a secular audience, to evangelicals, masturbation is quite serious. Even worse if the masturbation would include fantasies about a woman who wasn't his wife. According to evangelical logic, his sin would be my fault, since he wanted to have sex with me, his wife, and I was the one denying him—and he, a man with uncontrollable sexual urges, would be driven to pursue them elsewhere, outside marriage. In Christianity, self-control is considered an essential "fruit of the spirit," a mark of spiritual maturity—and yet somehow men are not expected to have it over their own sex drive. But I didn't know what was normal. When he threatened to sin if we didn't have sex, imputing all his guilt and all the blame at my feet, I would climb into bed dutifully.

Almost all the sex I had in my marriage would fall in a category Melissa Febos, in *Girlhood*, defines as "empty consent."* My own mother's advice to me was to *never say no*, advice I made the mistake of sharing with my husband, which Kyle proceeded to use against me on multiple occasions with a snide *You should take your mother's advice*. Given that he had relatively adverse feelings about my mother, I knew there was only one piece of advice he was referring to.

My mother was well meaning, of course. If you don't technically say no, you can talk yourself into avoiding the psychological rupture of being raped by your own husband.

✛

The appearance of conformity—of seeming the subservient biblical wife—was, to me, a compromise as I tried to work the system from the inside.

But when you are a woman pretending to play the game within a system that explicitly, expressly requires your submission and

---

* Melissa Febos, *Girlhood* (New York: Bloomsbury, 2021), 222, 227–29.

obedience, one that is designed to discredit you and is working with government institutions to turn religious practices into law, to believe compromise is possible is to play with fire.

Compromise, at the most micro level of this game, is entirely dependent on the husband's whims. And woe to the evangelical woman whose husband promises her equality but changes his mind.

✝

School was respite. I knew how to be a good student, how to throw myself into class, how to bury my emotions about what was going on at home under an avalanche of academic focus. Keen to avoid my already-burgeoning marital discontent, I relished the amount of coursework that came with being a first-year doctoral student, and that it kept me on campus most days a week.

For the first time, I was no longer the smartest, or one of the smartest, in the room. I was a small fish in a big pond—I was excited and intimidated, both.

So when another first-year who awed the shit out of me, Melissa, asked, *Umm, do you feel like you know what you're doing? Because I really don't*, about a month into the program as we were walking back to the train one day after class, a flood of pressure left my body.

*Oh my God. You too?* I asked, feeling enormously relieved. *Also, what are you talking about, you are so smart! I feel like the least articulate person in the room.*

*I feel that way too!* she insisted, her voice rising with a giddy glee as she flung her long, dark hair over her shoulder.

We talked all the way back to Porter Square on the train, then ducked into a Dunkin' Donuts in order to keep talking.

*Wait, so you and your husband go to church?* Melissa asked, looking at me with a familiarity that I hadn't yet seen in any of my other grad school peers. She chuckled to herself. *I grew up super evangelical.*

*Are you serious?* I asked. *No one out here knows what that word fucking means.*

*Oh yeah, my childhood was weird. New Hampshire, you know. I went to Christian school and everything.*

Sitting there in our coats at a wire table outside the Dunks with iced pumpkin spice lattes in the early-October chill, I started bonding with a new friend who understood the nature of my marriage and the tension that I was holding between academia and my faith.

*How is it for you, still doing the church thing and being in grad school? I cannot imagine doing both,* she said.

*You don't go anymore?* I asked.

*Not really. I try to go to more liberal churches sometimes, but like, evangelical-evangelical?* She made a face. *I can't. I'm honestly amazed that you can.*

I was curious about what going to a more liberal church would be like, the faintest hint of envy creeping in, though at the time I couldn't have begun to tell you why.

☩

The first Halloween of my married life, I dressed up in a cerulean shirt dress, pantyhose, and black heels. I bought a feather duster that looked as though, if it were to come to life, it would transform into Fifi from *Beauty and the Beast*. A dash of lipstick, a string of pearls. For my first costume party as a wife, I dressed as June Cleaver, that iconic 1950s housewife. Satirizing who I didn't realize I had already become. What I naively didn't think was possible an educated woman like me could be.

✢

I think a lot now about how Joanna Gaines, when finishing a job, just wants to be alone in the houses at night—without her husband, without her children.[*]

✢

For years, I convinced myself that what I wanted and what God wanted were perfectly aligned. Well, marriage was difficult. Wifely submission: that was difficult. But then, a godly life wasn't supposed to be a happy or easy one. As the Bible says, "Narrow is the way, which leadeth unto life, and few there be that find it."[†] I had a faithful husband who was okay with my having a career. What were the odds? I could and did bury any doubt that arose.

But then, reality was punctured by the possibility of a baby.

About ten months into our marriage, I had that most classic and common of experiences: a pregnancy scare. It was a confluence of unfortunate events. We'd had sex and I'd forgotten to take my birth control for several days running. A tale as old as time.

The fear involved in an unplanned pregnancy is implied by the name we have for that experience—it's a "scare," not a gift. But what I did not expect was the urgent feeling, spilling out of some hitherto unopened Pandora's box, telling me that it wasn't only that I couldn't have a baby *now*—I couldn't have a baby with my husband *ever*. The hypothetical far-off family I had always been taught to expect was the stuff nightmares were made of. If I had

---

[*] *Fixer Upper*, season 1, episode 1, 2013. "Looking Old but Feeling New." discovery+ on Amazon Prime, 36:12. May 23. https://www.amazon.com/gp/video/detail/B00JXD 16SU/ref=atv_yv_hom_7_c_unkc_1_1

[†] Matthew 7:14 (KJV).

a baby with him, I would be tied to him for life, and the feelings that arose in me, sudden and vicious, informed me that this was, in fact, impossible.

Was it because I knew, as I walked to the CVS to get Plan B, that I could not have a baby during graduate school, and that I would have an abortion, and that I would not tell him, because he was firmly pro-life and would say this baby was his, which, sure, yes, technically it was, but it was *my* body and he . . . did not see my body as mine alone? Was it because that moment broke that reckoning open for me, all the times that he'd obtained sex when I didn't want it? I finally recognized that he did not respect my body or prioritize my needs above his own, as some interpretations of Ephesians 5 insisted that the husband do for the wife. It was barely conscious. It was my body, pushed to the brink after twenty-four years of evangelical ideology, as I stood outside the pharmacy, tossing back a pill and chasing it with Starbucks cold brew. My body, which I had promised to a man, to God, which I had believed was not my own, revolted with a flood of pure adrenaline, a rushing river as great as the Mississippi breaking through the dam I had spent decades carefully building.

My body, dredging up from the depths of me the desire that had settled at the bottom of my soul, untapped and unearthed for years, saying:

*You are your own. You are a temple, and you belong to no one.*

# 5. MARTYRS AND SUICIDE GIRLS

The wild beasts of the desert shall also meet with the wild beasts of the island, and the satyr shall cry to his fellow; the screech owl also shall rest there and find for herself a place of rest.

—Isaiah 34:14 (KJV)

MY SISTER, JO, HAS ALWAYS BEEN ABLE TO TALK ME INTO THINGS I WOULDN'T do otherwise, like get matching tattoos of our initials when she came out to visit us in Boston that summer, the summer I took Plan B, the summer the fantasy marriage I had created started to fall apart. *Maybe we don't tell your husband*, she said, always seeing the cracks in me that I thought I'd kept hidden. She was in undergrad, partying heavily, with no time for the faith of our youth. But when it came to the nature of relationships with men, she had more insight than me.

We went to Redemption Tattoo on Massachusetts Avenue, where a kind-eyed wisp of a man tattooed JK on my foot and her shoulder. I drew the letters a dozen times before we got the lettering just right. I ignored the fact that my initials were legally three letters, that I was shunning my married name, that asserting JK alone, in my own handwriting no less, was a vehement act of defiance.

That small tattoo was the first inch toward reclaiming my own integrity, the kind that Alan Moore once wrote sells for so little. The church teaches that two become one, that marriage is the death of individuals and the birth of a new union. What is the self, then, within an evangelical marriage? A disappearance, an invisible woman.

My desires were unnamable, unspeakable. That summer, I started wrapping myself in leather jackets and soling my feet in cowboy boots, a cocoon in which to shed and grow a new skin.

✢

The last time we had sex, if that's what you can call it, I initiated. We had been having fights for a while, so reaching out to him was a bid for reconciliation. I knew he craved touch like water—not only sex, although he wanted that too. "Skin hunger" would be the term for what he had, and I felt guilty, so guilty for depriving him.

So I asked for sex as an attempt to repair. To show him that I was in this, still trying, even if my own heart and mind felt like a war zone. Even if I said awful, inexcusable, unforgivable things to him during our arguments, such as that I wished he'd just hit me already. This was me apologizing. This was me staying. Trying to convince him. Trying to convince myself, really, even if I had no idea what I was thinking or feeling half the time.

✢

Ask pretty much any woman I have ever slept with—I like rough sex. I like sex when it's pure fucking. I like being tied up and held down and choked out.

But I only like it when I ask for it.

✢

Lilith was cast out of the Garden for a lack of sexual submissiveness, Jewish legend tells us. The first woman created by Yahweh, by Jehovah God, was born of dust, like Adam—a signal of her equality that a misogynist creator would rectify with Eve the second time around.

The stories say that Lilith's sin was in wanting to be on top, but I sometimes wonder if she was exiled from Paradise for saying no.

One thing is sure: she is a woman of myth who prefers the eternal wilderness to marital submission, the solitude of a cave to sharing a man's bed—or obeying a god who would order her to do so, no matter that he was her maker.

✢

This is what I remember about that night:

I know that my face was shoved in a pillow.

I know that I said *you're hurting me*—in a bad way. In a *stop* way.

I know that he did not stop.

At the time, I figured that it must be hard to stop during sex. I did not have any experience with sex outside of him.

Now I am horrified that anyone could hear someone they are being intimate with express pain and not be interested in adjusting to prioritize that person's pleasure. To not care when that person says *that hurts*.

The lack of empathy.

The lack of care.

He did not stop.

His wife was in pain that he was causing, but, if a husband feels good inside his wife, it isn't sin. Can't be.

When he was done, he looked at me in a way I can only describe as sheepish, an embarrassment so mild that it seemed to say *Oh well* rather than *Oh fuck*.

I got out of bed as fast as I could. Fled to the bathroom. Turned the water in my shower up so high it was painful, scalding, turning my skin a vicious red. Stayed in there for I can't remember how long, not wanting to face him.

This is why my mother advised me to *never say no*—because once you say no to your husband, you find out who he really is.

+

I got saved when I was four and a half years old. I don't remember saying the prayer, but I can imagine the scene, because my mother wrote my sister and me poems to commemorate the dates of our salvation. Mine starts, "On August 20, 1992, I knelt by my bed / on a carpet of blue." My mother's journal, which expands on the evening, affirms many things—that I was precocious, for example, and (sort of) initiated my conversion experience by asking my mother to pray with me. For months, I had been listening to a tape called *Psalty's Salvation Celebration*, which tells children about heaven and God's plan of salvation. One day, I approached my mother and told her that I was ready to invite Jesus into my heart. My mother was ecstatic, as if the content she'd supplied for my tape player had nothing to do with it.

But I tend to prioritize conversion experiences I had when I was older—moments when I actively claimed faith for myself. At a middle school youth group event held in a loft in our small northern Wisconsin town, I cried quietly in the back, moved by the music from the rock band, by the youth pastor's fervent sermon on our need to understand how Christ would have hung on that cross even if it was for just one of us. I was twelve, and didn't feel worth it: *Hanging on that cross if it was only me, Lord?* A youth leader—a faceless, nameless woman—came over to pray with me through my tears. I left the building renewed in my devotion, in my belief in my need for Jesus, but also in my love for him. I continued to have similar moments of faith renewal throughout my teenage years and early twenties, where I came back to this core belief: that Jesus alone could save me from my own depravity and give me the grace I needed to get through each day.

But that first moment was the one that my mother has always considered to be the most significant, perhaps because it was the one she was a part of, the one she guided me through. Notably, according to my mother's journal, my father was also present, a detail she never includes in the actual retelling of my childhood conversion.

Jeanna's father was with us as we prayed. He sat quietly taking it all in, watching his 4 1/2 year old daughter commit herself to the Lord (a step he has yet to take)—and I can't help but meditate on Isaiah 11:6 . . . "and a little child shall lead them."

✛

Just as my mother hoped my faith would influence my then-apathetically Catholic father toward born-again evangelical devotion, the church has utilized its youth as soldiers for the cause for decades. "Train up a child in the way he should go," Proverbs 22:6 (KJV) says, a verse devoted parents take to heart. Christian homeschooling is a widespread movement in part driven by a mistrust of secular public school education, and in part by a desire to create children who will be "warriors" for the cause.

But warriors for a cause are only one step away from martyrdom. In its earliest days, Christianity was accurately identified as a death cult—a religion whose teachings revolved around death and eternal life, the willingness to die for one's faith a hallmark of its believers. Over the centuries, not much about this central ethos has changed, save the political power the church has acquired, which has made the frequency and necessity of martyrs rare, although the persecution complex remains central to the faith.

The white American church, arguably an even stronger nexus of Christian power than the Vatican, hasn't had a steady stream of martyrs on its own soil in a long time. (That's what missionaries are for.) Not the kind who can rally a nation to God, anyway. But when Rachel Scott, a seventeen-year-old white teenage girl at Columbine High School, allegedly answered yes in response to the shooters' asking, "Are you a Christian?" at the first major mass school shooting, in 1999, and was subsequently the first of twelve students to be murdered, evangelicals found a new rallying point. My elementary school was dismissed early that day; I left my fifth-grade class and linked hands with my sister, then a second grader, entirely unaware of what had happened as we walked to the car where Mom was waiting to pick us up, her eyes bloodshot. For weeks, it was *the* subject of sermons at church, the topic on Christian radio in Mom's car, the dominant national news story on our television.

Scott was memorialized as a modern-day martyr, called a "warrior" during her CNN-televised funeral by Pastor Bruce Porter, who called on the youth that were present to pick up the "torch" Scott carried, "a torch that was stained by the blood of the martyrs from the very first day of the Church's existence in the world nearly 2,000 years ago."[*] Cassie Bernall, an evangelical junior who had been murdered in the school library, was also instantly labeled a martyr. But when her church's pastor, Reverend George Kirsten, took to the pulpit after the shooting, he looked to the future rather than the past. Invoking the language of spiritual warfare, he likened Bernall to the martyrs in the Book of Revelation. "How long? How long will it be until my blood is avenged?" the reverend asked in anguish.[†]

Martyrs are often retroactively made. Scott and Bernall were clearly religiously devout teenagers, but the narrative that their horrific murders were directly caused by their faith has been strongly disputed by the evidence in the years following Columbine. There is no conclusive eyewitness testimony to the now-famous conversations and confessions of faith that allegedly occurred with both girls.[‡] But evangelicalism refuses to acknowledge any evidence that would cast doubt on the idea that the girls died explicitly because they believed in Jesus Christ.[§]

---

[*] Justin Watson, *The Martyrs of Columbine: Faith and the Politics of Tragedy* (New York: Palgrave, 2002), 52.

[†] Dave Cullen, *Columbine* (New York: Grand Central, 2009), 133.

[‡] Larkin, 48. See also Dan Luzadder and Katie Kerwin McCrimmon, "Accounts Differ on Question to Bernall: Columbine Shooting Victim May Not Have Been Asked Whether She Believed in God," *Rocky Mountain News*, September 24, 1999.

[§] Craig Scott, Rachel's brother, overheard a confession of faith in the library, which he initially attributed to Cassie Bernall. This has long since been corrected; the exchange was between the gunmen and high school senior Valeen Schnurr. However, Schnurr survived her gunshot wounds and was also Catholic, two facts that did not fit with the martyr myth evangelicals across the country immediately started spinning out (Cullen, 238–39).

The Rachel Scott and Cassie Bernall stories have long since become hagiography, the kind of idealized biography that can be used to proselytize and spread propaganda. Both girls' parents wrote books: Cassie's mom authored a book on her faith titled *She Said Yes*, which was reprinted by Simon & Schuster in 2000, and Rachel's parents published her journals and a biography entitled *Rachel's Tears*, published in 2000 by Thomas Nelson, the largest Christian publisher in the United States. Pastor Bruce Porter himself wrote a book inspired by Columbine called *The Martyr's Torch*. The cohesion of the girls' stories, disseminated so strongly across multiple media, became the source for talking points at youth groups around the country, as white evangelical youth leaders, parents, and pastors began to demand, *If you were confronted by a gunman in a school shooting who asked you if you were a Christian, would you be willing to die for your faith?* I cannot begin to tell you how many times I was asked this question in group settings—usually in rooms where everyone was white, where the odds of any of us actually encountering someone with a gun who was profiling us for any reason were nil to none. The strength of this foundational mythology of these girl martyrs from the first nationally recognized mass school shooting has persisted decades after their death; in 2016, a feature film called *I'm Not Ashamed* was released about Rachel Scott's faith and life, with an accompanying devotional tie-in.

For the price of financial backing from the NRA that keeps conservative evangelical Christians in power, politicians and voters are willing to sacrifice their own children to gun violence—at least they will become martyrs who can continue to rally the church.

---

* Immediately after the shooting, contemporary Christian artists like Michael W. Smith and Flyleaf recorded songs named after or even featuring sampled audio from Cassie Bernall.

Unregulated gun culture has created a new kind of martyr myth, one uniquely tailored for the rise of religious extremism in the twenty-first century: teenagers purportedly dying for their faith in school shootings, and also dying for their parents' so-called right to have automatic weapons, as per the Second Amendment.

✛

Christianity's oldest test is martyrdom: dying for or because of one's faith, or being targeted for daring to practice one's faith in public. But it is necessary to point out the obvious: white American evangelicals are not the most persecuted demographic in this country, no matter what their persecution complex would have them believe.

Black churches have a long history of being actively targeted by white supremacists—who are, more often than not, Christians—in this country. This antipathy and racist desire to control how Black Americans practice their faith goes back to the forcible ban on enslaved Africans practicing their own religious and spiritual beliefs. Indoctrinating them with Christianity was a useful tool for oppression, though it was deemed illegal to teach an enslaved person to read the Bible, or to read at all.

The history of one Black church shows how little has changed over the course of American history: Mother Emmanuel African Methodist Episcopal in Charleston, South Carolina, the oldest AME church in the Deep South, was burned to the ground in 1822 and then famously suffered a mass shooting in 2015, with nine congregants murdered by a white supremacist at a Bible study.

Black Christians murdered in these attacks have far more of a claim on the title of martyr in the United States of America than any white evangelical. They are killed in the house of God, their right to worship explicitly violated, their most faithful and their children targeted at Bible studies, while worshipping, when praying at Sunday service. And still, the survivors rebuild and continue to practice out loud and in public. When people talk about Christian martyrs, they should be speaking of Black Christians and their faithfulness and fortitude in the face of active oppression in every part of their lives, including their faith.

But the history of the Black church's persecution is too often ignored by mainstream denominations and white Christians and politicians in general. The persecution of the Black church in this country from past to present, and the refusal to acknowledge their martyrs, is part of the political agenda of evangelical white fascists, who continue to weaponize their faith in order to retain political power in the face of perceived threats to white supremacy.

I was a bad Christian. I did not feel "ready to go" at any time. Growing up at church, I listened as the Cassie Bernalls and Rachel Scotts of the world were lifted up, canonized in death. My mother and pastors talked about how "to live is Christ, and to die is gain."*

But I wanted to live. I did not long for heaven; I feared it. I had too much to do *here*. There was one sin I felt particular guilt for, sitting there as youth pastors railed about being willing to lay it all down for Christ: ambition. I really, really wanted to leave home, graduate from college, and publish a book before I died.

I grew up in a household where my mother was constantly saying she was *ready to go* whenever Jesus called her, a reminder that my

---

* Philippians 1:21 (NIV).

own primary caregiver was ready for death and seemed to desire it. My mom talked about heaven and its mansions and golden streets, about the jewels in her crown, about the loved ones she couldn't wait to be reunited with, about its lack of pain and worldly suffering. She did Bible studies on the Book of Revelation, and the Left Behind books, a *New York Times*-bestselling series that fictionalized the biblical End Times, were always prominent on our shelves.

Long-term planning is not necessarily conducive to Christlikeness—at least, not for working-class subjects who want to be Christlike. Why cling to your meager earthly possessions, or try to secure a legacy for your children, if a readiness to die for one's faith is the ultimate sign of devotion? If we're preparing for an imminent rapture? In this way, the evangelical fixation on "being *in* the world but not *of* it"* also facilitates the maintenance of the class system, of keeping people in their place not only because it's God's will, but because there's no reason to bother with accumulation if your *real* place is in heaven.

My mother is a Pisces. What seemed like her death wish—her mantra of *any time, Lord*—in hindsight strikes me as a profound disengagement with life in favor of the fantastic, the apocalyptic, and the beyond. Of course, my mother had also been a traumatized child raised in a home where domestic abuse and alcoholism were ever present, where the normalized level of violence was so high that, when my sister and I fought, she would tell us that we clearly loved each other because we weren't chasing each other around the house trying to stab each other with steak knives, which she had done to her sisters.

My mother's focus on the End Times at the expense of real-world

---

* A Christian phrase inspired by John 17:14–19.

accumulation wasn't just an affinity for Puritanical asceticism, but also a form of dissociation from the debilitating trauma of her daily life, of the harsh, unrelenting reality of our working-class living conditions. Through her, I learned that faith was the only way to find *something more*—a *something more* that only came after death.

✢

I did not want to be a martyr to my marriage.

And yet, I kept coming back to one fact: I had not only promised Kyle *till death do us part.* I had promised *God.* I took that vow seriously. Jesus doesn't say anything about being queer, but he says plenty about getting divorced—all of it quite damning. These are verses the many contemporary American evangelical churches, with so many divorced congregants, have conveniently decided to elide in their Sunday-morning messages. For those of us who interpreted the Bible literally and inerrantly, divorce was unacceptable.

If I divorced my husband, what was that saying about my relationship with God? That there was something in my life that Jesus couldn't fix? It felt better for me to die within my marriage than to try to leave it and discover if I could have a relationship with Jesus outside of those promises we'd made to each other during our wedding, till death do us part. The New Testament has plenty to say about people who refute the idea that Jesus is not enough. They're blasphemers of the Holy Spirit, and for Protestants, blasphemy is the one unforgivable sin. The one that will condemn you straight to hell.

*You know this is the twenty-first century,* a grad school friend told me as we walked through Davis Square on our way to Diesel Café one night, the Somerville air cold and crisp. *You* can *leave him.*

I fantasized about death, which seemed an easier end to my current predicament. I hoped my husband would die, or that he would leave me—that I could provoke him into leaving me. *A dead wife is better than a bad wife* was a phrase that cycled through my head, over and over, on repeat.

Walking into the ocean while I still had a modicum of faith to my name felt like a better option. I was in Boston, after all. The ocean was right there.

To stay in my marriage, I realized, would be to die, which would be to ensure a kind of martyrdom. Choosing to not save yourself when there is a clear way out is a kind of suicide, which Catholics may regard as a mortal sin, but which Protestants do not. Better to choose a death while in a marriage that is God-honoring than to turn away from him and become a blasphemer.

Edna Pontellier, the heroine of Kate Chopin's *The Awakening*, walks into the Gulf of Mexico, away from her family, from her life, at the book's end. She has tried to leave her husband, too—has left him, in fact. Has carved out a new life for herself. But the tendrils of sadness and ache persist. Leaving is not enough. In the sea, you are free from the pain of trying to reconcile your psyche with the reality of daily crisis.

I was drifting in a liminal space between life and death: or, rather, between desire and lack. Between freedom, and having my back against a wall.

The ocean always has purpose. The ocean can always carry you.

✛

We were eating dinner one night, sitting across the table from each other in a perfunctory performance of domesticity, the silence punctuated by forks scraping across a cheap dinnerware set we'd registered for at Bed Bath & Beyond. Words started tumbling out of my mouth, driven by anxiety, before I knew I was speaking.

What was I trying to say? That I needed time and space to figure out what I was feeling, what I desired? That I loved him, that I wanted to be with him—say the thing and you'll make it so—but that I also needed to figure out who I was as a person, as an individual?

He looked me dead in the eye, his mouth set in a straight line, and said, *You're not an individual. You're my wife.*

I froze. Fight or flight is the body's response to danger, some experts say, but there's another option—to freeze. To be still and unmoving, to try to blend and camouflage. But there is no camouflaging when the bear is sitting across from you, eating a dinner you've prepared for him.

Tears slipped down my face. I hated that I wept, that he could hurt me. That I had believed him years ago when he told me he loved my ambition, loved my difference from him, loved my independence. I was embarrassed, foolish for ever thinking a man like him would support a woman like me. I especially hated that a part of me still cared. Was it my fault for driving him back to the conservatism of his father and his youth?

Theologically, I understood what he was saying—that I was married to him, that I didn't get to operate like a single person, that as his wife who had promised to love him I had to consider him and his needs. That was fair. But there was a veiled threat in how he said "*my* wife" that reeked of possessiveness.

Because the other way to read *you're not an individual* is by its simile: *You're not a person. You're my wife.* A thing whose labor can be owned and exploited accordingly.

The historical erasure of a woman's legal personhood upon marriage is so well documented that it is practically rote to do so here. Part of the reason the evangelical context of "two become one" was revolting to me was because I was too aware of how white women had been historically subsumed under their husband's ownership, their husband's name, their husband's vote, their husband's property. It was exponentially worse if that woman was Black, Indigenous, undocumented, enslaved, indentured, or nonwhite in the United States.

But in a relationship where my husband had promised me a partnership of equals, to have him now say, cold and with utter confidence: *You are not an individual. You are my wife.*

Something snapped inside me, a loosening of the bonds.

✢

"Submission" is a word I still hate, no matter its context. "Surrender," too. The words are attuned too specifically to marriage. When I hear them, I feel like someone is reciting keywords to me in a lab, trying to activate the Winter Soldier–Stepford Wife within in order to reset my programming, those deeply ingrained neural pathways I've spent nearly a decade desperately trying to destroy.

I wonder if coding that goes that deep can ever be fully rewritten. It is conscious work every day to build my own ladder out of the pit that is the patriarchy-church. Some days, I feel like I have finally found the high ground. Other days, I wonder if I can ever truly be free.

✢

I walked miles and miles around Cambridge and Somerville in the weeks following that argument, hoping my body would figure out what to do if I just kept moving. I wanted to wear myself out from the heart-pounding anxiety that started up like the Daytona 500 every morning and didn't fucking stop. I wanted to not feel. I wanted to forget. The music I blasted through my headphones told me what I was feeling anyway. Music like Emmylou Harris's "Red Dirt Girl," which I listened to every day. In the song, the narrator talks about her childhood best friend, a girl named Lillian, who is the titular red dirt girl with big dreams. It's a folk song, a story song. Only one verse is sung in Lillian's voice, from her perspective, straining against the bonds of small-town living before life has had its way with her: "One of these days I'm gonna swing my hammer down. . . . /I'm gonna make a joyful sound." But Lillian ends up married to a man she doesn't love, with too many kids and a pill habit she can't kick—her dreams in the dust. The song ends with her suicide, at the tender age of twenty-seven.

In "Red Dirt Girl," I heard my story and my mother's story and my grandmother's story, saw so many women I went to school with back in Iowa and Wisconsin who were stuck in that loop. Lillian's song is the story of every small-town girl who did not get out, and even of small-town girls like me who got out physically but managed to trap ourselves in matrimony, in the church, in structures where we couldn't breathe.

These women—Edna Pontellier, Lillian—flirt with the edge, understanding themselves by struggling against the veil, by sometimes choosing to stop fighting against impossible circumstances, circumstances that are not destructive to their physical bodies, but to their souls, to their *selves*. To them, suicide isn't really death. They had been dead long before.

✛

In his letter to the Philippians, the Apostle Paul writes, "For to me, to live is Christ and to die is gain. If I am to go on living in the body, this will mean fruitful labor for me. Yet what shall I choose? I do not know! I am torn between the two: I desire to depart and be with Christ, which is better by far; but it is more necessary for you that I remain in the body."*

Within modern evangelicalism, this kind of Pauline eagerness for eternal life tends to manifest less as an explicit desire for death and more as a generalized fixation on the End Times and the "perfect" world that Christ purportedly promises upon his return to earth. After all, it's difficult to build long-term political movements based on leaving this world. Easier to establish your own ideal version of it in the here and now, one where everyone you hate has been consigned to hell.

But there is a contemporary political danger to the evangelical End Times fixation—most notably, climate change denial. It's not even so much that evangelicals don't believe in the science (although courtesy of Fox News, they may well not), but rather that the science of climate change *doesn't matter*, because they believe the Second Coming of Jesus is imminent, and that he will restore this sinful, fallen world to its heavenly intentioned glory. My entire life, my mother has fervently believed that there is a fifty-fifty chance that she will either die a physical death *or* be raptured in the Second Coming. (It must be noted that my mother is also a committed environmentalist and registered Democrat who believes that God's children are to steward and care for the earth *until* such a time as the apocalypse occurs. People are complicated.)

Within this framework, anyone who is actually worried about

---

* Philippians 1:21–24 (NIV).

climate change and what it holds for future generations is suspect, because why would you worry about the environment when Jesus is returning imminently? For right-wing evangelicals, their focus is not on the dying, sinful, fallen earth, but rather, on social issues like abortion and LGBTQ+ rights that, in their view, contribute to the increased spread of sin. Extrapolated out to other understandings of the world through the lenses of racism, misogyny, and homophobia (to name a few), this increasingly millenarian orientation may contribute to more empathetic evangelicals being unmotivated to do *any* work to better society. If Jesus is coming back, and he's gonna save us all and reset the world, why even try?

✞

The weeks around Christmas are usually my favorite time of year. In part, it's because I was born on the winter solstice. In part, it's because of my having grown up in the North—I love snow. But mostly, it's because the end of December feels like the New Year to me, a new beginning, an opportunity to reflect in the deepest dark.

However, the Christmas after Kyle's and my argument did not feel merry or bright, even though my sister had flown out to Boston to spend it with us. I hadn't shared any of my feelings with Jo before she arrived, hadn't told her any updates about my marriage since our August tattoos, but it was as though she had an inkling that something was wrong. We had joked about our "sister psychic connection" for years, but sometimes it was uncannily helpful. When she arrived, my feelings poured out of me, in that way that feelings do with the women in your life who you really trust.

Jo and I tried to go through the motions, cooking what is, for our family, a traditional Christmas Eve meal of tourtière pie. Kyle skipped out and went to our pastors' house instead. When he came home the night of the twenty-fourth, he agreed to open presents in the living room, just him and me, awkwardly exiling my sister to our bedroom, the only room in our apartment aside from the bathroom with a door that shut. I can't remember what I bought him. Our first Christmas, I had gotten him a nice winter coat. He had bought me a charm for a charm bracelet. This time around, I knew not to have expectations.

His gift for me for our final Christmas was a pink vibrator. *I hope we can use it together soon*, he said. This was his solution to the events of the previous month—to that last time. A sex toy I hadn't asked for and didn't want. A category of sex toy I didn't even *use*, and surely wouldn't use with a man who had done what he had done to me.

I didn't say anything, just got up off the floor, stepping over the wrapping paper, and went back into the bedroom where my sister was waiting. I crawled into bed with Jo, like we had when we were children sharing a room, and tried to breathe, anxious at hearing Kyle bang about noisily in the living room. The front door slammed—him leaving, presumably to go crash with our pastors.

*I don't think I can do this anymore*, I said, turning on my side to face my sister, whose expression was full of concern.

*Do what?* she asked lovingly.

*This.* I gestured at my body. *You know, just, like, this. With him. Living.*

She was quiet, but reached for my hand and held it tight.

*I love you*, she said.

I started crying. *I feel like Jesus has left me.*

Jo's grip tightened. *Jeanna, look at me. Look at me.*

I did.

*I will never leave you*, she said.

＋

I had not confessed my *better a dead wife than a bad wife* thoughts to anyone but my sister. I didn't even tell my therapist, who I started seeing shortly after that Christmas. During our first intake session, she asked me the question all therapists ask during intake, *Have you ever had suicidal thoughts?* and I said no. Which was a lie.

The thing was, I didn't make a concrete plan to kill myself. But the constancy of thoughts that began to circulate in my mind was enough to frighten me, enough to convince me to seek out a therapist in the first place, enough to make me begin to consider that divorce might be preferable to ending my life.

Intellectually, I knew that I did not *actually* want to die. But my life without Jesus, without Christianity, would be meaningless. How would I live on the other side of that chasm? I was terrified of walking away from everything I knew to be true. Who would I become without it?

*I think I'm suicidal,* I said to Kyle one night, when we were both sitting silently, reading quietly on opposite sides of the couch. In retrospect, I probably could have introduced the topic more gently, could have warmed up to it rather than dropping it like a bomb out of nowhere.

*No, you're not,* he said. *I would know if you were, and you're not.*

I shrank back into myself at his denial. What I said was frightening, to be sure. It must be frightening to hear someone you love say that she thinks life is not worth living. I understood that fear even as I pleaded with him to hear me.

The next day, after conferring with our pastors, he told me to never threaten him like that again.

✝

One day, when I'm at the Museum of Fine Arts in Boston, distracting myself from my failing marriage, I come face-to-face with Kiki Smith's *Lilith* (1994), a bronze sculpture depicting the purportedly demonic first wife of Adam. The woman who was cast out of the Garden, who cavorts with devils, who cannot be killed. Smith's Lilith is crouching, naked, perched upside down on the wall. Her eyes are a piercing blue and can only be described as ferocious. She is wild, feral, frightening to some.

To me, in that moment, she looks like possibility.

✝

Kyle wanted to take me to my doctor, because my disobedience had reached a point that, to him, indicated that I was sick. *You've changed,* he said. *You're not the woman I married. You're different. He'll fix you.*

He tried to get our four parents on board for whatever he was planning. Somehow, it had to involve my doctor; because I refused to go, no matter how much he pressured me, the plan fell apart. Also, my mom was unwilling to go along.

I've asked my parents in the years following what, exactly, Kyle's goal had been. *I don't even know if he knew,* my mom has said, although her memory of my husband's phone calls has dimmed over the years. *He wanted all of us supporting him, to get you to go to the doctor.* I don't know if, in mustering familial and medical support, my husband had been planning a simple intervention, or if he wanted to pursue something more extreme, such as an involuntary committal to a psychiatric ward.

Kyle had been particularly insistent to me, on multiple occasions, that I stop taking my migraine medication. He had fixated on the daily preventative I took to mitigate my chronic migraines (100 milligrams of Topamax, an antiseizure medication often prescribed off-label for migraine patients) as the cause of my behavior. Topamax can cause a number of side effects when one first starts taking it, but to the best of my knowledge, a sudden onset of queerness is not one of them. By the time he wanted to haul me into my own doctor for questioning, I'd been taking it for nearly a year.

Kyle was desperate.

He lived in a world where men were in charge, where our pastors and his father (also a pastor) were always on his side, and he clearly thought the visit would be to his advantage. For a time, I actually entertained the notion of going in to my doctor simply to disabuse him of it. To see my doctor's face when my husband explained why we were there.

On my first visit to my doctor, a man, I had a migraine so severe that I asked Kyle to accompany me, lest I pass out on the way there. Once we arrived, he accompanied me into the doctor's office when my name was called rather than remain in the sun-lit waiting room, which I didn't take note of at the time, because my head felt like someone was driving an icicle into my eye. He answered my doctor's questions both with and for me; I was in so much acute pain that I barely noticed until my doctor asked my husband to step outside and, after closing the door, gently, quietly asked me if I felt safe at home.

*Of course*, I said automatically, knowing exactly what he was asking and feeling caught off guard by the question. He gave me a long look, and we moved on. Over the course of that visit, he would get me started on my first-ever daily preventative for migraines. Shortly after, when I came in for a follow-up by myself, he would be the first professional in my medical history to clearly identify symptoms of depression and begin a conversation with me about it. I trusted that doctor implicitly. He took good care of me for five years, and it all started with him identifying a power dynamic in my marriage that even I had not noticed.

It is jarring that somewhere there is a file with my name on it in which I have been screened by my PCP for domestic abuse. To be clear: Kyle never hit me. He wasn't the violent, angry type. He didn't have substance-abuse issues. His temperament couldn't have been more different from that of my father. That was his appeal.

But I was so busy watching for symptoms that resembled my own father's behavior that I overlooked subtler flags that all was not well. Within evangelicalism, the "headship" and authority that husbands "naturally" assert over wives in the church often pings as abuse to people outside that system. It should make you question the system. The natural and automatic assertion of authority over the wife's body, as if it were your own, following her into such purportedly innocuous private places as her doctor's appointment, a place the evangelical husband perceives himself to clearly be a welcome arbiter—this is the unthinking reality, the result, of the ideology of male headship.

These days, I say I left my marriage because I was gay. This both is and is not true; it is, rather, a simplistic explanation that shuts down the person raising the question. These days, I don't disclose even to the closest friends I've made in the years since what the nature of my relationship with my husband was really like.

I did not wholly understand what I wanted then, but I did begin to appreciate the gravity of the threat of complete sublimation that lay before me if I stayed.

In "The Yellow Wallpaper," Charlotte Perkins Gilman's seminal 1892 short story, a woman who is married to a purportedly well-respected physician and is likely suffering from postpartum depression and psychosis is shut up in a house, away from loved ones and her own children, discouraged from all activity. Deprived of social company and intellectual stimulation, her singular source of entertainment is the hideous, titular yellow wallpaper. She begins seeing a woman—then, many women—trapped in the wall.

Depending on how you interpret the story, she comes to believe that she *is* the woman who is trapped in the wall. "I've got out at last," she says, "in spite of you . . . And I've pulled off most of the paper, so you can't put me back!"

*You can't put me back.*

It is a story of confinement and of escape. Not just of the internal mechanisms of self-regulation, but of the external mechanisms of patriarchy; of the dangers pressing so heavily on your life, enforced by all the people in your orbit, that they come to entirely define your reality.

I dyed my hair red, I screeched like an owl, I wandered in the wilderness until I created myself anew.

Back home, back at church, among my college friends and the folks who had known me—known *him*—to them, I became a Lilith, a terror, a nightmare, a demon wife: a woman possessed of herself, bereft of God and country, lost to all hope; a woman who had fled righteousness, whose example must be kept from your children and most especially your daughters. Hang charms around their necks and pray over them before they go to sleep lest their dreams take them to some faraway place where they, too, are inspired to flee the confines of the cross, where a strange redheaded woman, beautiful of face but snake of body, lures them away from the light of God and toward the shadows of themselves.

# 6. F/F

TAGS: author feels, angst, unresolved sexual tension, unrequited love, pining, just so much pining, one shot, jealousy, everyone has issues, gaslighting that is actually gaslighting, alcohol use, complicated relationship, you know how sometimes you think you're straight and then oops you're not, the butch/femme dynamics here are . . . problematic, religious themes, first kiss, emotional hurt/comfort, implied/referenced suicidal ideation, fake/pretend relationship, denial of feelings, the author regrets everything, the author regrets nothing

MY FIRST WEEK IN MY PHD PROGRAM, THIS IS ALL I HEAR, FROM ANYONE, EV-eryone: other graduate students, professors, administrators. *You have to meet Tony, you have to meet Tony, you have to meet Tony.* Everyone loves her, loves talking about her. To me, she is a ghost, an idea, an ephemeral thing; she has just taken her comps (comprehensive exams) that first week, and she's wiped, she's teaching some class on queer literature, she is always anywhere but where people are whispering her name in my ear, telling me about how we're both the same kind of small-town Midwestern and how because of this, we are bound to be good friends.

I don't meet her until two weeks into the semester. I'm standing in a doorway to an admin's office, when, as if summoned from the ether, Tony appears. Leather jacket, flannel, cowboy boots, jeans, Monroe piercing, big square black sunglasses that she takes off casually and, with a smirk that barely twitches into a smile, introduces herself. The tall butch of my dreams, though I don't know it at the time. Her long bleached hair is styled up into a loose mohawk, the sides of her head freshly buzzed; she has the kind of magnetic presence that pulls you in like a tractor beam in the dark.

To me, her Missouri drawl has the holiness and familiarity of church bells.

*Everyone has been telling me about the new girl from Iowa,* she says. *How are you holding up?*

*I'm Jeanna,* I say, her accent eliciting my own oft-suppressed nasally vowels of the northern Great Lakes states interlaced with my own barely detectable Plains drawl—inflections that, when I first moved to Wisconsin from Iowa, had my peers asking me what part of the South I was from.

She gives me a smile then, a real smile, and we lean in toward each other, each of our backs against a side of the slender doorframe, a tether of conversation strung between us, strengthening with intensity as we rapid-fire biography our way through the perfunctory first minutes of small talk, locking the others in the room out with each breath, the kind of spark that first lights when your energy hurtles toward another person and is reciprocated in kind, a boomerang rebounding back and forth between you. Or something sharper. Ulay and Marina Abramović's *Rest Energy,* the two of them leaning away from each other to create the tension to string a bow taut between them, the arrow pointed directly at her heart.

Before I know it, she's asking me, *What days are you on campus?* and *Do you want to get coffee tomorrow?* and something inside me unravels with what I, at the time, identify as the excitement of making a new friend.

In *Rest Energy*, the arrow is real.

✛

It is strange, to know that someone played a profound, defining role in your life when you were barely a blip in theirs.

✛

I didn't start wearing cowboy boots or reading comics till I met Tony. Didn't think I could write about fairy tales and Disney in grad school, let alone at conferences, until she took me seriously, ranting into the wee hours about academic fussiness and how I shouldn't let the faculty stop me from doing what I was passionate about. Didn't smoke until after her, when I missed her so bad that putting a Marlboro in my mouth felt like the only way to sate my longing. There are pieces of me that formed in direct response to her, to try to connect with her, in an attempt to get a reaction out of her and then just—stuck.

✛

She bought me my first comic, the inaugural issue of *The Fearless Defenders*, at Comicazi in Davis Square. We thought I was straight, then, even though I was starting to write fan fiction about women who could never be together and lost my mind over the image of Valkyrie kissing Dr. Annabelle Riggs.

I started writing femmeslash because she bet me a dollar that I couldn't.

✛

Friendship between women, between queers, is a category of relationship that has been historically dismissed in a society that has no utility for it, that cannot name what, precisely, the friendship "produces." The nuclear family produces stable citizens. Heterosexual marriage produces *more* citizens. Friendship between men, within white supremacist capitalism, can produce more businesses, the exchange of capital.

Friendship between women produces . . . what, exactly? Friendship between women is supposed to take a back seat when a woman marries, once a man becomes her priority.

Aristotle said that friends hold up a mirror to each other; given that he called women a "deform[ed]" copy of men, he likely wasn't thinking of us when he said this.[*]

✛

She becomes home, is home. I could live in her mouth, her wide lips, which exhale her slow drawl, cigarette smoke, late-night lectures on Foucault, and questions like, *My parents are in town, do*

---

[*] Aristotle and A. L. Peck. *Generation of Animals* (London: William Heinemann, 1943), Book 2, 737a.

*you want to come over for dinner with them?* and *You know I will always come get you, right?*

I am just her friend. This is clear by the number of times she calls me "dude," by the number of men and women she fucks, by the number of men and women she talks about fucking. I am every straight girl who is realizing that she's not so straight, who is maybe gay and maybe bi and maybe isn't sure, who is maybe leaving her husband, who is definitely depressed.

In an alternate universe, I go to a women's college instead of a coed one for undergrad and figure out my queerness a lot faster. There is no Kyle. Leaving God behind is one of the most painful and formative experiences of my life, but it doesn't entirely rip my life apart.

If my husband is the evangelical city boy who couldn't have been less like my father if he tried, then Tony is everything I grew up never knowing I wanted, a butch from shitkicker Missouri who can strut into a room full of Boston academics wearing cowboy boots and a flannel and spin a story that leaves them all in her thrall. The rural redneck, roughneck boys and men of my youth never felt right, but everything about the way she moves settles something in me like fresh morning dew on a quiet field. Her natural charisma reminds me of my father's, bright like the sun just before the eclipse shadow. She smells like every man in my family, all whiskey and tobacco, the kind a candle can never quite distill.

On her, the masculinity I used to think I hated is suddenly resplendent, a gravitational pull I don't want to resist. She fucks with gender on purpose, and when I tell her she is the best man I've ever met, she looks me straight in the eye and says *thank you*, the subtle twang in her voice reaching parts of me I thought I'd buried.

✣

Tony goes home to Missouri that first Christmas, and we spend almost every night on the phone. She calls me on her smoke breaks, describing the midnight sky, split open with stars across a wheat-planted field.

*I wish you were here*, she says, and it's as if I am.

✣

Wasn't I the Midwestern girl who was always going to choose God and husband over herself and her own desire? I thought I was safe. She thought I was safe, too.

✣

In an alternate timeline, I'm single, and Tony takes me home to Missouri with her that Christmas, where we hop in her pickup after dinner to go out on country backroads. We park in an abandoned field, go crawl in the truck bed, and lie down next to each other, her arm around me and my leg hooked in hers as our fingers trace the constellations in the sky above us together. And other things.

Her family thinks we're just friends, but we know what it means to be here together.

She likes to go on late-night drives. We make our way up the winding backroads of the North Shore for as long as she's in the mood for; all we do is talk and listen to country music. I set no boundaries; none for myself and none for her. I think this means getting as much of her as is possible, which is not true. She keeps vampiric hours, so I adapt and learn to keep the same. I meld myself to her, months before I am conscious of my feelings, ignoring the commitment that is waiting for me at home.

I take to staying at her house after class, studying and talking; she doesn't drive me home until two or three in the morning. I never text my husband to let him know where I am, though he asks. I am so caught up, enraptured.

✛

When it's just the two of us, she talks in hypotheticals about the future. Occasionally, we talk about raising kids together back home in the Midwest (platonically, of course), ignoring the fact that we're both in a tenure-track PhD program, entirely at the mercy of the market, and also how fucking gay that kind of conversation is. And that I'm married to someone else.

She peppers these postulations about life and family and love and relationships with lines like *if I ever fell in love*, to emphasize that she's not in love and never has been, and is always sure to show me her latest OkCupid profile update and messages from people who are interested in her. On the weekends at her house, when she takes a call from one of her parents, she always says, *Jeanna's doing well, she's right here, says hello*, because her parents have asked how I am.

I think we are good friends. This is what I tell myself for nearly a year, through spending hours on the phone with her through Christmas break, through late nights at her house, through night drives, through talking about her to my friends back home far more than I talk about my husband, through dressing up for classes I have with her, through my pregnancy scare that planted a seedling of a desire for autonomy, until—

We are about to take our first "friend trip" together—to a state fair for a country concert, because what else would two Midwest girls in Boston be doing?—and I think this is a brilliant idea for a short story, and would she mind if I write it as a sort of roman à clef? She texts me back BY ALL MEANS, so now I'm in a sun-soaked window seat at Bloc11 in Union Square, a queer-owned coffee shop with hot baristas and rotating indie art shows, and barely two pages into this story, I realize that the character who is supposed to be me is in love with the character who is supposed to be Tony.

I am a goddamn fool for not realizing it sooner.

It feels like the most obvious thing in the world, the most natural thing in this new world, where the only source of panic is the wedding ring on my left hand.

The existential dread that overwhelms me when I look at my ring comes from the fact that I still believe in God's will. I believe in an omnipresent, all-knowing, all-loving, all-seeing God, and I believe that my marriage to a man—this man—was part of his plan for me. But how could it have been, if I'm not straight?—a question that begins haunting me like an unfriendly ghost, day in and day out.

How could God have created me this way and allowed me to

marry *a man* when it is so clear that I don't desire him? And now I've gone and said, to Kyle and to God, those unbreakable vows that no one on earth can tear asunder. Queerness does not feel like a sin, but I absolutely believe that divorce is: One that Kyle and I promised each other we'd never commit. One of my parents' choices I absolutely do *not* want to repeat.

But I know the truth of myself now, and there's no way to un-know it.

✛

Tony likes married women, has a history with married women that she doesn't talk about to most people. Married women are safe because we're off limits, safe for the commitment averse like Tony to attach themselves to, because married women, like married men, so rarely *actually* leave their spouse.

✛

We go to the state fair, where we sleep in separate beds at the motel, buy straw cowboy hats, hold baby ducks, while I generally try my damndest to keep a lock on my emotions and not let on that I've had a world-shattering revelation.

There are carnival shooting games that Tony can't resist walking up to; she goes to a shooting range in Boston, and what can I say, I think it's hot, even though I have complicated feelings about guns. She holds the fake handgun she picks up at the booth with confidence, shoots with as much precision as is possible. She's fond of lecturing on pretty much every subject, but she never tries to explain country shit to me. Just pays for me to play. The inherent respect is attractive, something you tend to find only in folks who really understand where we come from.

My father did not take his daughters hunting, so my inability to properly aim the fake rifle I've selected is rather obvious, though Tony isn't paying attention, too focused on hitting her own target. The carnival barker starts explaining the gun I'm holding to me, trying to help.

*Dude, she's from Iowa,* Tony snaps, not looking up from her plastic quarry. *She knows what to do.*

I absolutely do not, but her defense of me and my nonexistent hunting skills makes me blush. I don't have the heart to tell her that this one single time, a man was not actually mansplaining, but trying to help. Now I am filled with the desire to hit a target to try to impress her, but my heart is racing too fast to focus on the scope.

I hit nothing. She has more success, and I'm hoping my sunglasses are hiding how turned on I am and also how much this is the kind of relationship I wish I was actually in, where we could toggle between talking about Romantic poetry and shooting together in the span of five minutes. My wedding ring glints brightly in the sunlight.

✝

In an alternate timeline, I have a sexual awakening at a youth group lock-in, like that one Semler song. The breakdown afterward is real, but perhaps one of my church friends has a similar revelation, and it turns out that we are all queer after we unhook ourselves from the drug cocktail that is evangelical shame and Midwestern repression. I don't feel as alone.

✝

When I get back from the state fair, I drop my bags off at home, barely able to look at my husband before bolting out of the apartment to go visit one of my closest friends in my grad school program, Kyley, a tall brunette with the warmest laugh you've ever heard. My emotions spill out of me in a panic once I step through her door, but Kyley takes my hand and tells me that it is, in fact, normal to have crushes during long-term relationships. This is the first time anyone has ever told me this, that anyone in my life has treated desire for a person who was not your partner as normally as going to the grocery store because you ran out of toilet paper. The evangelical part of me that screams *sin!* crashes in waves against the shore of me that feels staggering relief. Kyley pours me a glass of wine, trying to set me at ease as I fall apart on her couch, entirely nonplussed by the fact that my feelings are for a woman, and asks me to tell her all about it. I insist that this doesn't feel like just a crush, and my dear friend, who is familiar with Catholic guilt, spots my own shame as only someone with her own religious trauma can.

✝

In an alternate timeline, I find a more generous conception of God earlier in life. More unconditional love, less sinful depravity. Coming out doesn't entirely shatter my faith.

✝

The first time I hear "Same Love," the song from Seattle rapper Macklemore, I'm in the car with Tony, who cranks it as we're coasting in her beat-up sedan down Route 2. This is the summer of my pregnancy scare, the summer I realized I loved Tony, the summer we went to the state fair. The summer of all the cracks in the windshield.

I'm instantly struck by how purposefully religious the song is, musically. It gets my church-kid attention by opening with the low tones of an organ, the piano melody distorted over it like the speaker is a pastor pontificating onstage at the tail end of a sermon while the music leader plays an electric piano and throws in some synthy Christmas-style bells for extra emotional impact.

Tony likes the song—at least, she likes that a song that explicitly addresses gay rights is getting Top 40 airplay. Gay marriage is legal here in Massachusetts and in my home state of Iowa; nationally, it feels impossible. I'm catching some religious references in the lyrics, which I'm trying to listen to over Tony going off on yet another of her lectures on the history of gay rights in the United States. I know better than to interrupt.

But then Mary Lambert is singing "Love is patient, love is kind" from 1 Corinthians 13 over and over, repeating "Not crying on Sundays," and I am gone, head fully turned and staring out the car window, trying to hide the tears that are streaming down my face.

✛

My parents now also ask how Tony is on the phone. My dad, who had dinner with the two of us when he was visiting me in Boston, is fond of her, and reminds me to tell her hello for him.

✛

I am very much still crying on Sundays.

She asks me to be her plus-one at a local event where she's reading a portion of her dissertation. Her adviser is there, seated next to me, chomping on Goldfish throughout the whole thing, and what kind of entitled cisnormal white man do you have to be to loudly chomp your way through everyone's presentations on a child's snack at an Ivy League event? (It's really the ultimate sign of institutional belonging, though I don't realize it at the time.)

We go to an upscale dinner in Harvard Square with all the presenters and their advisers. We are dressed up. It's a lovely night of networking and one-upping and Tony and me being Tony and me, conspiratorially grinning and tapping each other's thighs through the evening when other people say the most ridiculous, pretentious shit.

One of the presenters asks us how we met. *We're in the same program,* Tony says casually, moving on to the next question.

Not even a week later, her adviser sits her down for a talk on how difficult dual-academic relationships are. He tells her to be careful. She relays it all to me. *Can you believe he thought we were together?* she asks, incredulous.

✛

Queer time is different from hetero time, the theorists say. Jack Halberstam reminds us that we do not "outgrow" certain things (like, say, clubbing) the way heteros do.[*] We do not have a sacred timeline;

---

[*] Jack Halberstam, *Gaga Feminism: Sex, Feminism, and the End of Normal* (Boston: Beacon Press, 2012), 2.

to be queer is to inherently step outside the hetero trajectory that society trains us to go down from the time we are born. Our spaces—our bars, our parties, our protests—are often multigenerational, and the same goes for our friendships and relationships.

But one kind of queer time Halberstam doesn't discuss is the gap that can happen when one person has been out for decades and the other person is just emerging from the shell.

I'm twenty-four, and she's in her thirties, which isn't a particularly notable age gap in and of itself, but add in my early-twenties evangelical naivete and the fact that she's known she was queer her whole life—

✝

I know it's an emotional affair, because I begin describing it that way to my closest grad school friends, who are dismissive of the concept in ways I do not understand. I can honestly answer *no* when my husband explicitly asks if Tony and I are sleeping together, a question spurred on by all the late nights at her house, our out-of-state trips, and my unhelpful confession of a crush, but the guilt eats at me.

Years later, I find that my emotional affair with Tony is essentially forgiven and glossed over by everyone in my life—*Well, of course you fell in love with a woman while you were married to a man; you're gay!*—in ways that still make me uncomfortable.

Just because it turned out that I was gay doesn't mean that I was automatically exempt from, say, telling my worried-sick husband where I was at two in the morning, or at least giving him the courtesy of letting him know when I would be home.

✝

In an alternate timeline, there is a version of me who feels too trapped to leave him, and she has been dead by her own hand for more than a decade.

✢

While my life is coming apart, Tony's dad receives a diagnosis that is supposed to be fatal. She flies back and forth between the Midwest and the East Coast, struggling to get her bearings in each place. We are tethered, and I serve as an anchor as she time-travels, transforming into an old version of herself every time she goes back, suppressing everything I love about her in order to be around the people she loves most.

I know how to do things that her family responds to, a love language that even she will understand. I bake cookies for her dad in the hospital—ones he's enjoyed before, when we all had dinner together in her apartment on his last visit. I organize a departmental card and flowers for her family. I talk to her on the phone every day while she paces outside the hospital, chain-smoking in the torrential Midwest rain.

I am a horrible wife to my husband during this time, but I can always pull out my inner church lady–Stepford Wife for her. I want to do things for her, anticipate her needs, support her and her family's grief. Any request from my husband feels like being asked to change a fundamental part of myself, but with her, it pours out of me, natural and unthinking.

She texts photos of her dad in the hospital with the whole bag of cookies I baked for their family. HE SAYS THANK YOU. I SAY THANK YOU, TOO.

✢

We drive ten hours for a rave in Toronto. These are the tacitly acknowledged rules of Tony and me traveling together (which we do, far more than we should, given the circumstances): Separate beds. No touching on trips. Really, barely any drinking on trips. We are stone-cold sober, even for a rave, declining dank joints in the pouring rain outside the venue until she breaks one of our cardinal rules and wraps herself around me, my head tucked under her chin, for the ostensible purpose of keeping me warm.

The rave feels like the biggest worship service I've ever been to. Thousands of people wordlessly swaying in unison, the collective effervescence of everyone in the room rising and falling together with the beat, as one. The cheers of exaltation. The solemnity of pause. The dissolve of self in the face of holy commune with each other. Tony's father is an elder in an evangelical church that she stopped attending early in life, and when I liken the experience to church on our drive back to Boston, she gets it.

This is what I mean when I say she feels like home—at that moment in my life, she is the only other person I've ever met who sits in all the liminal spaces with me: between the religious and the secular, between the pull of the wide open spaces of the Midwest and the opportunity we have on the coast, between everything our conservative parents wanted us to be—and queer.

*You know I'll come get you, right? I'll always come get you.*

When I feel like I am dying in my house, Tony makes the drive across town to pick me up and lets me stay at her place as long as I need: one night, two nights, three nights, four. She is the epitome of Midwestern hospitality. She cooks me biscuits and gravy, makes full pots of coffee at midnight so we can stay up late doing work, drags me outside to sit with her while she chain-smokes so I can lie back on the grass and stare at the stars and hope.

I spend whole weekends, whole weeks, sleeping on her futon alone, with one of her cats curled at my feet.

✝

It doesn't start right away, not until I'm fighting with Kyle (who is telling me that I'm not an individual, I'm his wife), not until my feelings for her are undeniable, not until I can't stand to be in my house anymore. I call Tony up one Thursday and say, *Come get me? Let's go out.*

And she does.

I don't know how it happens, that first night, kissing, it just manifests, how things happen when you're drawn into someone else's eyes and smile and skin. We're sitting at the bar, pressed up against each other, while Java, the Irish bartender, tells us about his lesbian babysitter, because of course the Boston Irish bartender has a lesbian babysitter, and somehow we realize that he thinks we're together, isn't that funny? so we start holding hands to sell a nonexistent act because we're holding hands underneath the bar where no one can see, so why is that happening? and somehow her lips find mine—or do mine find hers?—and we kiss right there in front of the bartenders and hold each other and it is brief and it is magic and I am gone, but that wasn't a secret. That was why I'd asked her to come get me in the first place.

We go to the back room where the band is playing, and she holds my hand in a way I interpret as fierce and protective, and we dance, our hips slotting into each other's like magnets. Then she pulls me onto her lap in a booth and asks me point-blank if I am in love with my husband, and I feel like I should say yes, so I do, but in that moment, I know I am not (was I ever?), just as much as I know that my feelings for her aren't a mere crush, that I am in love with her.

And in that moment, I am just as sure that I'm not going to do anything further about it except grind my hips into hers every following Thursday night to bad eighties music and hold her hand, fingers interlaced, as we walk through crowded back rooms and chug vodka tonics (me) and Jack and Cokes (her) like they're water.

I'm a goddamn hypocrite, and I know it.

✛

I tell Kyle that Tony and I kissed that night. I make it out to be a joke, which is obviously a lie. This intense kind of guilt is new to me. Guilt that I don't love Kyle like he loves me, guilt that I had kissed someone else I had feelings for. Curiously, I feel no guilt for kissing a woman. Perhaps it's because it feels so right; perhaps it's because my guilt for cheating on my husband is too overwhelming. Kyle is, predictably, furious, but in the quiet ways of his father, not the loud ways of mine.

I tell him in a public place, at a bus stop at the bottom of the hill we live on. He has never been violent with me, but my mother taught me well: sometimes, you have to tell your man hard things in public so he can't react in a certain way.

He doesn't touch me, just looks at me like I've betrayed him.

✛

She sends me lines from Richard Siken poems, calls me "kitten," buys me coffee when we're both on campus, wants us to duet to

Loretta and Conway's "Louisiana Woman, Mississippi Man" at karaoke. At least once a week, she can be reliably counted on to sing me the same damn Americana Bonnie and Clyde song where the narrator promises his lover *forever*, even if *forever* means undertaking an Orpheus-type journey to hell.

She also tells me about the men she gets off on topping and the women she melts for, and then she sings me a love song in the car, says she can meet me to go out dancing, and do I need to be picked up from the apartment I share with my husband?

I am young, and I am naive, and I am in love with a woman for the first time, and my frame of reference for a bad relationship is my dad throwing my mom down a flight of stairs, and Tony doesn't do that, and my husband doesn't do that, but I've never felt so strung out and strung along and physically sick like this.

Is this what being queer is like? Do I want this? Who would ever want this?

☩

In those months, I think Tony is the only one who really sees how much I am wrestling with not wanting to be here anymore, and she is doing whatever she can to tether me to this plane. She is my true north, though I also never know which way is up.

This is why I can't hate her. Because she helped me stay.

Kyley and Melissa tell me I give her too much credit.

☩

A little more than six months after that first kiss in the bar, I put on a pair of cowboy boots and a leather jacket and hop a bus down to the courthouse to file for divorce, and before I know it, our rules of engagement have changed. I start doing the things I wasn't supposed to do: I stop going to church with my husband. I leave him. I come out to my loved ones here in Boston but also back home in the Midwest. The cost is high; some people stand by me, but most don't. Tony watches me lose a life I had nearly died trying to hold on to—but now I am freer than I have ever been.

I come out to my father, something she has never done.

You would think she would be elated, but she is, instead, more cautious with me than ever.

Our relationship starts to tilt in a direction she does not seem to like.

I am changing, changing: ripping my body out of the cocoon, shedding everything that made me in an attempt to remake myself anew. She witnesses it all, an apostle to my resurrection, but she has no desire to testify or worship. She has no holy terror. She pulls away from the me who chooses herself, who does not put others above herself at all costs. I pretend I don't notice, even as I chase after her, grasping at what I don't think she is capable of giving.

✟

Once I move in with her (because of course I've left my husband only to move in and crash on her futon, temporarily), we stop dancing. We stop touching altogether.

✟

She goes out on a few dates, and I am overcome with a jealousy so severe that it runs through my entire body in a way I had never felt before. I literally sit in her parking spot, shaking, drinking hot coffee in the humid Boston summer night until she drives home at two in the morning, forcing her to look at me as she pulls in.

*How was it?* I ask, voice trembling.

This is not my best moment. We are not a couple, and she's allowed to go get laid, and I have no claim on her, and my possessiveness is entirely unfounded.

I know she doesn't love me, but I also know that our dynamic gets her off. I might have been a virgin on my wedding night but I have danced with enough men and enough women to know when dancing is just dancing and when dancing is a hell of a lot more.

✛

Once I move into my own apartment, we start going out dancing again.

On one of those nights, I kiss her.

She kisses me back, her hand sliding up my neck, fingers tugging on my hair, and I don't want this to stop, I never want it to stop. I let out the smallest of moans, and it is as if a spell breaks—

She pulls away and asks me what I am doing. (*This is your divorce, not mine,* my husband had said.)

She grabs my hand and leads me out of the bar, outside to the sidewalk. Lights a cigarette. I have enough time to regroup, to not lead with *I am horribly in love with you,* and reframe my attempt at a move as a simple, *We'd have good sex, so why aren't we having sex?*

She agrees: Yes, we have chemistry. Yes, we are essentially in a relationship without saying it's a relationship. (Her admitting that feels both like a hot-air balloon and like lead filling my stomach. So, she knows.)

*But if you have a choice between a once-in-a-lifetime thing that could be amazing but could blow up, and a normal friendship sandwich that you knew would be good every time, you'd pick the sandwich,* she says, like it's the most obvious thing in the world.

✛

Citing the source of the erotic in the Greek *eros*, born of Chaos, Audre Lorde writes in her essay "Uses of the Erotic":

> This is one reason why the erotic is so feared, and so often relegated to the bedroom alone. . . . For once we begin to feel deeply all the aspects of our lives, we begin to demand from ourselves and from our life-pursuits that they feel in accordance with that joy which we know ourselves to be capable of. . . . This is a grave responsibility . . . not to settle for the convenient, the shoddy, the conventionally expected, nor the merely safe.[*]

✛

I am not the kind of person who just picks the sandwich.

✛

We try to stay friends even after I say the quiet part out loud. She says she just needs time—like I used to tell my husband I needed time while I was prolonging the inevitable.

---

[*] Audre Lorde, "Uses of the Erotic: The Erotic as Power," in *Sister Outsider: Essays and Speeches*, rev. ed. (Berkeley, CA: Crossing Press, 2007), 57.

A *Dungeons & Dragons* spell invented by Matthew Mercer, a voice actor and *Critical Role* Dungeon Master, is Tether Essence, in which two creatures become magically linked so that any damage dealt to one creature immediately is done to the second. The spell is temporary.

An important detail: one or both creatures can voluntarily fail their saving throw, continuing to take damage in order to remain connected.

How many saving throws did I willingly fail in an effort to keep her in my life, no matter how much it harmed me?

✛

Tony and I break up. After New York Comic Con and days in the Javits Center, after going out dancing at a straight bar in New York where she tries to hit on guys in front of me, guys who keep gaping at me, verbally expressing their disbelief that we aren't together because she is butch as hell and too many straight men don't get that butches can be bisexual, but they *absolutely* recognize the possessive fury that is rolling off me, the fury she is oblivious to; after going to a drag show at Stonewall the next night, where she does a 180 and throws her arm around me and pulls me close, gives me bills to stuff in the queens' bras and garters, playing the butch daddy who is casually possessive of her femme as if she hadn't acted like she wanted nothing to do with me the night before—

At the end of the drag show night, so drunk that we are gagging ourselves over grates outside our Midtown hotel, trying to force our bodies to eject at least some alcohol so as to mitigate our inevitable hangovers, she looks up at me from across the sidewalk and says, *This is why we'll never have sex,* and it's nonsensical and out of nowhere and vulnerable, both of us with alcohol and saliva dripping from our mouths, but in my deliriously intoxicated brain, something finally—*finally*—clicks.

I didn't come out to live a half life chasing someone who doesn't want me, no matter how much she feels/tastes/sounds/smells/looks like home.

✛

I write her an email. This is not how I prefer to end things, but I'll lose my nerve otherwise. I don't trust myself to say what I need to say if I'm looking her in the eye, those eyes that are cold like the middle of an Iowa winter that will never end. Every time I've tried to bring shit up these last few months, she has talked me into staying, into playing this half game, this half relationship, stringing me along like I'm some lamb at the county fair who can't discern the difference between crumbs and a full meal.

✛

In an alternate timeline, I get accepted to a PhD program the first time I apply, during my senior year of college; I am gone, gone, gone, on the East Coast, meeting Tony or some other butch heartbreaker and I am coming out and breaking up with Kyle, who becomes merely an old college boyfriend, never a husband.

✛

*I never meant to impinge on your emotions*, she writes back, which is how I learn what "impinge" means.

*Take care of yourself*, she signs off. The trite, catchall phrase is the last thing I ever said to my ex-husband in person. The irony of her using it on me is not lost.

✛

Impinge: to have an effect or impact, especially a negative one.

Impinge: to advance over an area belonging to someone or something else; encroach.

Impinge: to strike.

She never meant to affect me; certainly never meant for me to fall in love. It was an accident, you see.

✛

*Divorce is like being skinned alive*, Kyle told me. I am mortified to realize that this is precisely how I feel about breaking up with Tony. Untangling my life from hers feels like peeling skin off; all the worse because she doesn't feel the same.

Growing up, my mother described sex outside of marriage as gluing two sheets of paper together and then trying to rip them apart. *Part of them will always be on you,* she said. *Don't have sex with someone you don't want to marry.*

But my mom was wrong. You don't have to have sex with someone to love them so ferociously that a part of them is always with you. Conversely, for me at least, you can have sex with people whose names you'll forget years later.

Sex is not a tether for everyone.

✛

In an alternate timeline, my mother doesn't convert to evangelicalism, doesn't raise my sister and me in such concentrated purity culture.

✛

In an alternate timeline, I'm born into a different family altogether, one that isn't so conservatively Christian, one that isn't trapped in a lower socioeconomic class, believing every source of systemic pain and violence to be God's will, one that does not teach me *I am not my own*.

✛

Alternate timelines are not useful to think about.

✛

What is there to say? For a few hours a week, there was a designated time on Thursday nights when I wrapped myself around her, where she clutched her fingers in my curls and buried her face in my neck and maintained that we were "just friends." For a few hours a week, it was like we crawled into our own gay Narnia where there were no gods and no husbands, just psychopomp bartenders and a room full of people who would happily ride their own personal pole to hell if it meant getting laid at the end of the night.

And then it was over, and I was told that none of it had been real or true.

＋

After months of silence, we try to restart a more casual friendship, catalyzed by the fact that we were driving to an event with other students in our program and needed to be able to put on a good face. This casual restart worked, sort of, up until the point I start dating a taller masc-of-center woman named Sam, an engineer who helps me begin to unpack everything I'd assumed butch and masc people are or can be.

Sam looks the part, sure—the short blond hair with a fade that, from a distance, is reminiscent of Abby Wambach or Megan Rapinoe, the men's clothing that, on a woman of her height and athletic build, means that far too many people do a double take when she walks into a multistall restroom. But she's earnest and brilliant and wears her heart on her sleeve, and her ready enthusiasm for me, for *us*, offers a balm I didn't know I needed. She makes me think that the stoic masculinity that historically ignites my body like a match is not only overrated, but destructive—that maybe I don't have to spend a lifetime chasing emotionally unavailable people trying to heal my mother's wounds. She shows me there is another way.

Sam and I are serious about each other, and Tony cannot stand to hear me speak of it, finds a way to exit the conversation anytime I mention anything to do with my new girlfriend. Or maybe she is simply uninterested and has no use for any relationship with me if my life does not revolve around her.

When I bring Sam to grad school parties, Tony refuses to be in the same room as us, vacating any room Sam or I walk into.

These are the things I think about when new friends and girlfriends ask, *You honestly don't think she had any feelings for you?*

✛

Okay, one more:

In an alternate timeline, there is no Tony; there is just me, in a world where I was not raised to repress and sublimate my feelings and desires, but to notice them, to respect them, to honor them. Where I had language for my experience.

In this world, I always knew.

### NOTES

*Dear Forgiveness, I saved a plate for you.*

        *Quit milling around the yard and come inside.*

               —Richard Siken, "Litany in Which Certain Things Are Crossed Out"*

---

* Richard Siken, *Crush* (New Haven, CT: Yale University Press, 2005).

# 7. THE QUEEN OF SWORDS

## 1.

The lights on the third floor of the downtown office building flicker as I step off the elevator. The hallway is long, full of faded, poorly labeled plaques for businesses. I knock on a discreet brown door, which opens to a room of 1970s-style carpet and thrifted, boxy furniture that looks like it belongs on an episode of *The Brady Bunch*, if *The Brady Bunch* were set in a frat house.

*So, you're here for a tarot reading?* someone says.

I am here because I am heartbroken, but not for the reasons I should be. I *should* be heartbroken because I just broke up with my girlfriend of three months. In actuality, I am not over Tony, or my divorce, or the fact that, for the first time in my life, I cannot hear Jesus' voice as audibly as a flock of birds taking off from a rustling field. I can't hear him at all.

*Ashley will be your reader,* the man at the front desk tells me, and a petite white woman with pixie cut brown hair wearing a men's button-down comes out to greet me. She's the only woman other than me in the room, and I can't articulate it at the time, but I do not want to be read by a man, do not want to sit with a man alone in a room ever again.

Who knows, maybe the man at the front desk can sense this. Or maybe she was simply the next available person.

Ashley sits me down at a private table, and I unload my emotions of the last almost two years like a trucker at the end of a cross-country haul. I understand, now, having sat on the other side of the table, how common this is, how raw, how challenging it can be to receive a client's unprocessed tidal wave. But she holds it all; she has an empathy and a gentleness to her spirit that shields me in a feeling of safety.

The first tarot reading she gives me, the first one I ever receive, is about Tony. The first card that comes up, the one that imprints itself on my psyche as the Past, as What Has Been Lost—as the grief of surrendered hope—is The Sun.

✛

Shortly after, my curiosity about the reading's ability to bring my emotions into sharper view piqued, I buy a tarot deck, chosen based on the fact that the internet tells me it's queer friendly and also that the aesthetic reminds me of Tony. She's still everywhere, in everything, for me, like that one Michelle Branch song I used to sing back when I was a teenager who didn't know where my obsession with my female friends came from. Now I do.

Staring at the blank page of my journal—the journals I most recently used to talk to God, to process the here and now—I have no idea how to write what I am thinking without turning it into a prayer: a petition, a question, a conversation in which the answer lies outside myself. If I am not ultimately directing my thoughts and questions toward God, who am I directing them to? A self? *Myself?* My sinful, depraved, untrustworthy self that I have been taught to check at the door every time I've talked to Jesus for my entire life? I am seeking something, anything, that will help me better comprehend my nascent emotions without turning toward a god who I cannot—and no longer want to—hear. There is no ghost—holy or literal—but his absence is overwhelming, the kind of haunting that, in Avery Gordon's words, produces a "something-to-be-done."*

I am realizing—for the first time in my adult life—that I do not know who I am, that I have no idea what I want, or how to think without an interlocutor and a set of guidelines.

I'm in therapy now, where I sit across from an older woman who waits out my long silences, who helps me begin to work my way through the all-too-recent past. After our sessions, the grief comes on like a flood, and the bus rarely gets me home in time to fall apart in the privacy of my own room. I get used to crying in front of strangers on public transportation.

So, tarot. A practice that turns the question around, in which I am trusted to have the answers that I seek. A foreign concept. Asking a question, pulling some cards, and using the close-reading skills I've honed all my life to craft a narrative out of the cards' imagery that applies to my situation felt much more manageable than simply journaling on my own, without Jesus there to catch me. Tarot cards are archetypes; they tell stories, in which the answer is coming from within oneself.

---

* Avery Gordon, "Some Thoughts on Haunting and Futurity," in *borderlands*, vol. 10 no. 2 (2011): 2.

Using a tarot deck only mildly obscures the fact that, for the first time in my spiritual life, I am profoundly alone. Save pockets of advice on the internet—Beth Maiden's Little Red Tarot, Theresa Reed's The Tarot Lady—that I stalk and stalk and never interact with, there is no human connection in sight. I couldn't fathom telling my grad school friends, the ones who couldn't believe that I went to church, why I was now teaching myself to read cards—that I used to hear Jesus' voice, that I missed him, that I was furious because I was realizing in its absence that there's more to spirituality than I had ever been taught, that I felt as raw as a newborn and would try anything at this point to feel my spirit wake up.

I flip cards in simple spreads on the white, leaning Crate & Barrel desk I found on Craigslist, in the small bedroom of a three-bedroom apartment I share with a few gay men in Somerville's Union Square. I don't go out in the common room. I stay in my room, even on Thanksgiving. I cry, and I drink, and I sometimes read tarot, and I never talk about it.

✛

In those days, I wonder if I am a fool. I wonder if I made it all up, if the conversations with Jesus I thought were real were simply all in my head, if I'm everything that my professors and peers in graduate school have said and implied that religious people are.

I wonder if, in turning to tarot, I am just the kind of person who is less intellectual than the rest, a weak mind comforted by spirituality, who isn't strong enough to survive on my own without believing in something greater than myself.

I wonder if the problem is, and will always be, me.

## 2.

Prayer had been a daily part of my life, a direct line to God. But it had also been a way of connecting with those closest to me. *Can I pray for you?* is a simple exchange between friends, or even strangers, to share an intimate moment before the Divine.

In undergrad, I would walk and talk with Amy, my maid of honor, and my best friends, most of whom were also believers, on the way to class, and some days, we would stop right there in the middle of campus on the pedmall, streams of students walking all around us, to pray for each other over something one of us needed that day. Praying for each other was as easy as breathing, as intimate and natural a thing to do for each other as hugging hello or goodbye.

Pain connects us more quickly than almost anything, and praying for someone is a way of sitting with them in their hurt while also offering support. It is a powerful thing, to speak the same spiritual language as your closest friends. To pray for someone is to show care, to offer someone consistent energy on their behalf—spending your time with God talking about them. Whether you are asking for their healing, for their comfort, or for their purpose to be revealed, to pray for someone else's need or want or grief when in their presence is the ultimate act of emotional and spiritual intimacy. It establishes a unique kind of trust.

✛

Reading tarot isn't the same as prayer. I like that it doesn't come with Christianity's shame, but it also didn't come with community when I began practicing. I had left a religion that had defined my old sense of self and purpose, had been the basis for most of my now-severed relationships. Could I ever belong again?

This question of belonging, of the process and trauma of leaving such a strict community, is central to *She-Ra and the Princesses of Power*, the Netflix reboot of the 1980s classic reimagined by ex-evangelical showrunner ND Stevenson and their team.[*] In the pilot, we meet Adora, the chipper, blond-haired, people-pleasing squad captain who constantly strives to be the best so as to be rewarded by authority. Her world collapses when she discovers that The Horde, the military authority who raised her, has been lying—that she has been raised by "the bad guys," as it were, that everything she assumed was true was a lie. That the inhabitants of Etheria, the queer, magical planet they are occupying, are not hostile, but simply people going about their lives, in complete terror of their colonizers.

Adora is horrified and mortified to have her worldview so profoundly, utterly shattered. Once she understands that The Horde is attempting to colonize the inhabitants of Etheria, she unquestioningly turns on it to help defend the planet. However, for Adora, the world has always existed in black and white, and flipping her allegiance does not mean that she automatically begins to question her default programming. Different beliefs, same fundamentalist methods.

I see so much of my baby gay, newly ex-evangelical self in Adora—the desire to do better and right the wrongs I have committed in the name of a god I no longer believe in, motivated by a wild, unacknowledged hurt and guilt that will only grow with time, plunging forward without stopping to take stock of how my former beliefs still inform the methods of thought and action I am employing.

---

[*] ND Stevenson, interview by Brian W. Foster, "Between the Sheets," February 20, 2019, https://critrole.com/qtvideo/between-the-sheets-noelle-stevenson-s2-ep4.

The person who is most hurt by Adora's newfound conscience is her best friend, Catra, the skeptical, sarcastic antiauthoritarian foil to Adora's idealism. Catra *lives* in moral grays, was well aware that The Horde was full of shit. Catra always saw through the propaganda, whereas Adora had bought in without questioning. But once Adora knows something, she can't unknow it, and she has to act in line with her convictions. She has to leave.

The pilot ends with Adora leaving The Horde—and, consequently, Catra, who feels betrayed by her friend. The series is set up against this tension: The Horde versus Etheria, grounded in and mirrored by the emotional tug that is the friendship/breakup/sexual tension/will they or won't they that is Adora and Catra.

When I was first watching the series as it aired, I despised Catra. She reminded me of too many people I had left behind but couldn't forget, caught up in the emotional stakes of betrayal and belonging. But was it really Catra I despised, or the faith that had driven a wedge between me and my friends?

In *She-Ra*, whether you are the one staying or leaving, the other person becomes a threat. Their choice reveals something about *you*. Thematically, the analogy between She-Ra's Horde and organized religion is not a hard reach. The Horde is precisely that: a hoard that creates robotic clones of its leader through a ritual ceremony that can only be described as baptism—in interviews, the show's creators said the mother ship was designed to resemble an evangelical megachurch. On Twitter, ND Stevenson expanded, saying, "Horde Prime is inspired by cult leaders. The idea of using something intended for love and community to oppress instead felt like it spoke to the heart of the show, so we drew a lot of inspiration from megachurches and modern church architecture"; they also shared moodboard photographs, pointedly including one of Joel Osteen preaching to his Lakewood congregation in Houston.*

The Horde cannot tolerate difference, and its structure is built on driving friends, family, and loved ones apart if they will not submit to its singular worldview.

✢

Shunning is a known practice of cults.

I lost almost everyone after the divorce, after I left evangelicalism, after my coming out. My Christian friends from before, as a collective and as individuals. Practically all the women from the women's Bible study I was close to. My closest friend from high school youth group, Chelsea, who I survived the cult church with, who could bend her conservative theology enough to support me through a divorce but not through my coming out.

Even Amy—my college best friend and maid of honor, my daily text those first eighteen months in Boston. I had been so grateful to be able to talk to her now that she was back in the United States after a year in rural Nigeria working at a nonprofit where it had taken days to coordinate one phone call. She would update me on the people she worked with, and how she had learned to butcher the chickens she bought at market, and the acts of God she was seeing in everyday life, and I would tell her my in-comparison pretty mundane wedding-planning woes. Her life story and family history were so similar to mine that we used to say we were destined to find each other, as if God had put us in each other's paths to support one another and be the found sisters we so desperately needed. Until

---

* ND Stevenson (@Gingerhazing), Twitter, May 22, 2020, 1:19 p.m., https://twitter .com/Gingerhazing/status/1263882205442437125.

we were sitting in her car in a parking lot in the middle of a frigid Minnesota winter as I told her I was queer, that I was thinking of leaving my husband.

*I think you're making a mistake,* she said, with the conviction only a woman of God can muster.

✛

Once Adora leaves The Horde, Catra treats her like the enemy. There is no room for nuance. No room for the love they shared, their lifelong friendship. This is a fight with lasting, world-defining consequences, one in which Adora has chosen the other team. Which, of course, must mean that Adora doesn't want to be with Catra anymore, even though she had reached a hand out and said "Come with me."

✛

I text Amy, reaching out across the chasm of her indifference. My words are a steady one-way stream over the years that gradually reduces to a trickle until her birthday—September 4—and Christmas. Eventually, nothing.

Christianity is, at the root, deeply strange: it sets up your faith family as your "true" family. Jesus denies his own blood family, as in Mark 3:31–35 (NIV) (a story repeated in other Gospels):

> Then Jesus' mother and brothers arrived. Standing outside, they sent someone in to call him. A crowd was sitting around him, and they told him, "Your mother and brothers are outside looking for you."
> "Who are my mother and my brothers?" he asked. Then he looked at those seated in a circle around him and said, "Here are my mother

and my brothers! Whoever does God's will is my brother and sister and mother."

Jesus prioritizes his found faith family above blood, above lineage, above inheritance. In Luke 14:26 (KJV), he says, "If any man come to me, and hate not his father, and mother, and wife, and children, and brethren, and sisters, yea, and his own life also, he cannot be my disciple." In many ways, the threat of early Christianity was that it destabilized the organized, law-affirmed order of the Roman household (and, by extension, the Roman Empire). Verses that now sound old fashioned—such as Paul saying, "Wives, submit to your husbands"—were, at the time, non-traditional. Paul broke custom by explicitly addressing churchgoing members of private households—wives, children, the enslaved—who were *not* the husband, father, or slaveholder, whereas contemporary Roman works of the time give instruction to the head of the house alone.[*]

It's an ambivalence that modern Christianity has trouble reconciling, between the biblical disruption of natal family for chosen family and the faith's emphasis on "family values." But Jesus' prioritization of faith family over blood family always appealed to me. Even though nuclear families[†] made up the majority of congregations I attended, I still internalized the implicit message around chosen family. Home was not safe, and my mother felt like the black sheep of her own family; it wasn't a stretch to interpret our churches in this way. While this was not overtly conscious in my youth, the adults I knew best and trusted most during my formative years were in church with me every week.

---

[*] Beth Allison Barr, *The Making of Biblical Womanhood: How the Subjugation of Women Became Gospel Truth* (Grand Rapids, MI: Brazos Press, 2021), 46–49.

[†] Itself a twentieth-century invention largely supported by late-stage capitalism.

As I grew older, my investment began to turn away from religious authority and toward my friends. When my sister, Jo, and I talk now about the fault lines of difference in our relationships with God—I was always all in; she was an antiauthoritarian skeptic who went to service because she had to—the first thing she points out is, *You always had church friends.*

The church was family, and friends in church were closer to me than non-evangelical friends could possibly be because of the spiritual intimacy. I was sparking to something, then, that it would take me years to identify—that, for me, finding friends who speak the same language as I do could create a network of family. I took the Bible seriously when it said that a true Christian would deny their father and mother; I believed that the friendships born out of a sharing of the Holy Spirit were familial in nature.

But I forgot the fail-safe of church "family": that inclusion was predicated on the perceived strength of one's faith. Once I was deemed a liability for my divorce and burgeoning queerness, once association with me became too much of a risk to my friends' reputations, I was cut off and ignored with the same ease with which Jesus denied his own siblings. My purported sins meant I was no longer part of the group; the friendships and any affection or love therein automatically rendered null and void—didn't I get the message? Just as there isn't room for the LGBTQ+ community in conservative churches or the "Don't Say Gay" Republican Party, those of us who come out individually to friends who have historically loved us are cut off, excised, and punished.

✝

I drank, and I went to church. Mostly, I drank. Being isolated from my faith community was hard, but, surprisingly, so was being single.

In the church, a woman's worth is found in coupledom. Even as I moved away from a straight marriage, I had trouble letting go of that desire to be attached or wanted. I had never really been single as an adult, and it was uncomfortable. My way of coping with that discomfort, and the insecurity it exposed as a newly out queer woman who had no idea what I wanted, was to down a bottle of wine most nights. My recycling bin resembled that of Goldie Hawn's character in *The First Wives Club*.

I attended a lot of new churches that summer, which was a challenging task. Anything remotely evangelical was off the table—the local Vineyard church, for sure. Anything that felt like it had been so much as *grazed* by the Baptists or Methodists or Pentecostals left a foul taste in my mouth. The church I knew best and felt the most comfortable in, by far, outside of evangelicalism was, ironically, the Catholic Church. I'd grown up attending mass with my dad's family, especially Grandma Kadlec, who lived in town with us for many years. I'd gone to monastic retreats in college, which my now ex-husband had been appalled by at the time. Something about the liturgy and ritual that had bored me in childhood, when I got stern looks from my grandfather for kicking the kneeler, spoke to me as an adult. But Catholicism was a nonstarter as a permanent community due to its similar patriarchal bullshit and rampant homophobia.

Given how many Protestant denominations there are in the United States, it seemed like finding a new church should be easy. But evangelicalism itself is not a singular denomination but an ideology, one that has infected numerous churches with its teachings around purity culture, biblical womanhood, and more. This left only a handful of options—the most liberal traditional Protestant denominations like the Episcopal Church, the Religious Society of Friends (a.k.a. the Quakers), and the United Church of Christ, which all embrace the ordination of women, accept LGBTQ+ people, and seek racial justice. These practices tend to make these churches unpopular among evangelicals. Thinking that the best remaining choice might be the Episcopal Church, which had a liturgy I was also somewhat familiar with due to its having been the lifelong spiritual home of my maternal grandmother, I tried attending—but the familiarity only made me feel more isolated, perhaps because my grandmother wasn't there.

Eventually, I made my way to First Church in Cambridge, a United Church of Christ congregation with a history dating back nearly four hundred years. The first Sunday I attended, they had an altar call for everyone in attendance who had ever been a deacon or an elder, and tears streaked down my face as scores of women approached the front of the sanctuary in a never-ending stream.

What would my faith have been if women had been visible and respected in this way, threaded through church leadership? If it was normal for me to see women in relationship with God like this? To see rainbow and trans flags planted proudly in the front lawn?

It was funny—the church plant I had been attending with Kyle felt called to Cambridge and Somerville because it is one of the least-churched populations in the country (which is, technically, true). "The darkness of New England," it's called. In my former pastors' minds, the non-evangelical churches there—in refusing to adhere to conservative gender roles of patriarchal white supremacist theology—were doing a terrible job. But First Church was a thriving congregation with elders, young families, college students, people of color, queers: a congregation that had served its community for literal centuries. That didn't look like failure to me. That looked like love.

*There are no love cards here,* Ashley says to me at my first reading, her voice gentle and lilting. I scan the tarot cards, searching for any imagery to counter her interpretation, and am unfortunately inclined to agree. Nothing here appears to indicate emotional connection, lingering intimacy, or interest.

The card that she thinks represents Tony is The Hierophant. *This card can be a teacher, a mentor, someone who is really dedicated to their studies,* she explains. *It sounds like she's someone who chooses her career in academia over everything and everyone else.* At the time, this strikes me as true.

This tarot reader is not telling me my future, as I went in thinking she would. She is telling me what I already know, the cards a third-party observer, reflecting back to me the intuition I had been so stubbornly ignoring for my entire life, that I had been trained to ignore. The intuition I am suddenly so curious to understand more about how to access. How to *hear.*

As I embark on my own study of the cards, I learn that The Hierophant in that initial reading may have more to do with my life than another person I used to care for. The Hierophant is sometimes called The Pope and is traditionally associated with religion, with higher education, with the wisdom traditions that become the institutional systems that so often oppress women and queers, legally and otherwise.

I also learn that it is my birth card.

I am resentful when I discover this. Why couldn't my birth card be more empowering like The Magician or The Chariot, more intuitive like The High Priestess, or more sensual and embodied like The Empress? No, I got the religion card.

But anyone who works regularly with the tarot knows that the cards reveal themselves to you slowly, over time. If you are willing to sit with archetypes and notice the patterns of your reactions and insights, you'll crack open a cleft in the rock.

The version of The Hierophant that helps me truly begin to unpack the archetype is from the So Below deck, which I don't purchase until the summer of 2015, more than a year and a half into my tarot-reading journey. In this deck, The Hierophant is a woman of color—the shopkeeper of a botanica who is helping a customer select herbs. She is a wisdom keeper, a teacher, a purveyor of ritual and traditions that are vital to her and her own culture. If you really want to put a queer lens on the card, you might assume she's casually flirting with the also-femme customer depicted in the image. As with all the women in this deck, you can safely assume that our entrepreneurial Hierophant is a witch.

I cried the first time I drew this Hierophant, much like the first Sunday I sat in First Church as streams of women elders and deacons swarmed the pulpit to pray over and anoint the new leaders joining the fold. The Hierophant doesn't have to be The Pope—she can, in fact, be a woman working outside the establishment. A woman making her own way, trusting her own wisdom, and guiding other women along the path. Gradually, The Hierophant comes to feel emblematic of my own journey of healing from religion, with how much work I know I have to do on myself—but with the knowledge that my own intuition could be a trusted guide.

✣

They call this journey that I undertook deconstruction. By "they," I mean other ex-evangelicals. By "deconstruction," I mean the process of excavating one's former faith to see if anything is salvageable. *The Deconstructionists Playbook* describes it as "a liberating process of surveying all the elements of one's faith in order to decide which to keep, which to reimagine, and which to completely throw away."[*]

The concept of deconstruction, used in conjunction with leaving evangelical Christianity, was not familiar to me when I was leaving my husband, or attending First Church, or reading tarot. In 2012 and 2013, Blake Chastain hadn't yet coined the hashtag #exvangelical. Chrissy Stroop, PhD, the creator of #emptythepews, wasn't yet a prominent ex-evangelical voice sought out for interviews and comment by major news outlets. Anthea Butler, a professor of religion at the University of Pennsylvania, hadn't yet written the essential *White Evangelical Racism*. There was no TikTok, let alone an entire community of ex-evangelical TikTokkers, such as Abraham Piper, one of the children of "biblical manhood and womanhood" co-creator John Piper, giving pithy breakdowns on evangelicalism, calling it "a destructive, narrow-minded worldview."[†] Joshua Harris, the author of *I Kissed Dating Goodbye*, hadn't yet denounced his work and his faith and immediately endeavored to pivot into a leadership role in the ex-evangelical movement, seemingly unable to take a seat for any meaningful amount of time.[‡]

---

[*] Crystal Cheatham and Theresa Ta, eds., *The Deconstructionists Playbook: An Anthology* (Philadelphia, PA: Bemba Press, 2021), 1.

[†] See Ruth Graham, "A Pastor's Son Becomes a Critic of Religion on TikTok," *New York Times*, April 12, 2021, https://www.nytimes.com/2021/04/12/us/abraham-piper-tiktok-exvangelical.html.

[‡] In 2021, Harris attempted to launch a course on deconstruction, charging $275 to "teach" unpacking and deconstructing evangelical faith to other folks leaving the faith, an effort that was heavily criticized by theologians and ex-evangelicals alike. See Carly Mayberry, "Josh Harris Launches Course on Deconstructing Faith, but Some Theologians Question His Motives," *Newsweek*, August 13, 2021, https://www.newsweek.com/josh-harris-launches-course-deconstructing-faith-some-theologians-question-his-motives-1619263.

In those years, I had no name for what I was doing. In those years, all I knew was that I felt entirely alone.

✝

I attend First Church on and off for several months, slide into a pew, unassuming and quiet, keeping to myself before service starts. I avoid eye contact and small talk at all costs. I don't want to get to know folks, don't want to "plug in." I have a feeling I won't be here long, that this is my last stand. Not for any fault of the church's, of course. Witnessing the services here, it's as if I see a second life, a retrospective of what could have been. How lucky these children are, growing up in a faith that is so much more accepting than the one I was raised in.

It feels like I come to church out of a desire to try to atone for a divorce I do not regret. I can't feel guilty for a decision that saved my life—for a decision that feels even more right with each passing day as I realize that I've been gay the whole goddamn time. How could a God who loved me let that happen? How could a God who loved *my husband* let that happen? Barring the God-loves-queer-and-trans-people argument: By evangelical standards, I did everything right. I was deeply faithful. I led Bible studies. I was a virgin on my wedding night. I had the kind of close, personal relationship with Jesus a lot of folks only talk about having. I walked the straight and narrow, and it wasn't enough. What more could God possibly have wanted from me?

*Total submissiveness*, is the answer that continuously comes to mind. *Church lady submissiveness.*

Old habits die hard. Here I am, still going to church, then reading tarot in my bedroom the same afternoon. *Witchcraft*, my mind whispers, as if I care enough to stop. I am going to have to give something up, and in choosing myself I've already crossed the rubicon—but how do you quit your home? Because that's what church had been: home.

A more progressive church was not the solution—after being raised in religious fundamentalism, it's a lens you always have, a language you always speak. I knew that I agreed with the ideas at First Church: how they framed the teachings of Jesus as those of a brown, Palestinian Jew, the son of refugees, the son of a teen mom whose testimony was not believed, a man who would in turn trust a woman with the testimony of his resurrection. The kind of Jesus who would look at me, a queer woman going through a divorce of my own making, and—this church said—treat me with loving kindness.

But that was not the Jesus I had grown up with. The Jesus I knew commanded us to go and sin no more. The Jesus I knew loved us, but not because he wanted us to be happy—but rather, because he wanted us to know that he was who he said he was and testify accordingly. "I am the way and the truth and the life. No one comes to the Father except through me."*

It's not possible for evangelicals, current or former, to self-describe as "culturally Christian," like it is for Jews who are "culturally Jewish" but not practicing. For us, there is no ritual without belief, no acceptance among church family if your participation is not oriented toward evangelism, toward the world domination and coming reign of Christ Jesus.

At the end of the day, the Jesus I was raised with was not a kind teacher, or a nice idea. He was—as C. S. Lewis's argument has been

---

* John 14:6 (NIV).

famously summarized—liar, lunatic, or Lord.* He claimed to be the Son of God. He claimed to be the only way to God. The point of Christianity isn't good works and charity. The point is John 3:16 (KJV): "For God so loved the world, that he gave his only begotten Son, that whosoever believeth in him should not perish, but have everlasting life."

If I didn't wholeheartedly believe this basic premise, if I could not say with absolute conviction that I believed Jesus to be the Son of God who had died for my sins, then why the *hell* was I still going to church? Why was I playing the part? It wasn't like anyone was watching.

Most Sundays, Kyle's last words to me echo in my head: *Beware ye who walk in the way of sinners.*

I come to church so I can try to feel something, but all I feel is exile.

÷

The church is often called the body of Christ. Inspired by the Last Supper, in which Jesus says of the bread, "This is my body which is given for you,"† the metaphor continues on, linking the church to the body in numerous New Testament passages.‡ To be a believer

---

* "A man who was merely a man and said the sort of things Jesus said would not be a great moral teacher. He would either be a lunatic—on the level with the man who says he is a poached egg—or else he would be the Devil of Hell. You must make your choice. Either this man was, and is, the Son of God, or else a madman or something worse . . . He has not left that open to us. He did not intend to." C. S. Lewis, *Mere Christianity* (New York: Macmillan, 1960), 51.

† Luke 22:19b (KJV).

‡ Romans 12:5; 1 Corinthians 10:17 and 12:27; Hebrews 13:3; Ephesians 4:12 and 5:23; and Colossians 1:24.

is to be of the body, to be able to connect to other believers intrinsically through faith. When you leave the church, when you leave your faith, you become disconnected from Christ, and from his body, other believers. You are no longer yourself; you are also no longer part of an intimate multitude. "Where two or three are gathered together in my name, there am I in the midst of them," Jesus says in Matthew 18:20 (KJV). Loss of access to other believers is also a kind of loss of access to Christ himself.

In "Save the Cat," an episode in the last season of *She-Ra*, Adora is trying to rescue Catra, who has sacrificed herself for Adora's new friends, who she has spent more than four seasons of the show resenting and feeling betrayed by. The group fights several clones and accidentally severs one of the clone's connections to Horde Prime.

"Where—am I?" the clone, dubbed Wrong!Hordak, asks upon his separation. "I cannot connect to the Hive Mind. I am alone. I am—*ALONE!*"

Wrong! Hordak's existential crisis serves as comic relief, but also provides a stark image of a believer violently shunned and excised from their community—of someone who must suddenly learn to live life outside the group and develop themselves independent of the rules and regulations of their former organization.

3.

I do not allow myself to be angry at God.

I am not reckoning with the roiling, furious rage and wrath that is rolling like a river inside me.

Anger still feels like sin, not like justice or righteousness. I am too embedded in grief and shame and the ideology of sin and repentance—instead, I try to ignore it, to distract myself.

I pull The Devil card over and over.

+

There is another kind of deconstruction, the first word I think of when those syllables are strung together, the only kind I knew back when I was sliding into the pews at First Church: Jacques Derrida's. His deconstruction is often accused of nihilism, because for Derrida, to deconstruct is to be willing to live in the tension of the unresolved, to risk never actually (re)*constructing*. But in the hands of the marginalized, deconstruction looks a little different. As philosopher and Derrida scholar John D. Caputo, writing about Derrida's Jewish identity, puts it, "The idea of deconstruction is to deconstruct the workings of strong nation-states with powerful immigration policies, to deconstruct the rhetoric of nationalism, the politics of place, the metaphysics of native land and native tongue. . . . The passion of deconstruction is deeply political."* It is a decolonizing of definition.

Language makes up power and institutions—the "rhetoric of nationalism," the "metaphysics of native tongue." Even Christians would agree on the creative power of language; it's right there in Genesis 1 (NIV): "God said 'Let there be light,' and there was light."

But *how* is the relationship between a word and what that word means created? When you say a word like "church," something happens: it invokes images in that space between what theorist

---

* John D. Caputo, *The Prayers and Tears of Jacques Derrida: Religion Without Religion* (Bloomington, IN: Indiana University Press, 1997), 231.

Ferdinand de Saussure calls signifier (the word) and signified (what the word conjures). However, depending on the person, the word "church" places you in a particular tableau. There could be pews or chairs and perhaps a choir or an organ or a rock band, perhaps holy water and people kneeling and relics on the altar and the smell of incense, or people praise dancing and waving flags in the aisles and that one woman who is always slain in the spirit, or the solemnity of sitting still for hours on end while the pastor thumps the Bible against the pulpit . . . or perhaps it's a big mystery of a building that you've never been inside but always hear politicians yammering on about. Some would insist that a *church* is not a building at all, that a church is, instead, the people who gather to worship. The space between signifier and signified constitutes, then, the immediate, deeply personal associations each person has when a specific word is invoked. Definitions are not, *cannot* be fixed. *Marriage, submission, wife, husband, sex, lesbian, queer*: each of these words invites associations that are personal to the individual who is speaking. Derrida calls this set of associations *trace* or, more famously, *différance*: an infinite, arbitrary unraveling of meaning.

When we talk about code-switching, doublespeak, and dog whistles, this is the phenomenon that we are identifying: the idea of *trace*.

Language is inherently plastic. This idea is in direct contrast to the current dominant theology of churches that call themselves evangelical and Bible-believing, whose uniquely American doctrine of literalism and inerrancy have served to prop up Far Right politics and fascism, where the assumed audience for their rhetoric is straight, white, able-bodied Christian men.

The dangerous idea that language is binary, that it's right or wrong, that all words and phrases, everywhere, simply "say what they mean" and can (and should) be interpreted the same by every single person, sans historical and cultural context, is supported by contemporary evangelical theology. When politicians say that the Constitution "says what it means," that we should abide by what the Founders intended, they are drawing a clear parallel to how evangelicals interpret the Bible and understand the will of God. Ironically, they're using their own *trace* to demonstrate how their own purported faith informs their governing—and their belief in how people *should* be governed.

✛

One of the most important contributions to the fascist turn that evangelical theology has taken in this country came from Charles Hodge, the reigning theologian at Princeton Seminary for much of the nineteenth century. His book *Systematic Theology* was published in three volumes from 1871 to 1873, just as American Protestantism was developing in light of Reconstruction, Darwin's discoveries around evolution were becoming accepted as scientific fact, cries for white women's voting enfranchisement were rising, and an influx of immigration on both coasts was resulting in a wave of xenophobia and the consequent passing of the 1882 Chinese Exclusion Act.* Across the country, white Protestant churches were at the beginning of a major schism that would bend some denominations toward a more modern, inclusive, social justice–oriented theology, and others toward a far more hardlining, fundamentalist isolationism.

---

* The Methodist, Baptist, and Presbyterian denominations all split over slavery shortly before the Civil War.

"The Bible is to the theologian what nature is to the man of science," Hodge wrote. "It is his store-house of facts."* It cannot be overstated how much Hodge's thesis, that the Bible was the completely inerrant, infallible word of God, was an astonishing break with Protestant church fathers and the traditional interpretation of the authority and limitations of scripture. Martin Luther, who had been a theology professor, used to acknowledge that the Bible contained contradictions and historical errors. Even the famously strict arbiter of human depravity John Calvin had been known to suggest that biblical writers were not particularly concerned with factual accuracy, keen to remind believers that the Bible's ideas about natural phenomena were clearly based on ancient understandings of the world. Two of the most revered theologians (including the leader of the Reformation), whose teachings Protestants had leaned on for centuries actively, publicly discussed the Bible's historical inaccuracies and contradictions†—and it did not seem to bother them or shake their belief in the least.

And yet Hodge, a name the vast majority of Americans would not recognize, set the tone for the conversation with his extraordinary assertion of biblical authority and accuracy in all matters (such as the insistence that God created the world in six days). In his own time, it had the immediate, unexpected effect of inspiring other conservative ministers to interpret the Book of Revelation literally.‡ His argument continues to define religious and political conversation in the United States to the present day.

This method of scriptural interpretation and the didactic

---

* Charles Hodge, *Systematic Theology* (Grand Rapids, Mich.: WM. B. Eerdsmans Publishing Co., 1940), 1:10.

† Frances FitzGerald, *The Evangelicals: The Struggle to Shape America* (New York: Simon & Schuster, 2017), 77.

‡ FitzGerald, *The Evangelicals,* 79.

approach to religious language has had stark and distressing consequences in the American political landscape, including our justice system. The foundation of Constitutional "originalism," which prioritizes interpreting the document as the Founders intended (no matter that, if we want to play by those rules, Jefferson said every generation should update the Constitution every twenty years),* has its origins in conservative white supremacist opposition to *Brown v. Board of Education*, during which point Hodge's ideas of biblical literalism and inerrancy were well within the conservative purview. The idea that the Constitution says what it means, means what it says, that it can be interpreted "literally" and "inerrantly"—with no unique *trace* or *différence*—is a twentieth-century invention by political conservatives influenced and supported by evangelical theologians working in the tradition of Hodge and his brethren.[†]

The way that some people read the Bible affects how they read the Constitution—and how they want Supreme Court justices to read it, too. The United States has the oldest active codified constitution in the world, and yet it also remains one of the most unchanged—a fact that is sometimes attributed to the influence of evangelicals' insistence on scriptural "inerrancy" that has come to inflect our founding documents. "One of the most malevolent characteristics of racist thought," Toni Morrison wrote, "is that it seems never to produce new knowledge."[‡]

But it's not just evangelicals who conflate scripture with law.

---

* Nicholas Stephanopoulos, "What Jefferson Said," *The New Republic*, December 1, 2008, https://newrepublic.com/article/63773/what-jefferson-said.

† Defenders of constitutional originalism point out that originalism demands fealty to the text regardless of its moral quality, separating it from evangelical fundamentalism—but then, there is the obvious point that originalism is a judicial position only ever taken by the most conservative justices.

‡ Toni Morrison, "The Trouble with Paradise," in *The Source of Self Regard: Selected Essays, Speeches, and Meditations* (New York: Knopf, 2019), 273.

According to a 2020 Pew Research study, half of Americans, far more than the white evangelical population alone, think the Bible should influence US law. Nearly a third—28 percent—insist that strict adherence to Christian scripture should supersede the will of the American people.* This is the theocracy the Puritans dreamed of, not the so-called "land of the free." Consider that the Bible gets trotted out in the law, wielded against LGBTQ+ folks, especially children (Florida's "Don't Say Gay" bill; trans kids in Texas, Arkansas, Alabama, Iowa, and elsewhere); against people who get abortions; and against immigrants seeking asylum.

This is evangelicalism today: the civil religion of white fear, of brittle ego, of sameness that cannot abide any difference whatsoever. It is predicated on the cruel optimism of denial: Christianity continues to believe its own underdog hype even as it achieved world dominance. The January 6 terrorists said they felt like they were losing their country, even as they stormed the Capitol building with the president himself a collaborator—with innocent children still in cages on the border, with trans folks worried for their lives as bathroom bills were introduced, with *Roe* teetering on the brink only to fall a year later under a conservative Supreme Court with three Trump-appointed justices.

Where, precisely, is the persecution white evangelicals claim? Where lies their suffering? Can an itemized list of losses be supplied? They have the resources to travel to the Capitol, to stay in hotels and take military-grade weaponry to "protest." They aren't isolated from each other. They are united in their hatred, in their purported faith, in their purpose to make their country great again.

---

* Michael Lipka, "Half of Americans Say Bible Should Influence U.S. Laws, Including 28% Who Favor It over the Will of the People," Pew Research Center, April 13, 2020, https://www.pewresearch.org/fact-tank/2020/04/13/half-of-americans-say -bible-should-influence-u-s-laws-including-28-who-favor-it-over-the-will-of-the-people/.

They count politicians and police and even a former president among their number. They show their faces on national television with no fear of retribution. They say the quiet parts out loud.

World domination is in their grasp, and the Second Coming has always been nigh.

☩

*Systematic Theology* is one of my ex-husband's favorite books. Red flags I ignored early on: his perpetual insistence that a word could only mean one thing, and that its meaning was bound up in his own worldview and life experience. That if someone did not live as he did and make choices he approved of, they were a sinner condemned to hell for all eternity. That even within the wide and vast umbrella of Christianity, only some people had the right idea, and the rest were idolators, Democrats, homosexuals, abortion advocates, false prophets, Mary-beseeching goddess worshippers who would all burn.

☩

In my Moleskine planner from 2013, the year of the divorce and Tony breakup, I have notes in the back—notes on the trip to New York Comic Con, notes for tattoos, a timeline of the French Revolution, and also a random, undated paragraph—

> Time as useful for constructing timeline: event vs. experience. Days as jour vs journée. What does it mean for time, historically conceived, to seem compressed into a day, to hear it constituted as a journée? How do we, looking back, evaluate // consider something as an event or an experience?

In French, *le jour*, the masculine, is a precise unit of time—the day, the hour—whereas *la journée*, the feminine, indicates a duration, a length of time. This distinction speaks to the difference between an event and an experience: a specific event, a moment or unit of time, as opposed to an experience, an ongoing feeling that can extend into the present day.

It can be hard to describe to folks outside the faith that "leaving the church" or "leaving God" is a *journée*, not a *jour*—and is, in fact, an experience that is ongoing at any given moment. Yes, there was a day when I stopped sliding into a pew. But the feelings did not stop. The grief did not stop. Has not stopped.

There is no "it is finished." No final breath on a cross. Healing is not finite. I am resurrecting myself without a guidebook.

I am angry at God, and so I do not read my Bible, and I do not pray, and I show up at church on Sunday mornings hungover from going out on Saturday nights, from stomping home down Somerville Avenue several miles in my cowboy boots, alone and wasted at three in the morning after going to shows and staying out late at my favorite Irish pub, getting home untouched and in one piece somehow, miraculously, with what I can in hindsight only describe as the grace of some kind of deity—but at the time, I do not see it that way.

Sometimes, I feel like the anger is just beginning.

✝

Millennials have left Christianity in record numbers—church attendance in this country is at an all-time low. We are the most LGBTQ+-identified and least religious adult generation in American history, or at least, we will be until Gen Z grows up. Millennials attend fewer religious services, pray less, and believe in God with less "absolute certainty" than Gen X, Baby Boomers, or the Silent Generation.

The questions reveal deep generational uncertainty about what it means to be "religious" or faithful. The significance of faith is clearly in a state of renegotiation, one in which the traditional markers of religious devotion (service attendance, congregational membership, daily prayer and scripture reading) are not necessarily as relevant as cultural or familial association, prayer, or other emerging kinds of personal devotion.

Church is community, but it is also ritual: an organizing principle for life and community that structures the week and gives order to the people involved. The loss of church, and organized religion generally, has created a major shift for younger adult generations—a contributing factor to the increasing centrality of work to people's lives.

In *Can't Even: How Millennials Became the Burnout Generation*, Anne Helen Petersen cites the prescient work of political scientist Robert Putnam in discussing the rapid and stark decline of nonfamilial social groups in American life in the new millennium. Since the year 2000, Putnam argued, "American participation in groups, clubs, and organizations—religious, cultural, and otherwise—had precipitously dropped, as had the 'social cohesion' that sprang from regular participation in them."[*] A follow-up study in 2011 by Putnam's critics ironically confirmed continued significant decreases in both familial and nonfamilial networks.[†]

---

[*] Anne Helen Petersen, *Can't Even: How Millennials Became the Burnout Generation* (New York: Houghton Mifflin Harcourt, 2020), 199.

[†] Petersen, 199.

The general decline in social infrastructure is yet another contributing factor that Petersen cites in discussing the lack of social cohesion found in millennials and Gen Z. Such an infrastructure, she writes, consisting of spaces "public and private, from libraries to supper clubs and synagogues . . . made it easy to cultivate informal, nonmonetary ties. These places still exist, but they have become less central, and less vital, and, most importantly, less accessible."* A lack of public funding is a factor, as is the rise of the internet, social media, and the impression of constant connectivity, and an increasingly burnout work culture with a lack of social safety nets.

Millennials, the last generation to grow up with memories of analog life, and Gen Z, the first fully online generation, were both raised in the wake of 9/11. Millennials' adulthood has been marked by two major economic recessions, one spurred on by a global pandemic. We have more debt and fewer safety nets in place than our parents did, and an imminent climate crisis on the horizon, one that will affect us but most especially our children. What unites millennials and Gen Z alike is a devastation of institutional trust, one that clearly extends to religion.

Recent studies on belief and religion reflect this, indicating that millennials and Gen Z are either stunningly atheist *or* are leading some kind of spiritual revolution, one that decenters and deprioritizes an insistent certainty in belief in one god beyond any shadow of a doubt.† Certainly, the rise in popularity of metaphysical sub-

---

* Petersen, 200.

† See Christel J. Manning "Gen Z Is the Least Religious Generation. Here's Why That Could Be a Good Thing," *Pacific Standard Magazine*, May 6, 2019, https://psmag.com /ideas/gen-z-is-the-least-religious-generation-heres-why-that-could-be-a-good-thing and Jana Riess, "Gen Z is lukewarm about religion, but open to relationships, study shows," *Religion News Service*, December 21, 2020, https://religionnews.com/2020/12/21/gen-z -is-lukewarm-about-religion-but-open-to-relationships-study-shows/.

jects like tarot, astrology, and witchcraft speaks to the power of the latter. But then, interest in the occult usually tips over into the mainstream during times of cultural crisis: most recently, in the 1970s, during the Vietnam War, numerous social justice movements, the passage of *Roe v. Wade*, and Nixon's insidious "War on Drugs" (which was blatantly targeted at Black Americans). The rise of the occult in the 1970s also occurred simultaneously with the first emergence of evangelicals as a political powerhouse back when movement leaders like Billy Graham and Jerry Falwell Sr. were alive, which would ultimately catalyze the conservative political backlash of the 1980s.

The metaphysical often arrives as medicine when institutional trust is in the toilet but people aren't willing to give up on spirit. But the metaphysical is also often not a movement, particularly once it is absorbed by whiteness, by a capitalist, "take what you want, leave the rest" mindset that relies on the privilege of personal utility and issues no centralizing, community-based call to action. Many alternative modalities, especially in New Age circles, have yet to move beyond an isolating focus on the individual; there is healing to be found in decentering traditional models of hierarchy and leadership, to be sure, but there is also healing to be found in coming together.

These days, community ritual work is largely the bailiwick of organized religion.* I firmly believe that the evangelical church's political power is found not only in its financial connections to the Republican party, but also in the spiritual work it does on behalf of

---

* Which is the purposeful result of colonization. The legal and cultural repression of Indigenous traditions, rituals, and ceremonies (such as the Dawes Act of 1887) is but one example in the United States where a long and awful history of white colonial control has resulted in the Christian church's consolidation of power.

the GOP: its ability to connect the individual user experience to a collective, community goal. Coordinated group efforts in worship services, through song and prayer, harness the power of individuals together for a united purpose; it's the kind of spiritual ritual I was practiced in when I was still actively participating. Say what you will about evangelicals—they know how to collectively call down spirit in a church service and do the kind of energy work that many Instagram witches can only talk about. This is also part of the shame and pain of leaving: knowing the ways in which I have enacted, and been a part of enacting, spiritual work that harmed others who I am now in community with.

✙

I will never forget the first time I watched Bobby Berk of Netflix's popular *Queer Eye* refuse to walk into a church; how much he normalized what so many of us, what I, felt. In the season 2 opener, "God Bless Gay," the Fab Five are tasked with renovating a church community center for a Black woman named Miss Tammye, whose gay son is attending their congregation's homecoming. During the episode's first act, Bobby declines to go into the sanctuary; his colleague Karamo teases him, saying, "You look like the gay that's scared they're gonna burn when they cross the door."

But Bobby's response is not born out of inexperience or misconception, but out of trauma. "There wasn't a day I wasn't in church," he later says to Miss Tammye. "It was my life. Those people were my family. And I knew from a young age that I was gay, and I'd be down there at that altar just crying and begging God to not make me gay. Once everyone there found out, they completely turned their back on me. . . . I was so hurt."

In response, Miss Tammye, or "Mama Tammye" as the Fab Five come to call her, looks Bobby straight in the eye with compassion. "You're God's son," she says, tears rolling down her face.

In a moment of vulnerability, there is a specter, where compassion is facilitated through the language of the church. Miss Tammye's pure acceptance is meaningful, but the ghost of the social violence done to Bobby looms, casting its eerie shadow.

✚

The binary way of thinking on which evangelicalism thrives precludes the membership or participation of those who leave, of those whose *trace* or *différance* would break, snap, or otherwise stretch to accommodate other associations outside the predetermined set of meanings.

4.

Stalker cards, they're called—the tarot cards that come up in reading after reading in such a way as should be statistically impossible. Within a few months of beginning a personal tarot practice, I have one such stalker. She comes up constantly. No matter the subject, she is there, asking me to show up for myself, relentless in her pursuit.

The Queen of Swords.

The suit of swords is often called the suit of sorrow. Associated with the element of air, it's about the ways we get in our own way; many of its cards depict the results that come when you're trapped in your own mind or worldview. The court cards—The Page, The

Knight, The Queen, The King—are about how you learn to embody and process anxiety and mental blocks, how you make your mind work for and with you rather than against you.

I understand The Queen of Swords as a woman who has learned how to set boundaries, who is a truth-teller, who wields the sword of justice decisively. She's often interpreted as a divorced woman, as a woman who has seen some shit. She feels like someone I could learn how to be.

She came to me almost every day while I was building myself anew.

These days, she only visits when I need a reminder that I am on the right path.

✣

I never thought I would find another spiritual family, never imagined that spiritual connection with people outside organized religion was possible. I didn't grow up with models for it outside of the evangelical church, and depictions of the occult in pop culture (*The Craft* and even *Charmed*) often show highly insular, less than healthy group dynamics.

This was the price of walking away, I figured. There are consequences you have to live with for some choices in life, even choices that are good for you. Giving up on the prospect of any spiritual community was one of them.

Eventually, my comfort in my new life settled, as did the cards in my hand. I started casually mentioning my tarot and journaling practice to close friends, who asked me questions, wanted to know why and how it worked and, also, maybe, could I read for them? Sometimes—to my great surprise—my friends even read cards themselves. They hadn't wanted to share their practice, either. We were in graduate school; we were supposed to be rational, reasonable, objective. *I mean, I don't believe in it,* one friend in my program maintained, even as she gave me sharp, incisive readings with her Rider-Waite-Smith deck in the tiny apartment she shared with her wife.

Slowly, emboldened by community, I started to read, and even volunteer to read, for others. In public, even. I read for Kyley and Melissa over dinner at The Independent in Union Square, at Diesel, at Bloc11. By the time I moved to New York City, when I was accruing even more friends—tarot readers, astrologers—who were openly into the occult, I was reading in coffee shops and breweries and wine bars, pulling my tarot deck out of my purse with the casualness that others pulled out a wallet to pay the bill.

My friends and I read cards for each other about relationships, crushes, people with whom we were breaking up; about new career choices and our books; about coming out to different people. But conversations tended to circle back to how we ourselves were in charge of our own lives, our own desire, in contrast to the way prayer was a petition to seek the will of God. Our tarot practice affirmed our own and each other's agency. *You can see what the cards are telling you,* a friend might say. *You know what you need to do. You just need to fucking do it.*

In my life, tarot has come to possess a similar function as that of prayer, individually and communally. A key difference, however, is this: the common acceptance of Derrida's *différance*, the free-flowing knowledge that many decks are different, that all readers bring their own perspective and their own interpretation. Within tarot reading, the *trace* a reader brings—your own personal associations—are welcome.

✛

Millennials have left the church, but we are still seeking spirituality. What are our options when the secular doesn't always feel sufficient but the traditionally religious doesn't feel safe? How do you learn to re-create a self, to trust an intentional and sacred community after experiencing the trauma of authoritarian extremism?

In the last decade, alternative spirituality has experienced a boom, with interest in witchcraft, tarot, astrology, and the occult at an unprecedented high.* There has been a swath of media coverage of how young people, particularly women and LGBTQ+ folks, are looking for forms of spiritual expression that embrace us, that validate our identities, and that offer opportunities for connection without condemnation.

Much is made of "Instagram witches," of how theirs represent "new" explorations; they do not, of course. There is a strong and extraordinary history of animist and occult practices in the Americas dating back centuries. There were Indigenous religious systems, as well as traditions brought over with enslaved Africans; those were integrated with the imposed Christian religion to create new forms such as Santeria and other African diaspora religions that are often mistakenly lumped together under the name "voodoo." However, there is a key difference: this turn to witchcraft and the recovery of alternative spiritual practices is happening at a cultural moment when millennials, ourselves a now entirely adult generation

---

* See "The US Witch Population Has Seen an Astronomical Rise," *Quartz*, October 4, 2018, https://qz.com/quartzy/1411909/the-explosive-growth-of-witches-wiccans -and-pagans-in-the-us/ and "'New Age' beliefs common among both religious and nonreligious Americans," Pew Research Center, October 1, 2018, https://www .pewresearch.org/fact-tank/2018/10/01/new-age-beliefs-common-among-both -religious-and-nonreligious-americans/.

occupying much of the workforce, are the least Christian-identified generation in American history. *That* is new.

However, even as there is a resurgence of alternative modalities, there is often a stigma in liberal and progressive circles associated with recognizing any kind of other-than-human influence or higher power at all. Many of us flee from the conservative orthodoxy of evangelical Christianity only to encounter a similarly orthodox commitment to Enlightenment rationalism and "objectivity," itself rooted in the denial of intuition, emotion, and other knowledges that are coded as feminine and therefore less than. There is a rich opportunity, then, especially in queer communities, to interrogate the oppressive structures that devalue our experiences, regardless of whether they are rooted in organized religion or secular philosophy. These lessons in emergent spiritual seeking can offer a path toward integrating intuition, emotion, and spirit alongside reason, logic, and a healthy skepticism.

✣

These days, I'm extremely out, as it were, about reading tarot. It's my party trick for celebrations in the West Village and picnics in Prospect Park. But I've also brought my cards to company retreats, reading for groups of mostly cishet men and introducing them to the collaborative power of the unknown (*Holy shit, you were right,* more than one exclaimed in the weeks after). The cards also come out to play on upstate retreats with my all-women, mostly queer writing group, where those of us who are familiar with tarot take joy in pulling cards for each other over wine at the end of long, creative days.

Today, when friends share a difficult thing happening in their lives and I know (or suspect) they might be receptive, one of the first questions I ask is: *Can I pull a card for you?* Not because I think the cards have the answer, exactly. But because the cards open up an opportunity for more dialogue, for more questions, but also for intimacy, for connection—for relationship building. They offer those I love the comfort of knowing that I'm here to support them, however I can.

Much as I used to do with prayer, all those years ago.

# 8. THIS IS MY BODY

I DESIRE THEREFORE I EXIST," ANGELA CARTER WROTE.* I NEED TO DISCOVER what I desire in order to understand my existence. I need to desire to remind myself that I exist.

Once my divorce is legally finalized, shortly after Tony and I end things, I sign up for OkCupid: to distract myself, to soothe my broken heart. I was in no state to be dating, but I was also not searching for any deep kind of connection.

The woman I start going out with regularly, the first woman whose heart I will break, is also femme, with pale skin, blue eyes, and black curly hair that trails down her back in waves like a mermaid. She's from a big Irish Catholic family in western Massachusetts, near the Connecticut border, which any New Englander knows is just as redneck as the rural Midwest. On our second date,

---

* Angela Carter, *The Infernal Desire Machines of Doctor Hoffman* (New York: Penguin, 1972, rev. 2010), 220.

she asks for my advice about buying a new truck—I'm still reeling from Tony and my divorce, but now I'm hooked. She's a nurse who paints, and she is the least career driven person I've ever met. *My work doesn't define me,* she says, and her ability to be so present and unattached to the future intrigues me. I don't meet many people like her, whose immediate goals—painting more, hiking the Pacific Crest Trail—have nothing to do with productivity and monetary "success." She takes me to dive bars where we shoot pool badly, with George Strait and Johnny Cash singing in the background. On our third date, two guys come over to hit on us, interrupting our pool game, thinking we are friends or sisters. Our matching curls are cute, did we know? (We did.) We're in a white working-class part of town that's more akin to old parts of Southie than Cambridge, the kind of place that obstinately reads two women holding hands as family. We book out of that bar early to go back to her place to watch *Hocus Pocus* and don't even make it ten minutes before we're horizontal on the couch.

That first night, I know from the time she pulls me in for a kiss to the time we are in her bed, clothes coming off, her leg between my thighs, her nails scratching into my skin, that this is what everyone has always talked about—*this* is what the church warns about because it is so good, so holy, how could anyone ever want to be anywhere but here—

Her hands and mouth are on me, making a storm of my body, pulling sounds out of me I did not know I carried.

I wake up at her place under a wall-length painting of a naked woman hung over her bed frame (hers, of course), giddy with desire. I decide to skip class, and she calls in sick for work, and we spend the day in bed, only occasionally getting up for food.

I've never had casual sex before, having been taught that it's a sin, that it would be subpar and unsatisfactory and empty. But it is revelatory. This is standard third-date fucking, I assume, and it's already the best sex I've had in my entire life. When she says, *I've got you*, the whole world falls away.

In my marriage, I hated giving up control in the bedroom, always on edge that something wasn't right. But here, letting go feels like release. Like safety. Freedom.

(*And this is sex with someone I don't love*, is a thought that faintly flickers through my mind, unhurried. *What's it going to be like when it's with someone I do?*)

✝

In the 2021 video for his hit single "Montero (Call Me By Your Name)," ex-evangelical Gen Z rapper Lil Nas X traverses an Edenic garden, a judgmental heaven, and a sensuous hell. He is the innocent, genderfluid Eve *and* the tempting snake (potentially an ode to Lilith, the woman on top). He is the pink-haired twink in chains, the blue-wigged angelic dandy who is judge, jury, and executioner in a Romanesque colosseum. Finally, he is the thigh-high-clad, hell-bound, pole-dancing gay who literally rides Satan into an early grave and assumes the throne for himself.

He is everyone, everywhere; he is surveilling himself, judging himself, ultimately freeing himself—the religious gaze and the unrepentant sinner, both.

The video plays with a delicious irony: that Lil Nas X is an openly gay artist—and an openly flamboyant, makeup-wearing bottom, at that, in a part of the music world where a particularly dominant, often toxic patriarchal form of masculinity is celebrated and any admission of submission or femininity is decried, an industry where the f-word is freely flung. This kind of homophobia in rap is consistent with the homophobia of white and Black evangelical churches. Lil Nas X, whose father is a gospel singer, told British *GQ Style* that, growing up, he'd understood his desire for men as "a test. A temporary test. It's going to go away. God is just tempting me," but he also noted that he couldn't recall exactly where the belief came from—that the religiously inflected homophobia "was never really talked about, but it was always around me, constantly."[*]

The shame is a pool that young queers raised in the church may not realize we've been born into, brought up completely submerged in—it manifests in the fear of discovery, the pressure to keep silent or pray the gay away. The pervasiveness of homophobic rhetoric in faith communities has been the subject of recent work ranging from the conversion therapy memoir (and film) *Boy Erased* by Garrard Conley to the story "Eula" in Deesha Philyaw's PEN/Faulkner Award–winning *The Secret Lives of Church Ladies* to singer-songwriter Lucy Dacus's *Home Video* album.

For Lil Nas X, the *Montero* album is a declaration of grievances, an exorcism of shame, and a baptism of new healing. Throughout the tracks, fear shifts from the fear of discovery toward the fear that accompanies any kind of fool's journey.

Major Protestant denominations are often in the news, announcing that they are splitting or otherwise dividing over LGBTQ+ issues—over ordaining us as clergy, over accepting us as members in the congregation, or over allowing our marriages. United Methodists, Presbyterians, Lutherans (ELCA), the Reformed Church, the African Methodist Episcopal Church, and even the Episcopal

---

[*] Jamal Jordan, "Lil Nas X: 'At first I felt a sense of responsibility. But now I just don't care,'" *British GQ*, May 10, 2021, https://www.gq-magazine.co.uk/culture/article/lil-nas-x-interview-2021

Church have all come to internal blows in recent years.* There have not been this many schisms among Protestant denominations since the years leading up to the Civil War, when churches split over slavery.

Lil Nas X, having grown up in the church's cesspool of homophobia and transphobia, was ready for the outcry around the video by Christians who argued that it was promoting homosexuality. He tweeted:

> i spent my entire teenage years hating myself because of the s*** y'all preached would happen to me because i was gay. so i hope u are mad, stay mad, feel the same anger you teach us to have towards ourselves.

The "Montero" video includes a separate spoken introduction: "In life, we hide the parts of ourselves we don't want the world to see. We lock them away. We tell them no. We banish them. But here, we don't. Welcome to Montero." The framework for the visual story is one of bringing what has been repressed and shamed into the light, into active participation, into liberation.

Evangelicalism builds a prison inside a person, but the truth will set you free.

Lil Nas X calls this place of truth Montero, his given name. Here, he is his full self—a gay Black man from the Deep South, who sings and raps about his relationship with his parents and religion and

---

* Some denominations, such as Methodists, have fully split, and others, like Presbyterians and Lutherans, have allowed individual churches to break off or determine policy. The African Methodist Episcopal General Conference continues to deny individual churches the right to perform same-sex marriage in their congregations, but the issue has been increasingly contentious within the denomination.

bottoming on the same album. Who kills the god-devil he's been taught is the keeper of his soul. Who becomes his own keeper, who refuses the system and the prison of established norms that others are so content to live in. Who names his whole world after himself.

I look down at my sister tattoo with my initials, JK, on my left foot, as I write this. Kadlec, alone. The names we choose for ourselves, and choose to reclaim for ourselves, have power.

✢

As if there is not queerness in the Bible:

> The soul of Jonathan was knit to the soul of David, and Jonathan loved him as his own soul.
>
> —1 Samuel 18:1 (KJV)

As if when Lil Nas X sings about wanting a guy who will snuggle with him all night, he's not talking about something David and Jonathan definitely did:

> Thy love to me was wonderful, passing the love of women.
>
> —2 Samuel 1:26 (KJV); David, on the memory of Jonathan

✢

I am in my body for what feels like the first time, awake with want and need. I am slow, methodical in accessing my intellectual and spiritual desires through tarot and journaling, but physically, sexually, I am ravenous. Human skin is the largest organ in the body, and mine has been starving for attention from someone whose touch I truly craved.

But there is a double-edged sword to desire: waking it up means also reckoning with the shame that has been entwined with it.

Brené Brown, a sociologist and researcher, defines shame as the belief that we are flawed and unworthy of love and belonging, that we are undeserving of any connection itself.[*] Shame is different from guilt; it is not productive or useful, and its ability to isolate us from each other is profoundly degenerative to the human condition. According to the findings of Dr. Brown and her team, the antidote to shame is simultaneously simple and complex: empathy.[†]

"If you put shame in a petri dish, it needs three things to grow exponentially: secrecy, silence and judgment," Brown says in her most famous TED Talk, which has been viewed more than seventeen million times. "If you put the same amount of shame in a petri dish and douse it with empathy, it can't survive."[‡]

Within the confines of evangelical Christianity, empathy was only available to me, a depraved sinner, because Jesus loved me. And because Jesus loved me, I could love other people. Without this framework, I had to find new ways to discover compassion and empathy for myself. Therapy helped. So did the routines of tarot and journaling, and my friendships—most notably with Melissa, Kyley, and my sister, Jo—where I could say the quiet parts out loud and learn that I can be truly loved, anyway.

---

[*] Brené Brown, *Daring Greatly: How the Courage to Be Vulnerable Transforms the Way We Live, Love, Parent, and Lead* (New York: Avery, 2012), 68–69.

[†] Brown, *Daring Greatly*, 81–82.

[‡] Brené Brown, "The Power of Vulnerability," https://www.youtube.com/watch?v=iCvmsMzlF7o&t=1115s&ab_channel=TED.

Empathy now also means learning to be kind to my flesh, to the curve of my breasts and lower belly, this physical vessel that I have been taught from childhood is my enemy, a sinful source of temptation for others, a thing to be abhorred. After years of dressing myself in clothing that was ill fitting and modest, to avoid accusations of tempting my brothers to sin, I start dressing to make myself happy. After two years of avoiding the lingerie I'd always coveted, I started buying it for myself.

Forty Winks is a small lingerie shop off the main roads in Harvard Square. It's not the most accessible, tucked away off a patchy brick sidewalk. There are quite a few stairs to climb to reach the entrance, but its elevation does helpfully deter any creepy passersby.

My first time in Forty Winks is my first time in a lingerie boutique this nice. Growing up, I felt fancy going to Victoria's Secret with my mom—"Vicki's," she called it. She let me pick out fun, playful prints from the 5-for-$25 bin when I was a teenager. Given that I'd quickly grown past Victoria's Secret's bra sizing and was relegated to the, at the time, relatively limited, drab selection of 34Gs from Kohl's and JCPenney, shopping with my mom at Victoria's Secret felt like the height of luxury.

But I hadn't let myself experience *this*—a store decked out not in shocking pinks and blacks but, rather, in pale neutrals, with chaise longues in the front and gold-knobbed drawers to hold extra stock. I felt out of place, not because of my size—I had checked online before—but because of how elegant it was. This was the kind of store my mom could never have afforded to shop in, and I was a newly divorced but broke-as-shit grad student, just walking in there, thinking I was going to drop the equivalent of my monthly utilities on underwear?

Did I deserve to spend this kind of money on myself? On an

item that had no greater purpose than my own pleasure, than feeling good against my skin, that wasn't for the intention of serving someone else's needs?

The store was narrow, with two aisles. In the center was waist-high custom cabinetry that both held and displayed knickers; the racks of bras were on the outer walls, with a small curation of loungewear in the back. I gingerly touched the different garments, allowing myself to inspect them (*Look, don't touch*, had been my mother's constant admonition in stores like this). I felt the different fabrics: the laces, alternately soft and scratchy, the polyester satins, the velvet, and the most luxurious and expensive—silk. Any color I could imagine was available, but I wanted to feel grounded, secure. Sexy, but safe. Black it was.

One bra caught my eye above all the rest. It had a molded cup—I hadn't yet discovered the joys of unlined bras for full busts—with straps across the top. When I tried it on and really looked at myself in the mirror, shirtless, black strappy bra and black high-waisted jeans and cowboy boots, I felt a kind of power wash over me that I didn't know was possible. In this bra, I felt my attitude shift from a desire to constantly cover what I perceived as my least-flattering features into a desire to scream *Fuck it* and run around half-naked in Harvard Square. I hadn't known clothing could do that.

"I'm sorry someone was mean to your perfect belly," ex-evangelical poet and singer Mary Lambert writes.[*]

The price—$125—made my heart skip a beat, but I was rebuilding from the ground up, and anything that helped me feel like I could do battle was worth it.

---

[*] Mary Lambert, "Jesus Loves My Crop Top," in *Shame Is an Ocean I Swim Across* (New York: Feiwel and Friends, 2018), 32.

That bra was the first of many. Next were matching sets from Simone Pérèle and Panache, then stockings that said WHIP ME BITE ME EAT ME TEASE ME from Agent Provocateur on Newbury Street.

I gradually accrue pieces from independent designers: A harness from Karolina Laskowska. Robes from Dear Bowie before they go out of business; one particularly dazzling silk number from Harlow & Fox, which makes me feel like a goddamn princess. I wrap myself in lush, sensuous fabrics I never would have allowed myself under the ascetic religious beliefs both my ex-husband and I grew up with.

I am reminding myself that I have a body, and that it is good and deserving of pleasure, that my curves are not sinful. That I am beautiful simply because I believe myself to be.

*I've come to dance the shame out of my childhood, I've come to win back my joy.*\*

✛

Because I first experienced her in Boston, where, unbeknownst to me, she had been on loan from the Met, I was surprised and delighted to accidentally stumble upon her years later once I was living in New York and regularly going to museums. My best friend and I were wandering through the modernist section when we walked up a stairwell, turned a corner, and found her. Kiki Smith's *Lilith*. Possibility herself.

I was so surprised to see her there, so many years later, just *perched* on the wall staring at us, that I shrieked with delight— which, I think, is an appropriate greeting for Lilith, the screech owl,

---

\* Lambert, "Jesus Loves My Crop Top," 33.

made all the more so by the fact that it is decidedly uncivil behavior in the storied Metropolitan Museum of Art.

In the months after, I would make regular visits to the Met for the express purpose of sitting with Lilith in that back-corner stairwell, journaling and meditating on her, staring at her as the light streamed in through the floor-to-ceiling windows that backlit her. The light was beautiful, although the situation was less than ideal. It was only a matter of time before a museum guard approached me with a *Miss, you can't sit here,* but sometimes I could get a solid ten or fifteen minutes with her before getting kicked out.

How I wished she wasn't in a stairwell, that there was a bench where I could sit and write and meditate on her for hours. I appreciated the shock value of the placement, of Lilith's display in a liminal space where she greeted travelers who were only ever on their way somewhere else. But it also felt like the stairs dishonored her. It's not that stairs cannot be a majestic home for a work of art—the Louvre's Daru Staircase, which houses the Hellenistic Winged Victory of Samothrace, comes to mind. But I sat with Lilith often enough in this back staircase of the Met that I witnessed how many people simply passed by, how few really took time with her, shocked and awed by her ferocity, by her piercing gaze, which asks you just how invested in freedom you are.

Or maybe it was simply that a weirdo redhead in a leather jacket was quietly crying on the steps.

✢

Jewish tradition tells us that Lilith was exiled from the Garden for wanting to be on top, for wanting to ride Adam into the ground beneath her.

Topping is one aspect of Lilith I do not relate to. I am on top and in charge in most areas of my life, but when it comes to sex, I want to be fucked by women who want to ride me into the ground—and who never wanted to be in Paradise in the first place.

✛

There is a tall, femme woman with dark hair I dance with at a party. We dance, the kind of dancing that leads to fucking against a wall in a private corner. Her mouth is on my neck and her fingers are inside me and it's rough and it's glorious and she is asking me if that's too hard and I'm telling her it's not hard *enough*, and *yes there*, and *please more* and soon enough I'm bent over with my hands up against the wall just the way I like it, which is apparently just the way she likes it, too.

I don't find out she's a priest until days later—entirely by accident, because the queer community is small—and the question presents itself: If I had known she wore a collar, would I have let her wrap her hands around my neck, eagerly sucked the same fingers that administer the Eucharist?

✛

There is a healing component to the erotic—the kind that Audre Lorde advocated for in her famous essay "Uses of the Erotic." Lorde writes:

> There are many kinds of power, used and unused, acknowledged or otherwise. The erotic is a resource within each of us that lies in a

deeply female* and spiritual plane, firmly rooted in the power of our unexpressed or unrecognized feeling. . . . We have been raised to fear the **yes** within ourselves, our deepest cravings. . . . †

For Lorde, the erotic is craving. Purpose. Motivation for living. The erotic includes sex, but it is not *just* sex. In *Conversations with Audre Lorde*, she continues, "We tend to think of the erotic as an easy, tantalizing sexual arousal. I speak of the erotic as the deepest life force, a force which moves us toward living in a fundamental way."‡ Part of Lorde's argument is that the erotic has been corrupted through white supremacist capitalism—from people becoming detached from our own capacity for intuition and empathy. Purity culture—both religious and secular—also disconnects us from our own bodies, all so that we can become consumers of the machine that sells us back to ourselves.

Coming out helped awaken me to my own erotic, but it wasn't just about having sex with women, though that was essential to rewriting my story about pleasure. It wasn't just learning to be in my body, though that was essential to revising my story about my own value. The erotic was ultimately about finding friendship and community with other queer people. It was engaging in the mundane nature of spirituality. It was rebuilding my life from the ground

---

* Trans and nonbinary writers have long been in conversation with "Uses of the Erotic" around how it approaches gender, among other subjects. See "Letter to Audre Lorde from the Future," available in both English and Spanish, by Tito Mitjans Alayón, July 10, 2020, https://www.centerforthehumanities.org/distributaries/letter-to -audre-lorde-from-the-future.

† Audre Lorde, "Uses of the Erotic: The Erotic as Power," in *Sister Outsider: Essays and Speeches*, revised edition (Berkeley, CA: Crossing Press, 2007), 53, 57.

‡ Joan Wylie Hall, ed., *Conversations with Audre Lorde* (Jackson, MS: University Press of Mississippi, 2004), 99.

up, not just trying to add gay sex into an existing framework of fucked-up religiosity and capitalist striving.

Shame is lucrative for the people making money off our self-hatred, off oppressive systems, off bigotry. Lorde's erotic and Brown's exhortation to empathy are essential correctives if we are ever to get free.

It is vital that we begin or continue the process of shucking off the old lessons and messaging, that we examine the internalized systems that put us on autopilot when it comes to our relationship with our own bodies and desires and what we believe we're capable of. But there is an absolutely vital, second component to Lorde's essay that is often forgotten: the erotic is to be claimed, recognized, and—most important—shared. Lorde continues:

> The erotic cannot be felt secondhand. As a Black lesbian feminist, I have a particular feeling, knowledge, and understanding for those sisters with whom I have danced hard, played, or even fought. This deep participation has often been the forerunner for joint concerted actions *not possible before*. . . . Recognizing the power of the erotic within our lives can give us the energy to pursue genuine change within our world, rather than merely settling for a shift of characters in the same weary drama. [Emphasis mine]*

The erotic is deeply communal and community oriented. It's how we connect with others, divesting from white supremacy, from heteronormativity, from capitalism, from the systems that would keep our lives small. Tapping into our erotic energy is how we can build a more loving and reciprocal and just world, together.

---

* Lorde, "Uses of the Erotic," 59.

✝

There is a woman who I dance around the kitchen with while she's cooking us dinner, who I read tarot and cast spells with, who was my best friend for years before we were like this; who now chokes me out and fucks me into the earth like we are about to be cast out of Paradise—or like we've found it. *Why haven't we always been doing this?* I ask her, the first night I kiss her, the night she sinks her teeth into my thigh, claiming me like a succubus, leaving marks that bloom like a sunset for days.

This is what the church wanted us to fear, but it is, in fact, the erotic that *they* fear, women and queers and people the world over imbued with the force of its grounded confidence and power. Tenderness and joy and pleasure can be found outside the Garden. Lilith's daughters are skilled at making a communal oasis in what appears, to others, to be a desert. We always have been.

> Intreat me not to leave thee,
> or to return from following after thee:
> for whither thou goest, I will go;
> and where thou lodgest, I will lodge:
> thy people shall be my people, and thy God my God:
> Where thou diest, will I die, and there will I be buried:
> the Lord do so to me, and more also, if ought but death part thee
> and me.
>
> —Ruth 1:16–17 (KJV) (Ruth to Naomi)

I was right, all those years ago. When it's with a woman you truly love, it's holy.

# 9. COMMUNION

FIVE YEARS AFTER MY DIVORCE AND COMING OUT, I REGISTER FOR A-CAMP, AN exclusively queer camp hosted by Autostraddle, the internet's leading independent media company for "girl on girl culture," for the most obvious reason: I like a girl, and she's going.

That flirtation fizzles out long before camp starts, but our conversations piqued my interest about the camp itself—a community for queer women and trans folks that springs up in the woods, magically, for five days a year. For me, a femme-presenting lesbian who refuses to get an undercut or a septum piercing, or to wear most types of clothing that would register as legibly queer, the idea of being someplace where I'm immediately seen, where I don't have to come out to someone new for a whole five days, sounded nearly utopian.

One of my dearest friends signs up to join me. I have other friends from Boston who are going, and a whole host of queer Twitter who I've never met in real life is descending on the camp as well.

The schedule is released a few weeks ahead of time. Among

dozens of workshops, there are dance clinics (yes), crafting events (no), Disney Princess sing-alongs (hell yes), and a Dana Fairbanks Memorial Tennis Tournament (hard pass). There's a Shabbat on Friday for Jewish campers. Also of note? A Gospel Brunch on Sunday morning, described as a service for those who were faithful, seeking, and "running from" the church.

I'm living in New York these days, so I reconnect with Boston friends who are attending, and it doesn't take long for Erica, a kindred spirit, and also a fellow nerdy redheaded femme, and me to end up on the subject of religion. Our conversations always go there. After all, we're both in the "running from" church category.

*We probably aren't the only two people at camp who are ex-fundie,* Erica says. *There are definitely more of us. We should put a meetup on the board.*

I scribble a quick note: "Ex-Religious and Fundamentalist Lunch Meetup—1:45pm Saturday, Cabana," and pin it to the "Missed Connections" board, where lunch meetups for Saturday are already springing up.

The next day, Erica and I host a group of ex-fundies in a conversation at a picnic table in the open-air cabana. There are fewer than ten of us, and a meetup that is supposed to last forty-five minutes goes for nearly three hours, all the way through the first workshop block of the afternoon.

We each introduce ourselves by name and pronouns and launch into detailed recountings of the faiths in which we were raised, of what we've experienced, as queer people within faithful families, of what we've lost.

*I'm a lesbian, but I grew up really conservative and really Christian, and I've got an ex-husband,* I say.

*I've got one of those,* another lesbian in the circle says, and we laugh in recognition, seeing—really seeing—each other's pain in a way virtually no one else can.

In spite of having different backgrounds—some from cults, some LDS (Mormon), some ex-evangelical Christian (like myself), some ex-Catholic, some ex-Muslim—everyone at the picnic table shares similar traumas around sexual purity, rigid gender roles, authority and authoritarianism, and literal interpretations of religious texts. We're all wounded, bitter, searching, healing.

None of us are practicing any even adjacent forms of the religions we grew up with. All of us have issues with our natal families; many of us have been cut off and are struggling to find ways of staying connected. Many of us feel too hurt to even try any form of spirituality and are skeptical of the queer community's embrace of alternative forms of spirituality. I'm one of the few who have embraced practices like tarot and astrology, albeit more as a form of self-healing, of rebuilding my own identity outside organized religion.

That night, I eschew the afterparties and stay up talking in the common room with my cabinmates, especially one—Lauren, a short, soft butch with glasses. It turns out that she and her partner are both ex-evangelicals, that she grew up in the South around the kinds of churches I had.

*It's so hard, with our queer community here,* I say to Lauren. *They don't understand how much of a loss the church is.* It can feel like our LGBTQ+ community doesn't take our trauma seriously because we should be glad to be out of the church, because Christianity is so damaging that we shouldn't mourn its loss.

For hours, Lauren and I talk religion and God and church and family and identity, finishing each other's sentences, starting to explain the words we're using and then realizing we don't have to, because we're talking to another native speaker of our own first language.

The next morning, it turns out that I'm not too tired from staying up talking late into the night with Lauren to go to Gospel Brunch. I show up at the windows-on-all-sides room, dubbed the "Fishbowl," with my breakfast plate—mostly blueberries, raspberries, blackberries, and strawberries—and sit at a random table.

The only person I recognize in the room is Ari, the Autostraddle staff member who is leading the service.

The feeling of isolation in church is familiar, practically comfortable. But there is orange juice and champagne on the tables for mimosas. That's different.

A girl sits down at my table with her plate and pauses. *Should we pray before eating?* she asks, the question seemingly directed to all of us. I pause midbite. I haven't prayed before a meal in years, haven't even stopped to consider the question.

It only then dawns on me that some folks here haven't lost their faith, have found a way to hold their queerness and God simultaneously. I knew that was possible, intellectually, but now I really see it. A small engine of anxiety starts up in my stomach, that gnawing feeling that I don't belong here.

Ari is praying, and there are readings from scripture.

Why did I come here? This isn't me anymore. I don't believe in sin, don't believe that Jesus is the only way to God, don't even know if I think he's an option on the path to God.

My mind is reeling, and practically on cue, Lauren and her partner come in and sit down next to me. I feel a little less alone because I know they're in the same category as me—"running from" God—even though we ended up here, in church at queer camp. But then, Ari starts reading an unfamiliar poem from Natalie Diaz—

*isn't this what God felt when he pressed together*
*the first Beloved: Everything.**

—and I split open like a seed, tears falling from my eyes uncontrollably. The words are balm, and Ari's voice is rainwater. Something starts growing, or maybe something starts healing. What are these words doing in between readings from 1 Peter and Acts? It is magic, indefinable, except it is entirely definable. This is the kind of thing that used to happen for me in church, that I used to call the Holy Spirit—back when I still believed, back before I knew I was queer.

*If you'd like to take communion, we're going to have it,* Ari says. *We've got cinnamon bread and champagne—*

At this, laughter.

*And there is absolutely no pressure. But if you would like to come up, come on up.*

I am out of my seat instinctually. Lauren is, too. We look at each other in an unspoken agreement.

I had stopped taking communion long before I stopped going to church. To me, communion symbolized that you were and *wanted* to be right with God, and even when I was still trying to go to church, I wasn't sure what I wanted. Depending on where I was attending that week, I passed the communion plates, didn't go up to receive.

But I know that here, I want to. Here, no judgment. Here, safety. Here, family. Queer family, full of bisexuals and lesbians and gays and queers and trans and nonbinary folks, all of whom are coming

---

* Natalie Diaz, "These Hands, If Not God's," in *Postcolonial Love Poem: Poems* (Minneapolis: Graywolf Press, 2020), 7.

from their own place of religious trauma or questioning or even, most remarkably to me, groundedness. All beautiful.

We stand in a circle, and Ari starts the prayer chain. I hold Lauren's hand tight, a lifeline, as people pray aloud, the prayers making their way around the circle. Lauren squeezes my hand, signaling that she would rather not pray aloud, that if I want to, it's my turn. Back when I attended church, I was never the person who passed the prayer, who declined to pray in a group setting. I always had something eloquent, emotional to say. But here among my family, the truest spiritual family I have ever felt, I have no words.

I squeeze the hand of the person to my right, passing it on, silent. I don't know their name, and they don't know mine. They pass the prayer, too, and it is as though we can feel each other's wounds through our palms, like Christ's palms, bleeding as we hold each other's hands.

Someone speaks up, a person who I would later learn was also ex-evangelical, the child of Pentecostal preachers: *Hi, God. It's been a while.*

After, the champagne-and-cinnamon-bread communion is passed around the circle, as we had with the prayers.

When it gets around to our side of the circle, Lauren turns to me and says,

*The body of Christ, broken for you,*
*The blood of Christ, poured out for you.*

We're both crying as she gives me communion, as I eat the bread and drink the champagne. I turn to give communion to the stranger who feels like family on my other side, and I repeat:

*The body of Christ, broken for you.*
*The blood of Christ, poured out for you.*

And for the first time in a very, very long time, saying these words does not feel false and they do not feel trite; they do not feel forced. Not because I believe, but because I feel something else— whole?

# 10. THE PROMISED LAND

The homunculus green carves a keyhole through which a cathedral
can be seen.

About those tragic moments.

—Selah Saterstrom[*]

**W**HERE I LIVE IN BROOKLYN, I CAN HEAR CHURCH BELLS RING. THERE IS THE
singsong melody that chimes on the quarter hour while I'm editing
on my pink sofa in the middle of the afternoon, the full hymn that
electronically plays at six p.m. while I'm sipping wine on my balcony at the end of a workday. The rhythm offers a familiar comfort
and structure.

---

* Selah Saterstrom, *Ideal Suggestions: Essays in Divinatory Poetics* (Berkeley, CA:
Essay Press, 2017), 162.

It would have been hard to live here even a few years ago.

I used to not be able to walk by a church without wanting to cross the street, without a deep anger stirring. It's not that I've made peace with God, or with the church, or even with what happened. I now acknowledge that the grief comes in waves, that losing the part of me that was once all of me leaves the kind of scar that is unlikely to fully fade. I no longer think it means that I haven't "healed" if I get angry or even if I have a day when I miss worship with other believers so badly I can barely speak—when I crave Durkheim's "collective effervescence," which I used to experience most Sunday mornings. Scripture is a language I will always understand; the familiar hymns I hear my neighborhood Catholic church play every day are ones I catch myself humming along to in recognition. Sometimes, I resent the musical intrusion into my daily life. Other times, I am grateful for its familiar company.

I am often told that I have "replaced" Christianity with tarot, with astrology. That what I do now is a "substitute" for the church. But I don't need anything to fill the vacuous hole left by the hot mess that is organized religion.

This is also true: nothing and no one can replace Jesus, just as getting a new best friend or girlfriend doesn't "replace" the old one who unexpectedly broke up with you. Jesus remains what Avery Gordon calls a "seething presence"* in my life—a third rail, a live wire I cannot bear to touch, an absence that interacts with me more than I purposefully interact with him.

---

* Avery Gordon, *Ghostly Matters: Haunting and the Sociological Imagination* (Minneapolis, MN: University of Minnesota Press, 1997), 8.

My new spiritual practice is not a replacement for Christianity but, rather, a redirected conversation that asks the questions *Why are we here? What is this life for?* Questions that follow a thread of acknowledgment of a spiritual realm beyond our understanding that I no longer consider through a Christian lens, but still believe in.

There are some uncanny coincidences and similarities between the organized religion I grew up in and the New Age "witchy" circles I find myself around. There are numerous "spiritual" concepts borrowed from Christianity, usually around an ascensionist, "let's meditate our way to a new earth" mindset, which sometimes seem directly lifted out of a "this world is not our home" End Times–focused evangelical Christianity. There are just as many crystal-loving folks trying to use spirituality to disengage from their lives as there are evangelicals.

To me, corrective spiritual medicine is learning to be present in the body—affirming that this world *is* our home. That my body is my home. That I am aware of what's going on in the world around me, of the damage being done to the people in my community, to the land that I live on, to the climate at large.

✛

A common topic of conversation among ex-evangelicals is that of "coming out" to our faithful families. For me, it happened slowly, over time; in many ways, my parents have had a harder time accepting my loss of faith than they have my sexuality.

It has been particularly painful for my mom, whose commitment to learning and growing in her sixties challenges every stereotype about boomers—but then, she's the one who brought me to church as a child, the one who knelt by my bed when I was four years old and first accepted Jesus into my heart. Her affirmations that my beliefs are my own are punctured by moments of profound evangelical panic: of asking me on a sunny walk through Central Park if I'm a witch, of begging me to not take the Mark of the Beast in the final days once the church has been raptured, of telling me point-blank she thinks I've lost my salvation.

My dad sends me devotionals and writes Bible verses in birthday cards, but his efforts never hit the same way as my mom's. As of this writing, he still hasn't been a Christian for as long as I was, and I didn't grow up with him as a spiritual authority the way I did my mom. I find his attempts to lecture me on the Bible well-meaning but misguided; it's hard to take him seriously when I'm aware that I know scripture better than he does. It's hubris, but it's also a lack of empathy on my dad's part—he had no idea what my faith meant to me, how difficult leaving was, and he has shown little interest in understanding more about the pain of that process.

The only time my mom and I came to blows over my departure was a few years ago, while we were walking up to eat at a restaurant in Minneapolis, the first time I was getting ready to tell her about this book. It was also one of the first times we were talking openly about how I had left the church, and she was explicitly wrestling with competing drives—her love for me and her desire to respect my decision alongside her decades of devout faith in a God who she believes is always there. *The church is full of broken people,* she said. *The church makes mistakes. I just think that if you knew Jesus—*

*I* do *know Jesus, Mom,* I said, cutting her off abruptly, furious at the insinuation. *That's the problem.*

When I hear anyone say that evangelicalism's embeddedness with the GOP has undercut what they see as "true" Christianity, say that they have a problem with the church, with Christians, but not with Jesus, the hairs on the back of my neck stand on edge. My spirit riles up. *I knew him*, I want to scream at folks—including my mother—who suggest to me that I didn't know him well enough.

Even when I left the church, I knew atheism was never an option. The everyday reality of my life and my experiences with too many profound, otherwise inexplicable phenomena made it impossible for me to leave the concept of a spiritual realm behind. I have a personal grudge against Jesus, you could say—a spirit I feel abandoned by. I hate that I am told by psychics and akashic records readers that, in addition to my ancestors or whoever else they are sensing, the God called Jesus or Yahweh or Jehovah is also there, lurking. Haunting me.

✝

Since that fateful Christmas, Jo and I, consciously or not, have made it a point to spend many of our birthdays with each other. (*I will never leave you.*) Recently, I spent mine, which bleeds into the Christmas holiday, with my sister at her home in Texas. At one point, we land at an indoor-outdoor honky-tonk, our Midwest asses perpetually marveling at the ability to be outdoors in merely a flannel and a leather jacket at this time of year.

We saddle up comfortably to the bar. Jo is sober now, and she orders a club soda. I keep it simple; these days, chronic migraines have me on a rosé diet. No hard liquor for me.

The older we get, the more we talk about our childhood. So much of it—Dad's anger, Mom's codependence—shaped us in similar ways, but the religion got to us differently. Even we marvel at our divergent approaches to faith, given the conservative, fundamentalist incubator we were raised in. Call it temperament, birth order, the distinction between a Capricorn and an Aries—same family environment, polar-opposite outcomes.

*I was never as all in as you,* Jo says to me as we take our drinks outside to sit at a wooden bench near a heat lamp on the cement patio, the sound of folks line dancing and two-stepping to George Strait, Dolly Parton, and Brooks & Dunn pouring out into the night. *I think doubt has been pretty normal for me throughout my life, so I've had to be flexible with things around faith. That's probably why I still believe in God,* she continues. *I started praying again. I talk to him. But I don't think the Christian version has to be it for people. I think we can find answers in a lot of places.*

I look up, and the Texas sky is so big, and I think of what an old writer friend once told me—that I was too orthodox to be a Christian. *Honestly, Jo, I envy that. I was so rigid,* I say, kicking my boots up on another chair. *This is something I see with a lot of folks I meet who are ex-evangelical—we were so all-or-nothing that, in the end, once it became clear that having it all wasn't an option, it had to be nothing. There wasn't any room for grace.*

Jo scootches closer to me and leans her head on my shoulder. *Well, I hope you can find some.*

*Thanks, honey.* I take a sip of my wine. *I get it elsewhere these days.*

For years, there was no regular, ritualistic group activity I was involved in that did not have a professional component. After I started working from home full-time in 2019, my weekly writers' group was the only thing that came close. But then, I started playing *Dungeons & Dragons*.

*Dungeons & Dragons* is a tabletop roleplaying game (TTRPG) in which you construct a fighter or magical character and act out what is essentially an adult game of make-believe.* In the 1980s, the game helped fuel the Satanic Panic, a media frenzy that centered on abuse that purportedly occurred during "devil worship" and that cast a looming shadow over anything that could potentially be a nexus for cultists, such as heavy metal music and *D&D*. For evangelicals, who interpret even thoughts as sins, a game like this is full of opportunities for sinful stumbling—any "fake" thing you do in the game, like murdering enemies or flirting with a bartender, is, in an evangelical worldview, still committed by you as a person.

When I was approached about joining a campaign run by my friend Smita, who was going to write, plan, and run the game sessions as the Dungeon Master (DM), I asked if it would be all right to create a character with rough religious backstory. They said yes. I created an orphaned character who had been raised in an abusive, controlling religious environment—specifically, in the largest temple of the capital city of the world we were playing in. I designed a character who had made a pact with the queen of hell to escape, had gotten involved in a criminal syndicate for a while, and for the last few years had operated as a vigilante/terrorist (depending on who you talk to), running her own crews to blow up the temples of state-approved gods whenever possible. And yet, she lives in an apartment a mere stone's throw from the temple she grew up in, where she still volunteers so that she can keep an eye on the kids who are kept there under lock and key. Her name is Delilah,

---

* These days, *D&D* and the multitudinous TTRPGs it has inspired elicit less evangelical ire and are more in the mainstream, as evidenced by the success of streaming shows like *Critical Role*, whose adult cartoon adaptation of the prequel to their first campaign was acquired by Amazon Prime Video.

and whenever the subject of religion comes up, she gets a little un-hinged.

Delilah helps me access—and release—a chaotic fury I have been burying in the deepest vaults of my subconscious for decades. She cusses out priests (*Make an intimidation check*, Smita the DM laughs) and interrogates the religiously devout fighters our group encounters about their beliefs. For three to five hours every other week, through the joy that is improvised roleplaying at the table with my friends, I get to dig in. Sometimes, we're fighting monsters. Sometimes, we're flirting in a make-believe strip club that Smita had to invent on the fly, because we need to blow off steam. Some-times, our crew is having a charged emotional conversation. And sometimes, Delilah is dealing with her religious trauma—which is different from mine, but which allows me to process emotions my repressed Midwestern ass has not allowed myself to feel in years.

I had figured it would be fun to build a character who was an-gry about religion. I did not anticipate how much it would help me process. But I can only process because of the vulnerability and creativity within the group—because all of us are respectful and generous and supportive and invested in listening and collaborat-ing. Because we are building this group together: not only the re-lationships our characters have in-game, but also the relationships we have as friends.

You can't have roleplay without trust from everyone sitting at the table. Guests who have played with us, such as my dear friend and fellow writer Austen (who has also DM'd games I've played in), have commented on the vulnerability in our game, on how easily we slide between humor, battles, flirtation, breaking into song, and an outright in-character fight, often in the scope of the same three-to-five-hour session. When the game ends, we engage in what is essentially aftercare: hugging, processing what happened, and continuing to check in on Discord in the days following.

The level of communication *has* to be high in order for us to engage so vulnerably with each other. I am perpetually struck by the transformative power of witnessing and participating in this kind of care, follow-up, and consent check-in—an intentionality that never happened in any church or Bible study I ever attended, or led.

✛

I am not particularly interested in rediscovering or reclaiming Christianity or Jesus. For months, I told my writing group, my girlfriend, my therapist, that I was terrified of reconverting while writing this book, that my greatest fear was somehow falling back into the old, unthinking ways of my youth. On the other hand, I knew it wasn't possible—that I now loved and accepted myself too much to possibly revert.

There *was* more awaiting me spiritually while writing this book and reprocessing my relationship to evangelicalism—but instead of reverting my brain to the sense of restriction I felt growing up, something in me broke open—something deep and tender. Helped along, I think, by the concurrent excavation of anger that I was processing through *D&D*; the external unfurling of that fist of rage I had kept closed for so many years, allowed free reign in Delilah's furious fire magic, made room for something else.

✛

I believe in spirits, but I'm not a psychic or a medium, and seeing spirits or the dead or other phenomena is not a part of my normal life. So in early 2021, when I was in the middle of drafting this book and Jesus *walked* through one of my apartment's walls and into my kitchen while I was preparing dinner, I startled. I may have screamed, even, before dismissing him with a firm, verbal *No, not today!* He turned, exiting as quickly as he'd come in.

At first, I doubted myself. But slowly, I remembered to trust myself. To trust my own experience. To trust my body, my instinct, my intuition. *You're fucking kidding me*, my ex-evangelical girlfriend said when I told her a few days later.

*I wish*, I responded.

A few months after, I was working on this book at my writing desk, the afternoon sunlight streaming into my studio apartment through the enormous windows. I glanced over at my pink velvet couch, and Jesus was sitting there in a leather jacket, ankle over knee in a figure four, long, dark hair spilling over his shoulders, arm casually slung across the back, smiling at me. I groaned.

*Fine*, I said. *But I'm not talking to you.* I turned the classical playlist up louder to prove the point.

He hung around for a few minutes before leaving. I haven't seen him since.

✝

These days, I consider spirituality to be connection between yourself and other people, or with nature, or with the other-than-human in a way that acknowledges that all those things are inextricably interlinked. Living in a spiritual way means that a conversation is always going, which includes listening as much as speaking.

In the year after I got the book deal, I began doing ancestor work (*Don't talk to spirits you don't know*, Mom always told me when I was very young, a lesson I quickly internalized). I was curious about how faith had been passed down to me—something I had never really thought about in the decade since leaving the church but that I was suddenly struck with an urgent interest in and yearning for. I took classes, bought books, and researched.

These days, you can find me lighting candles for my beloved dead in the morning and reciting the Hail Mary on Sundays in honor of my Catholic grandmother as well as different Psalms for the many, many Protestants (and Puritans) I descend from. Not because I believe, but because I now interpret prayers as blessings; because it's powerful to remember and, as a white American, to remediate. I'm finding ways to hold the texts, ideas, and people of my upbringing in ritual space, in ancestral honoring, in being in community with the other-than-human. If I'm writing on my couch, look out the window and start talking to the birds that happen to be visiting my balcony, and feel my grandmother's spirit and presence—it's all part and parcel of the same moment. Spirituality is a mundane, integrated way of living.

There continues to be a certain synchronicity, a certain familiarity, between the evangelicalism of my youth and my new approach to spirituality. I grew up in a household where God was all around us. In the rural Midwestern countryside, this meant that God was in nature—in the animals in our yard, in the trees, in my parents' gardens. In the small country church my family attended alongside numerous farmers, the cycle of the seasons were the pastor's metaphors, and the earth was regarded with high respect as God's creation. I grew up talking to the world around me, a practice that has lent itself toward the slow development of my animist worldview.

Growing up in a rural part of Iowa, I always knew what crops were in season, could tell ripeness at a passing glance in the car, knew how a drought or hailstorm would affect our neighbors' yield, just by being around adult conversation. I knew what vegetables we were growing, which birds were singing, could easily identify the local wildlife at a distance. I didn't know the scientific names for the fauna and flora, but I could shuck an ear of corn picked from our neighbor's field pretty damn fast. At church, we prayed for rain, and for safety during tornado season, and that the harvest would be bountiful.

During my process of deconstruction, I've realized that I have had a mundane attitude toward the spiritual aspects of life from the time I was a child, seeing God and spirit in the land, in the animals, in the passage of seasons. It's just my framework that has shifted.

✝

The church is broken. It cannot be fixed from the inside. Evangelicalism is rotten, shot through to the core with the kind of infectious hatred that cannot be undone one person at a time. The institution is designed to work against women, against queers, against anyone who isn't white, against anyone who wakes up while still plugged in; it's designed to press on us until we are crushed within it, unrecognizable to ourselves.

Leave it behind. Burn it down. Go build something new. And know this: You aren't alone. You were never alone. The damage the church has done is extraordinary; witness the wake of its destruction, of its spiritual abuse and political maneuvering.

Human beings are driven by belonging, by hope. The urge to believe in and belong to ourselves, to each other, and to something greater is real and profound—and the harm that it has caused in the past need not continue in the future.

There are other systems. There are other ways.

✛

The joy of the Lord was talked a lot about in church; namely, the continual exhortation that "the joy of the Lord is [my] strength"*— that the comfort that comes from knowing and trusting God is a source of strength. So, too, is there much talk of the "freedom" that comes from knowing Christ Jesus—purportedly, freedom from the sin you are constantly repenting from.

Today, there's another kind of joy that gets talked about a lot in my friend circles—queer joy. Queer joy is different from the "joy" I grew up with, the kind that is emblazoned with Christmas colors on holiday towels. The Latin root of joy is *gaudere*, to rejoice. Joy is not simply a feeling one settles into, like a warm blanket; it is active, perpetual movement—a state of being that is cultivated with others. "I want to attempt toward joy," Ashon T. Crawley writes.[†] Queer- ness isn't just a sexuality. It's a way of life that requires active and intentional daily work to decenter the normative and recenter our community, our safety—and our joy.

Queer joy is not hierarchical. Queerness is the freedom to be- long to yourself and others without societal restriction, without the bonds of natal family, hierarchy, and the state pressing on you. "Queerness's ecstatic and horizontal temporality is a path and a

---

* Nehemiah 8:10 (KJV).

† Ashton T. Crawley, *The Lonely Letters* (Durham, NC: Duke University Press, 2020), T-IV.

movement to a greater openness to the world," José Estaban Muñoz writes.* Queerness is getting to invent the communal structures that best serve your beloveds in real time.

Queer joy is found in Audre Lorde's erotic. Queer joy is waking up with the woman I love and going to meet friends for a picnic in Prospect Park or on a rooftop without any obligation to church or institution or blood family. Queer joy is listing each other as our emergency contacts, showing up when crisis plunges our beloveds into homelessness and health emergencies. Queer joy is found in my all-queer *D&D* games, in the explicit, collective commitment to decentering and deprioritizing cishet men and heteronormativity, to putting friendship and the collective of chosen family at the center. Queer joy is dressing in white and gathering with our people, thousands of us, at the Brooklyn Museum to march for Black lives. Queer joy is understanding that, as artist Micah Bazant wrote on their now-famous poster honoring our Black trans foremother Marsha P. Johnson, "There is no Pride for some of us without liberation for all of us."†

✢

Something in me resists the idea that we are our own gods—but what is a god but a creator, a source, and what are we, queer people, but the creators of our own lives?

I broke out of the prison that I, my family, and institutions had built inside me from infancy through childhood. I chose myself at the crossroads.

---

* José Estaban Muñoz, *Cruising Utopia: The Then and There of Queer Futility*, 10th anniversary ed. (New York: NYU Press, 2019), 25.

† Micah Bazant, "Marsha P. Johnson," https://www.micahbazant.com/marsha-p -johnson

Learning to choose myself has not been easy. It has upset a lot of people who have historically benefited from my subservience and lack of self-knowledge. But it's true what they say: When you say no, you get to say yes. I have let the *no* fill my mouth like a sacrament, like Job 38:11 (KJV): "Hitherto shalt thou come, but no further." When the no drops, a gate slamming into the ground, everything that *no* has made room for becomes clearer. More space. More presence. More love. More mindfulness.

Less bullshit.

✢

In *Body Work: The Radical Power of Personal Narrative*, Melissa Febos calls "the power of telling my own story . . . a gospel with the power to cure."*

The English word "gospel" comes from the Latin *evangelium*, which, as any current or former Christian knows, means "good news."

The healing power of our personal authority is good news, indeed.

✢

On what would be my ten-year wedding anniversary, I am hosting a pandemic-delayed housewarming in my apartment.

My friends bring bottles and bottles of wine. One bakes a vegan chocolate cake; another brings the quintessential Junior's New York cheesecake, and over the course of the evening, the two are mixed together to create an entirely new delicacy. There are

---

* Melissa Febos, *Body Work: The Radical Power of Personal Narrative* (New York, Catapult, 2022), 123.

offerings of dried lavender, fresh pink cockscomb flowers, bundles of sage wrapped in dried roses, numerous herbs, a nice bottle of bourbon for my girlfriend.

The apartment is full of queer and trans folks—friends, couples, folks from my *D&D* game, folks from my writers' group, folks I first met in the lingerie and fashion world, and the one friend from my old college evangelical days who stuck by me through it all. The concentric circles lap and lap: almost half the people in the room went to A-Camp, well over half are writers or work in publishing. There are conversations about books and much fangirling, between readers and writers, over my resplendently glamorous lingerie industry friends, Twitter mutuals, folks who haven't seen each other in years reconnecting after a pandemic apart. I have an extended conversation with the single representative man in the room—a friend's husband—about calling Missouri "Missour-*ee*" or "Missour-*uh*," as one does with other Midwesterners at a Brooklyn housewarming after several glasses of wine.

Halfway through the evening, a fellow member of my long-running writers' group pops a bottle of champagne, the light catching on her signature gold-and-silver rings, and the whole room erupts in spontaneous cheers and applause. This ignites a conversation about sabering the bottle and how all my deeply lesbian apartment is missing is a sword, and it turns out that a handful of the queers milling around my kitchen island simply *happen* to have swords, because of course they do. A quick moment of joking turns into me announcing *Well, it* is *my wedding anniversary* to more applause and whoops and hollers.

I'm hosting: constantly scanning the room for empty hands and glasses, walking around pouring freshly uncorked rosé and distributing sweating ice-cold bottles of Topo Chico, refilling the cheese board, putting out forks for dessert, trying to ensure that every-one here has gotten some amount of one-on-one attention. But a few times, I pause to take it all in. People from almost every im-portant part of my life are here, and so many who couldn't make it sent flowers and spices and other sweet gifts, and this feels like a culmination: the gifts, a ceremonial blessing; everyone's presence, a ritual way-opening. Having so many people I care about in one place, talking, laughing, finding points of connection. This kind of togetherness is all I ever wanted.

I look around, and I know—whatever home is, I have found it.

✝

Coming out and leaving the church was a death: of an identity, a worldview, everything I thought I had known about myself. Like so many queer people before me, I lost friendships, family, com-munity.

But there is a secret that the church does not want those of us who have left to remember. There is a love that is as strong as death—the love you discover for yourself when, as Audre Lorde once wrote, you define yourself for yourself.

I buried my old self years ago. Do not look for her; she is not there.

This is the truth about queer people: We have resurrected our-selves. We are born again.

Our tombs are empty.

We are risen.

# ACKNOWLEDGMENTS

Sᴇᴄᴛɪᴏɴs ᴏғ ᴄʜᴀᴘᴛᴇʀ 2 ɪɴɪᴛɪᴀʟʟʏ ᴀᴘᴘᴇᴀʀᴇᴅ ɪɴ "ᴡʜᴇʀᴇᴠᴇʀ ᴡᴇsᴛ ɪs," originally published with Autostraddle. Sections of chapter 7 initially appeared in "After Leaving the Church, Tarot Became My Salvation," originally published with *NYLON*. Chapter 9 is excerpted from "I Found God at Queer Summer Camp," originally published with *Narratively*.

✛

To Jenny Xu, my brilliant editor. This book was waiting for you. I did not know how absolutely vital it would be to work with someone who also spoke the language of evangelicalism and wintered Midwesternness—but of course it was. I feel deeply lucky to have had you as a creative partner and advocate through such a roller coaster of a year, to have had this project in the hands of someone I trusted so wholeheartedly from our very first phone call. You envisioned the perfect structure for this book and raised it to a level I never thought possible.

To Dana Murphy, my agent and fellow pragmatic, business-brained Capricorn moon. No one will ever top your inbox slide. This book was such a journey, and you fought for me at every step. Thank you for being the best of cheerleaders and champions. I am so glad to be in this with you.

To Liz Velez, for making sure none of the balls—no matter how small—got dropped. Books simply cannot get made without editorial assistants, and you are the best of them.

To the rockstar Harper team: Robin Bilardello, Elina Cohen, Kelly Doyle, Frieda Duggan, David Eber, Diana Meunier, Becca Putnam, Beth Silfin, and Lydia Weaver for designing, producing, and otherwise making sure that this book was the best it could possibly be before going out into the world.

To my Wonder Women of a writer's group: Angela Chen, Lilly Dancyger, Deena ElGenaidi, and Nina St. Pierre. I am so grateful for what we have built together and for all the ways y'all make my life better, personally and professionally, every goddamn week. Thank you for being the ultimate sounding board, the best possible team of creative midwives.

To my beloveds, writers and nonwriters alike, who read drafts of this project over the years, were generous with their professional advice, pulled tarot cards for me, co-worked over Zoom throughout the pandemic, counseled me off more ledges than I can count, brought me books and coffee and wine and meals, and told me that they believed in me when I did not, or could not, believe in myself: Natalie Adler, Kendra Austin, Keenan Caldwell, Kendra Clarke, Ella Cerón, Frankie de la Cretaz, Melissa Faliveno, Cora Harrington, Michelle Hart, Heather Hogan, Haley Houseman,

Lyz Lenz, T Kira Madden, Austen (A.E.) Osworth, Siri Plouff, Kayla Prestel, Bailey Schroeder, Arabelle Sicardi, Marisol Sternke, Kirstin Wagner, Esmé Weijun Wang, Mecca Woods, and Ryan Yates. I love you all.

To Rachel Kincaid, for a wonderful class on craft and hauntology that broke some important things open for me at just the right moment in the revision process (and also for publishing my first-ever personal essay).

To my earliest editors, especially Kristin Iversen, Alanna Okun, Jess Zimmerman, Rachel, and Lilly, for nurturing and encouraging my work when I was just starting to touch on subjects that I'd develop here. For always treating and respecting me as a whole person, rather than something to be mined for parts, and in so doing, teaching me how it was possible to survive in this industry.

To Diana Rose Harper, for the uncanny Saterstrom bibliomancy and especially the astrological support at some truly pivotal moments in Book Year.

To Steve Wall, for naming Kyle. I could not adore you more if I tried.

To my *D&D* family—Michelle Marchese/Artie, Nicole Sam/Zinona, Meg Jones Wall/Zayla, and most especially our brilliant Dungeon Master, Smita Patankar—for creating the most incredible story to collectively dive into from week to week. To Kate/Sindri, for the time we had together. Thank you for letting me work out so much of my religious shit through Delilah—for allowing our game to be a soft place to land while I was writing this book. Thank you for trusting me to write about our Tuesday nights here. I love you all so dearly, and I can't wait to see where our adventures and shared nerdery take us, both in and out of game. Long live Old Tree.

To Emmylou Harris, for songs that helped save my life and articulate a way forward.

To my therapist, S., for more than I can possibly put in a few sentences. This book would not be possible without the years I've spent sitting in your office (and on Zoom). I'm so grateful for the work we've done together, for how you've supported and advised me through the strange and particular emotional landmines of this project. Thank you for helping me learn to be more gracious with my past self.

To my parents, for your consistent support of my writing and especially this project, even knowing what it entailed. Thanks especially to Mom for sharing your journals and bearing with me through all of the fact-checking phone calls.

To the doctors, nurses, and staff at Brooklyn Hospital Center, whose wisdom and compassionate care were so desperately needed when my body decided to come crashing down around me in the final weeks (weeks!) before my book deadline. (And the weeks when Omicron hospitalizations in the city were skyrocketing, at that.) The most special of thank-yous to the Emergency, Surgery, Radiology, OB-GYN, and Neurology departments, most especially to Dr. Irene Lou, Dr. Natalie Best, Dr. Athena Hsu, Dr. Saba Gilani, Dr. Obiakor, Dr. William, Dr. Ocasio, Dr. Qureshi, Dr. Julian, Dr. Chai, Dr. Alexander, and Nurse Primus, Nurse Gayat, Nurse Kevin, Nurse Hakeem, Nurse Robinson, Nurse Edwards, Nurse Gauthier, Nurse Gaby, Nurse Marcelle, Nurse Sultana, Nurse Landais, Nurse Ng, Nurse Sonia, Ms. Lydia, and Ms. Chan. Also, thank you to Ms. Morgan, who had the timing of a guardian angel.

To everyone near and far, acquaintance and internet stranger, who found ways to materially, emotionally, and spiritually support me and my partner during those terrifying weeks I spent in the hospital—from the bottom of my heart, thank you.

To Sam, for encouraging me to keep the flame alive back when *Heretic* was barely an idea. I will always be grateful.

To Melissa-Leigh Gore and Kyley Caldwell, for showing up for me during the events of this book and for being my family ever since: *A cord of three strands is not quickly broken.* As Melissa once said, "Thank you for traveling with me to every place my heart has needed to go." You have shown me so much about the nature and meaning of love.

To Meg: Thank you for always being my *very* first, most generous reader. You made this process so much gentler, so much more spacious and loving. If only our younger, closeted evangelical selves could see the queers we have become. I think they'd be properly horrified—and perhaps a little inspired. Our friendship is so rich, and adding romance has unlocked a kind of intimacy and trust that this lifetime will not be enough to explore. The next one, perhaps.

To Jo, for being the Sally to my Gillian. This book is only possible because you went into the furnace with me and held me when the flames were strongest. If there is a higher power, I'm so, so glad they put us in the same family. You are everything that is good and hopeful in this world; how lucky am I, to be your sister, to get to witness the many chapters of your life in all its richness.

To every woman and queer who wrote their story down, who knew that their life—in all its holiness and terror—was worth the telling. You helped so many of us stay in the game. Thank you.

# ABOUT THE AUTHOR

JEANNA KADLEC is a writer, astrologer, former lingerie boutique owner, and recovering academic. Her writing has appeared in *ELLE*; *NYLON*; *O, the Oprah Magazine*; *Allure*; *Catapult*; *Literary Hub*; *Autostraddle*, and more. A born and bred Midwesterner, she now lives in Brooklyn. *Heretic* is her first book.

mans.' A German truck had broken down nearby, she explained, and the Germans, six of them, came here on foot through the mud. The villagers took their guns and shot them, killed all six.

"And it was true. When we left the village, we saw six pairs of feet sticking up out of a ditch.

"Olga and I kept on walking. We avoided villages by day, because you never knew who you might run into. But we always headed in the direction of the thunder, the rumbling that was like a sound from home.

"Listening to it, I said, 'That's our people, coming to save us.'

"It became easier to keep going. In the evenings we risked entering a village for the night. It was a time when many people were homeless, when many were on the road, and it was more natural to let strangers into your home, despite the lice and occasional thieves, than it is today. People lived as if everyone were trapped in a fire or some other catastrophe, and life was too dangerous for them not to help one another.

"After three days and three nights we arrived in the village of Grishkovtsy, and the first thing we heard was, 'The Russians are here.'

"Vlasov's anti-Soviet army, I thought, because there were units of his troops in some of the villages. But I soon realized it wasn't them, after all. The men we saw were very young, all of them eighteen years old. They were stopping everyone who wore good boots, pulling them off, and giving their own soaked felt boots in exchange. 'You're staying, but we have to keep going,' was what they said.

"They didn't touch my boots, which were felt, but took Olga's. Just then a nurse passed by, and Olga turned to her to protest. The nurse snapped, 'Shut up, you whore. While we were at the front shedding our blood by the bucket, you were having your tits nibbled by German bedbugs.' From the woman's accent I guessed her to be a Siberian of some kind.

"The gibe struck home, and I was pleased by the sight of Olga in soaked felt boots sloshing through the mud. Greed and treachery get their just desserts, I thought. To her I said, 'Those are our people.'

" 'They may be our people,' she retorted angrily, 'but those were my boots.'

"As soon as we reached our town, I turned my back on her and never saw her again.

"I went straight to my old room, opened the door with the key I had kept all this time in my rucksack. If Nikolai Pasternakov had ever been here, there was no sign of it. All my belongings were exactly as I had left them, right down to the few pieces of kindling stacked beside the little stove. I lighted a fire and piled on some turf. The room warmed quickly and was soon pleasant. Thank God, I thought, the worst is over now. I'm still young and have time to catch up on all I've missed.

"And a lot of people thought this at the time. We welcomed the return of the Soviets with the same joy as we had welcomed the arrival of the Germans. Because, with the kind of life we had lived for so long, change, any change, was what our hearts desired. Even our old people became young, for the expectation of change is a youthful thing. When the Germans descended on us from an unknown Europe in the summer of 1941, we had no idea what they were. So there was reason to hope. We knew our own people all too well. Now we hoped that the regime of 1943, which was advancing, would be better than the one that had retreated in 1941. After so much bloodshed, we couldn't imagine a return to things as they had been before. After all, a man who has recovered from a mortal illness is a changed man. But we were wrong: the clock was turned back, to every last detail.

"Not everything in the past had been bad, of course, and not only the bad things were restored. Under the Germans, for example, the streetcars hadn't run at all, and to get to one end of town from the other had been a major undertaking. But within two weeks of the Soviets' return, the streetcars were running again, making life a lot more pleasant, if a lot noisier. People would climb on and ask the fare. 'You've forgotten already?' the conductor would say. 'Twenty kopecks, just as it used to be.'

"The streetcars had been reassembled out of scrap iron, spare parts, and odds and ends found in the ruins of the depot. While rummaging among the pieces of metal there, workmen unearthed a bronze statue of Pushkin. I remembered that when I returned from Chubintsy the first time I'd left town during the occupation, I happened to be walking past the Teacher Training School where I had attended Bisk's literary group, and saw that the pedestal out front was empty. Now I learned about the statue's recovery completely by chance and from an unexpected quarter.

"Late one cold, windy evening, there was a knock on my door, a tentative knock, the knuckles of a beggar, not the fist of the State. Who could it be, I wondered. It was still wartime, and there was a curfew, with military patrols in the streets. Although gone, the Germans kept up their air raids, and had destroyed the station and bombed a hospital train that was standing on the tracks there. The town had held a mass funeral for the victims. It was an uneasy time, yet slowly life was returning to normal, and I had my old job, drayman at the soft-drinks plant. The knock at the door came as I was about to have supper.

"The only personal friend who ever came was Leonid Pavlovich, but he would not show up so late, having no pass to be out after curfew, and no bread ration either. I tried to help him and his blind sister in little ways, trading beer for bread and buckwheat, which I brought to their home. He was embarrassed to accept help, but I felt indebted to them, and was hopeful that things would soon improve. The theater was not open, of course; the building had been sealed up, and Gladky had disappeared. But the head of the local nursing school wanted to organize, along with a motorcycle class, a drama group. He was one of Leonid Pavlovich's prewar fans, and promised him a job with the group that would entitle him to ration coupons. Still, I was subject to sudden attacks of anxiety, and this late-night knock put my heart in my mouth. The idea of opening the door frightened me, but so did the idea of not opening it. Suppose it was someone who wanted to warn me about something?

"I unlocked the door, and there was nobody there. My mind is playing tricks on me, I thought. Then I heard a voice from out of the gloom. 'Let me in,' it said. I squinted, and saw that it was old Saltykov. This doubled my fear. The old man was on the run; if I let him in, I'd become his accomplice. I stood there, silent, and old Saltykov understood my silence. There was no way to misunderstand it.

" 'Just for tonight,' he pleaded. 'Until the curfew lifts in the morning.'

"He looked terrible, soaked to the skin, bent over from the cold, and clearly ill. I took pity on him. 'You can stay until morning,' I said.

"I gave him something to eat, poured him some beer, and put his clothes near my little stove to dry. He ate as though he was starving: stuffed his mouth, shoveled more in before swallowing what was already there.

" 'Why didn't you leave with the Germans?' I asked.

" 'I couldn't,' he said. 'This is where Masha's grave is. Besides . . .' He began to tell me about the discovery of the Pushkin statue. 'We were waiting for saviors from Europe, and they tossed our geniuses into the garbage. That statue of Pushkin was erected before the Revolution, in front of First City High School, which became the Teacher Training School in Soviet times. It's the work of a well-known sculptor. Pushkin, you know, as Gogol said, was very Russian. As a young man I often went there to look at the statue. And in Soviet times too I went with Masha. We'd stand and look Pushkin in the face, and it would soothe my soul. But Europe, with its Beethovens and Schillers, tied Pushkin to a tank and dragged him from his pedestal.'

"Since he was so weak, old Saltykov quickly got drunk on the beer, and went on talking, and wept shamelessly, as a child weeps when his favorite toy is broken.

" 'They pulled him down with a tank, tied him to horses, and dragged him through the streets,' he sobbed. 'They pulled him over the stones while stupid, heartless people laughed. Masha and I accompanied Pushkin on his final journey, along the sidewalks to the town market, the place of execution. There, the German savages'—at this point, the old man's voice broke, and he spent a long time blowing his nose and wiping his eyes with a rumpled, dirty handkerchief—'the German savages began to rock the statue from side to side, trying to smash it. But the metal was too strong for them, all that pre-Revolutionary bronze. The only damage it sustained was scratches, scratches on Pushkin's bronze curls, on his wonderful face. . . . It was after this crime that Masha took to her bed; she never got up again.'

"I gave Saltykov a cup of tea sweetened with saccharine. He gulped it down noisily, holding the cup in trembling hands. He fell silent for a while after his tea, seemed to calm down a little, and was at last able to speak without tears, though there were tears in his voice.

" 'I wanted to write the German Gebietskommissar

and tell him that this kind of action by the German authorities only made the job easier for Soviet underground propaganda, but Panchenko dissuaded me. Then, later, I saw a set of instructions from Alfred Rosenberg to his subordinates. They said that the Russians were animals, that the Bolsheviks had turned them into beasts of burden, and Germans must work them all the harder. I continued to work in the town hall, but from that day on I had only one desire: to be rid of the Germans, but without letting the Judeo-Bolsheviks back in. Our crazy Russian hopes . . .

" 'The Bolsheviks are back, but they have changed. Perhaps the war taught them something, after all. They haven't laid a finger on the Orthodox churches that were reopened under the Germans; the army people have badges of rank again. And the Pushkin statue is being restored. As if the Bolsheviks are becoming more and more Russian and breaking off their ties with Judaism. If this is really true, then our country may yet, by some miracle, be reborn. But why should it be a miracle? Wasn't the Russian nation able to draw strength from the period of Mongol oppression, using the Mongols to unite the separate principalities into a single state? In the same way, the Russian nation can use the Bolsheviks, once they are purged of Yids. . . .'

"I made up a bed for him on the floor with some old blankets and gave him my jacket for a pillow. He lay down, but didn't sleep. He sighed and wheezed, and kept turning over, keeping me from getting any rest before work the next day. At dawn he left. Two days later, I read in the local newspaper, *Lenin's Way*, that the body of the traitor Saltykov had been found in the town cemetery. The article said that in his terror at the prospect of much-deserved punishment he had poisoned himself. I think he swallowed the poison at the grave of Maria Nikolaevna.''

# 10

"ON ANOTHER OCCASION I read in *Lenin's Way*, which had disappeared in 1941 but was revived in 1943, an announcement for a paid lecture to be given at Red Army Hall. Its subject was "Hitler and His Close Associates: The Kind of People They Are." The lecturer was a certain Battalion Commissar Bisk. Could it be Saul Abramovich himself?

"Under the German occupation, Red Army Hall had been turned into an officers' club, and entry had been restricted to Germans. Perhaps that was why so many came in spite of the five-ruble admission fee. I sat in the middle of the hall, and throughout the lecture I couldn't take my eyes off the speaker. Was it Saul Abramovich or just someone with the same name? I kept asking myself. It was hard to tell, because of the partisan beard that reached down to his chest. Was this officer, grown fat on army-headquarters rations and wearing a squeaky-new leather belt, the same frightened Saul

Abramovich who had been evacuated to the east on a flatcar piled with rusty machinery, with his wife, Fanny Abramovna, distracted by fear, in her housecoat? Yes, it was. I recognized his voice, the gestures he used to hammer points home. He had the audience in the palm of his hand.

" 'Hitler, the son of a poor civil servant, became a capitalist when he took power,' he said. 'He owns a Nazi publishing firm, and has made over three million dollars from the sales of *Mein Kampf*, which all Germans are required to buy. He personally owns two castles in the mountains, and has yachts. And Göring has a gold-tiled bathroom, and all the plays and films in German have to have Goebbels' approval.'

"After the lecture Bisk answered questions written out on pieces of paper. I wrote: 'Dear Saul Abramovich, do you remember me, Sasha Chubinets? I would like to talk to you. Greetings to Fanny Abramovna.' The chairman, a representative of the Party town committee, placed the pieces of paper in a heap before Saul Abramovich, who picked them up one by one, unfolded them, and answered the questions. Afterward I waited for a long time; the audience left, and still I waited. Finally Bisk appeared, wearing a fine officer's greatcoat with badges of rank and an astrakhan cap with crimson trim. He marched out in military fashion, accompanied by the town committee representative, and his salt-and-pepper beard gave him that grandfatherly look the young soldiers all admired. He looked as if he would burst into song at any moment and give a rousing rendition of 'My Only One Is My Field Gun,' which the returning Soviet soldiers had brought back with them and often sang, even when marching to the municipal bathhouse with their toilet kits.

"At the sight of this new Saul Abramovich, I was overcome with timidity, but nevertheless I went up to him and said: 'Saul Abramovich, I'm Alexander Chubinets. I was at your lecture and sent you a note.'

"He strode past me without even turning his head—the head of a sage from the shtetl, wearing a cossack cap instead of a yarmulke. But his glance took me in, from the corner of his eye, and I knew he had recognized me and had read my note. Without a doubt, this was the Saul Abramovich Bisk who at the Teacher Training School had spoken of August Bebel and proletarian literature in a way that resulted in the accusation that he was a Trotskyite. As I followed him with my eyes, his back seemed to accuse me. It said, 'Chubinets, you and that traitor Saltykov looted my apartment in 1941. You broke my mirror and ripped my books to shreds.' 'No, I didn't,' I replied in my mind. 'I didn't break anything. All I did was take what was mine, and you gave me permission to do that as you were leaving on the train.' But his retreating back continued to condemn me: 'You engaged in cultural collaboration with the German occupation, and the Gestapo allowed your play to be produced.' I replied: 'My lip still has pus coming from it because a German whip hit me when I tried to help some Soviet prisoners. My premiere took place only after that, and not on a stage but in a dressing room. So what am I guilty of? What are we all guilty of—Leonid Pavlovich, Lelya Romanova, and the others? Of the fact that not everyone in the town was hanged when you abandoned us for Moscow or Tashkent? So, you ask, who gave shelter to the traitor Saltykov? All right, I gave him shelter. Is it a crime to put a sick old man up for the night before he dies? He was a traitor, yes, but he's dead now, his suffering is over, and his rage is extinguished. No, Comrade Bisk, I am innocent.'

"But in those days, when someone said he was innocent, you knew he was already a condemned man. So after that lecture of Bisk's, my conscience gave me no rest, and I wasn't surprised when they came for me a week later, at night. The knock of authority, and a voice thickened by a cold, announced yet another stage on the forced march of my life: 'Open up! Military police.' "

"I'm sorry," I interrupted. "But that name, Bisk, is familiar. I think I know the man. He writes about the connection between fascism and Zionism. Do you happen to know where he is?"

"No," Chubinets said, "but I heard that he too was jailed for something or other at the end of the war."

"Well, then it can't be the same person. Wait . . . the one I'm thinking of was Wanschelbäum, not Bisk. Former spy, now writes spy stories—you know the kind. At a literary gathering once, he shouted at a brother writer, Kirschenbaum, who was about to leave for Vienna with an exit visa to Israel: 'You and I have nothing, nothing in common! I'm a Soviet patriot, and you, you're a rotten Zionist!' Not the same man at all, and the name is totally different. Wanschelbäum, Bisk—but for some reason I thought they were the same. Maybe because of the way just changing clothes on mannequins can change their future—a fancy life-style or time in a prison camp."

Chubinets and I were both worn out. We had already passed Rakitno and Berezanka, and I was thinking how nice it would be to get some sleep, since there were another three hours to go before dawn and one and a half hours to Kazatin. Kazatin is noisier than Fastov, more brightly lighted, and has two platforms: one for the line from Kiev and the other for the line to Shepetovka and Zdolbunov. It seemed like a good idea to catch a few winks before Kazatin, because after that we'd have no peace. Forty minutes after Kazatin comes Berdichev, and at Berdichev West Ukrainians would climb onto the train, reeking of salt pork and onions. In the east, for some reason, Ukrainians tend to eat their salt pork with garlic; whereas in the west they eat it with onions. The onion habit probably comes from the Poles. The odor of garlic, if unacceptable in company, is at least aromatic, but the smell of raw onions evokes phony Polish gentry and uncouth peasants. I'll bet the entire SS Galicia Division stank of raw onions.

Their smell and behavior aside, Ukrainians, it must be admitted, are closer in spirit to the Poles than to the Russians. And if it turns out that they can't be independent, they would be better off with the Poles. The Poles have historically drawn Ukrainians into Europe; the Russians have sucked them into Asia. Poles and Ukrainians together number sixty or seventy million people. Had they somehow bypassed the age of bar-

barism and kept their sovereignty until the nineteenth century, who knows how they might have influenced the history of Europe and of the world? After all, if Catholics and Protestants can share Germany, why couldn't the western Slav Catholics and the Orthodox have shared a unified Polish Ukraine or Ukrainian Poland? Thus buffered, and cut off from German spiritual and material influence, Russia might even have been spared her bloody destiny.

My thoughts were interrupted by a sudden roar: a freight train clattering past on the other track. Freight cars, tank cars, freight cars again, flatcars, cars carrying crushed rock, stone, coal, and tractors. Outside our window, the night was as dark and impenetrable as before, but the muffled noises of night were now drowned out by ringing wheels and a hollow hurricane of what sounded like wet sheets slapping. Then suddenly all was quiet after the caboose flashed by, its windows lighted like a hut, a man in a canvas slicker at the rear holding up a lantern.

"So I was shoved into solitary," Chubinets went on, "with no explanation. But during my interrogation I figured out that I had been accused of Ukrainian nationalism. They kept asking about some Ukrainian nationalist whose name I had never heard before. The main interrogator was a tough character, who whacked me across the face with a ruler because I wouldn't answer. When the ruler hit my infected lip, I nearly fainted. But the pain gave me courage, and I began to scream at him that I would write to Comrade Stalin, to Iosif Vissarionovich himself. That they had no right to beat me. That I had my constitutional rights. The man stopped hitting me. One day, when I was being led out for interrogation, I saw Ivan Semyonovich Czech in the corridor, but he quickly turned away and disappeared behind a door. He was apparently not there as a prisoner or as a witness. Then I realized that he—not Bisk—was the one who had informed on all of us.

"I learned that Leonid Pavlovich, and Gladky and his wife, had also been arrested and accused, just like me, of Ukrainian nationalism—and Gladky's wife, Manya Gurevich, was Jewish. In the newly liberated Ukraine, this was the most common indictment, and the Soviet authorities applied it left and right. One of the accused, a seventy-five-year-old peasant, later shared a cell with me. He said:

" 'When the Russians came back, we were overjoyed. My friend and I—he's the same age as me—celebrate by getting drunk at my place. After we've had a few, we start singing. We don't know any Soviet songs about the Ukraine, so we sing "The Ukraine Has Not Yet Perished." Just then the door swings open and in walks a Soviet officer, and he says: "You are singing the Ukrainian national anthem." We were dragged off. I haven't seen my friend since.'

"Another prisoner was a priest. He was accused of establishing a Ukrainian church under the German occupation and of conducting services in the Ukrainian language. He said his church was 'autocephalous,' whatever that means. And he tried to convert me. In those days I didn't believe in God and told him so. After what

I'd been through, I said, the only thing I believed in was the Devil. The priest said that every nation had to have its own religion. The Armenians, for example, had the Gregorian rite, and it set them apart from other, more powerful, peoples. But what did we Ukrainians have to set us apart from the Poles and the Russians? Orthodoxy, he said, has strengthened the Russians but destroyed the Ukraine.

"It was useless arguing with him. Even the interrogator couldn't beat this out of him. I learned afterward that the priest was sentenced to twenty-five years. Meanwhile, they were still trying to get me to sign a document that said I was a Ukrainian nationalist. As part of the strategy, they brought me face-to-face with Leonid Pavlovich. I looked at him: he had shrunk, had lost his good looks. And he had been such a handsome man, with such marvelous diction, an acrobat, and an actor with the divine spark. I wanted to ask him about his sister, but the interrogator forbid us to talk to each other directly. He produced two posters. One of them advertised the play about collectivization in which Leonid Pavlovich had played Otava, the son of a kulak; the other was for *A Ruble and Two Bits.*

" 'Are these your family names?' the interrogator asked.

"The name on the poster was not Semyonov but Semeniv, which is how Leonid Pavlovich's name was spelled in Ukrainian. And my name too was written in Ukrainian, with an extra letter: Chubinetsy.

" 'You are Ukrainians,' said the interrogator. 'Confess to your crimes.'

" 'Yes, we are Ukrainians,' we said to him. 'As for the crimes, we don't know what you mean.'

"The interrogator began speaking about the play, and I realized that the play was the crime. Leonid Pavlovich then spoke well, though he looked terrible. He said that the mayor had forced him to act, threatening to send him to a concentration camp if he didn't, and that he only agreed to take the role for the sake of his blind sister, who would have died without him.

" 'And you, Chubinetsy,' said the interrogator, 'why did you write a comedy for the Germans? To entertain the enemies of the Fatherland?'

" 'It wasn't a comedy, it was a tragedy,' I replied. 'Like my life. I was writing about my life.'

" 'Very well. Perhaps some time spent in the company of others will make you less stubborn. Perhaps they will teach you how to behave.'

"So Leonid Pavlovich and I were put into a large cell with ordinary criminals. I was well dressed and clean, and Leonid Pavlovich even more so. The prisoners immediately demanded that we swap clothes with them. Without waiting for our reply, they showed us how to conduct ourselves. They asked an army officer, who was wearing calfskin boots and a clean uniform, to swap clothes with them. When he refused, they beat him over the head with the heel of an old boot. When he was unconscious, they stripped him of everything, even his underwear. When my turn came, I asked only for something warm. They left me my old sailor's jacket. Leonid Pavlovich, in return for his overcoat, suit, and underwear, received a sweater, torn quilted trousers, and canvas boots. They told us we were smart to be so cooperative. Soon we were removed from the cell with the criminals and thrown back into solitary, because the interrogations were to continue.

"One day, the door of my cell opened, and a beautiful, appetizing woman walked in. She wore bright red lipstick and had large breasts under her Red Army tunic. Her large hands and face smelled good too, like she'd just washed with toilet soap. For the first time in a long while, my heart began to beat in a most unprisonlike fashion. I became dizzy. She looked at me sweetly, smiled, and said she was a lawyer. She asked me to tell her my life story, because, she said, she was going to defend me. I took a long time in the telling, and she wrote down every detail. When she finished, she said that the most they'd give me was three years. I was overjoyed, and began to await the trial impatiently. They put me back in the common cell just before the trial, but this time without the criminals. And there I met Leonid Pavlovich again. Gladky wasn't among our group, but, to tell the truth, I wasn't sorry not to see him. Our trials didn't take long. Those who were found guilty and sentenced were soon back in the cell with their stories. Some got twenty years, some twenty-five. The old man who had welcomed the Soviet army by singing the Ukrainian national anthem got ten years for nationalism. He had a great sense of humor, and when he came back to the cell, he said, 'I've just had ten years added to my life. I was getting ready to die soon, because I'm seventy-five, but I can't now; the court won't let me.'

"We all laughed. It was strange that morale in that cell was so good. If they had simply executed people or thrown them into a concentration camp, like the Germans did, we'd have been terrified. Yet because the letter of the law was being followed, it was more like a game.

"Leonid Pavlovich and I were tried together. A panel of three heard our case—one judge flanked by two assessors. I looked for the beautiful lawyer who was to defend me, but she wasn't there. Nor was the prosecutor. We were both tried on political charges: anti-Soviet activity and nationalism. The evidence against us was the play about the expulsion of the kulaks and *A Ruble and Two Bits.* One witness, an elderly actress from the theater, had nothing but praise for Leonid Pavlovich, but she wasn't so kind to me, claiming that before I was employed by the company, I had been a Polizei in my home village. I protested, saying that the Germans didn't accept cripples in the Polizei. But one of the assessors remarked that some traitors had been known to be lame. The second witness was Lelya Romanova. The moment I saw her, I became deaf to what the assessor was saying. She looked wonderful: was fashionably dressed, and had the face of a woman who has slept and eaten well. I found out later that Vitka, her pilot husband, had not turned up after the occupation ended, and that she had lived with the colonel of a tank regiment, and when his unit moved farther west, moved in with a doctor at the army hospital.

" 'What can you tell us about Semyonov?' I heard the judge ask her.

" 'He's a good man. He stayed behind because of his

153

blind sister. He worked in the theater because he didn't want to be forced to go to Germany.'

"Asked about me, she said, 'An honest, feeling boy,' and she told of the incident with the Soviet prisoners that she had witnessed.

"Speaking in his own defense before the sentencing, Leonid Pavlovich said: 'I am guilty of acting in the show, and I am still more guilty of staying alive. I should have hung myself. I went on living for the sake of my sister. But there was no ideological motive behind any of my actions.'

"I was asked if I had anything to say for myself, but I was thinking about Lelya Romanova and remained silent.

"The judge asked, 'Does the accused refuse to testify in his own behalf?'

"I answered yes.

"At this point the assessor who had spoken of crippled traitors spoke up. 'Chubinets, why didn't you defend the Fatherland?'

" 'I'm a cripple,' I said, 'and unfit for military service.'

" 'But you have hands,' said the assessor. 'You could have strangled Germans with them.'

" 'My hands are weak,' I said. 'I have a weak grip.'

" 'Then you could have torn out their throats with your teeth.'

" 'I'm squeamish,' I said. 'I couldn't stand someone's throat in my mouth.'

"Seeing Lelya Romanova again had made me high-spirited, defiant. Suicide comes in many shapes and sizes. Some weep when the end draws near, but some rejoice. And for us the end was drawing near. The court officers retired to confer. Three or four minutes later, they returned with their verdict: Semyonov, ten years' hard labor in a northern camp; Chubinets, six years in a local camp. But when the next group was assembled for dispatch to the far north, I somehow got thrown in with Leonid Pavlovich. Two weeks later, after riding in a freight car with common criminals, we reached the camp.

"I remember the visits we were allowed with close relations after the trial. Leonid Pavlovich's blind sister was brought to the prison by a neighbor's daughter. She was twelve years older than her brother, and when she heard his sentence, she burst into tears and said, 'I will not live that long.'

"Aunt Steffie came to visit me from our village. She too had her share of woes. The Soviet soldier she'd been hiding had been arrested. The army doctor at the military hospital signed an affidavit saying that the soldier's wound from a shell splinter should not have prevented him from walking the thirty-five kilometers to what had been the Soviet front at the time. But Aunt Steffie had some good news too. She had received a letter from her husband, Mikola Chubinets, written at the front. So if she couldn't have her soldier back, at least she could wait for Mikola. Aunt Steffie had always been the practical one in our family. That was why, when collectivization began, she went to work with the Young Communist League to help build a new factory. After I was sent to the labor camp, she and I corresponded for a while. Then suddenly her letters stopped. Perhaps mine were not being delivered. Or maybe she no longer felt like answering them.

"I don't care to say much about my time behind the wire. I know that these days it's fashionable to talk and write about such things, but personally I find it boring, like the conversations patients have in hospital wards, going on and on about their illnesses. Besides, I signed a paper promising that I wouldn't talk. All I'll say is that the ones who survived were either the healthiest or the most unscrupulous. Occasionally—very occasionally—someone survived through sheer luck. I owe my own survival to the fact that, as you will recall, I chose a Serbian, not a Gypsy, to tell my fortune, and she said that I would suffer in good times but do all right in bad times."

# 11

---

"I SPENT SEVEN years in Arctic prison camps. For four of them, I was unlucky, having to work in the forests cutting timber with the forced-labor gangs, but the last three years were easy; I worked in a group that cooked yeast to help keep the prisoners from getting scurvy. We were located in a sturdy wooden hut on a stone foundation, and the place was very warm because of the heat from the caldrons. There was a lot of light too, through six large windows, and I learned how to grow tomatoes and flowers by them. My good fortune began with those flowers, and with the camp library.

"Despite everything, I hadn't given up hope, and I turned to reading as a way to keep myself from becoming an animal. I remembered certain books from my past, including ones that old Saltykov had recommended, and managed to find one or two by Gogol and Pushkin. But I couldn't get into them. Our minds receive only what our bodies allow them to, and my body was no longer up to that kind of reading. I found a book by Maupassant, but it reminded me too much of Lelya Romanova. In my present situation, out all day in the numbing wind, felling trees with a heavy ax, I didn't want to think about Lelya. Then I stumbled on a book about growing flowers and vegetables in the home, started reading, and couldn't put it down. I made boxes out of scraps the carpenters left, found some soil, and begged manure from the stables. It was more difficult finding seeds, but I finally got some from the free exiles we came into contact with. The exiles kept flower gardens and grew vegetables during the brief Arctic summer. But in the hut where I worked, flowers and vegetables could grow all year round.

"In the Ukraine, flowers and vegetables are everywhere, part of everyday life, but up in the Arctic they were occasions for joy, and welcome guests not only to us prisoners, but also to the guards and prison bosses. The sight of a flower was like a reunion with a dear friend or a sudden whiff of air from our homes in the south—and above the Arctic Circle everyone is a southerner. Winter in the Arctic lasted from September to June, with blizzards and temperatures of minus-forty degrees Celsius; summer is short, chilly, and wet. Huge ice floes were constantly forming in the river and usually didn't melt until May. Snow stretched as far as the eye could see. But in that wilderness I created the Ukraine on a windowsill.

"This got me out of the forests and into the yeast shop, where I had my own corner, shielded by boards.

I put my cot there. Years later, I could still picture that warm, cozy spot I had made for myself.

"In November 1949, during the anniversary celebrations of the Revolution, I was told I would be released in a month's time: I had served out my term. I had hardly any money from my work inside, since they paid so little, but I was given three hundred and twenty rubles and a ticket to Molotovsk, a town being built on a swamp. There I was assigned to work in a local prison camp, but this time outside the wire and without guards. Once again I was lucky in the work I got. It was in a place where they washed out barrels of waste fuel oil; my job was to stack the empty barrels. Even luckier, I stacked with a former actor from Krivoy Rog. We became friends and talked a lot about the theater, and told each other our life stories. He was released before me and immediately wrote me from Krivoy Rog, where he was again working in the theater. So when I finally got my release, in 1951, I went to visit him, intending to look for work as a theater administrator in Krivoy Rog, since I was denied the right of residence in the main cities of any Soviet republic. He had no home of his own and was living in the makeup room at the theater. I stayed with him for two weeks, but then I caught cold and went to look for work elsewhere. Besides, I might have caused him trouble by staying on. Both his and my identity papers were stamped with the ominous number 37, which said that we were former political prisoners.

"I was now completely on my own. Aunt Steffie had

died, and Mikola Chubinets, her husband, had taken over our house and started a new family. After reading in a newspaper that its theater had vacancies for administrators, I went to the city of Aleksandriya, in the Donbass. But that theater was shut down soon after I started work there. Everyone was given two weeks' severance pay and a new job, but because of the 37 in my identity papers, I got nothing.

"After thinking things over, I went back to the area I had come from and knew well. But it was only to discover that I had no friends or relatives left. I walked those streets that were so familiar to me, and wept and sighed, and finally went to the town theater, which took me back as a junior administrator despite the 37. They paid me a miserable salary and gave me no place to live, so I slept in the theater, curling up wherever I wouldn't be disturbed: on the stage at night, or in the corridor beneath the stage, or down in the boiler room. Once I even spent a night in the dressing room where long ago Lelya Romanova had been my leading lady at the private premiere of *A Ruble and Two Bits*. A sleepless, uncomfortable night."

"Yes, I can imagine," I said, looking out at the lights as the train approached the next station. They were only a blur, because my eyes were filled with tears. We had passed Chakhovaya and were coming into Kazatin.

Before the Revolution, Kazatin was a small town southwest of Kiev. Despite a population of only fifteen thousand, it had its own girls' high school. The boys apparently had to travel to nearby Berdichev for their education. Before the Revolution too, the Kazatin station was the biggest in the area, with a large train yard and a huge freight business. But despite the importance of the railway, Kazatin remained a small town, and the contrast between town and trains persists to this day. Although there are connections here to Kiev, Rovno, and L'vov, and even to Moscow to the east, Odessa to the south, and Leningrad to the north, the nearest city is Berdichev, and it is Berdichev that takes the lead in the district, culturally and economically if not administratively. From the crack of dawn, commuter trains leave Kazatin for the forty-minute journey to Berdichev, supplying labor for that city's industries. And during holidays and weekends, young people escape to Berdichev's five restaurants, its dance halls, or its cultural center, particularly when entertainment personalities come from L'vov or Kiev. Such stars wouldn't be caught dead in Kazatin.

But if the people of Kazatin take advantage of the economic and cultural opportunities of Berdichev, they laugh at the larger town, as do the inhabitants of other anti-Semitic Ukrainian and Soviet towns. Everyone knows about Berdichev's Jewishness, and in Omsk, Tomsk, and Novosibirsk, they jeer at it, although in actual fact both the town's name and its origin are Lithuanian. Jews once formed eighty percent of Berdichev's population, but the efforts of the Bohdans and Adolfs have seen to it that Ukrainians and anti-Semites now form the demographic majority. I distinguish between the words *Ukrainian* and *anti-Semite*, even though very few Ukrainians are not anti-Semites. One day, perhaps, this will change. As time goes on, there will either be fewer anti-Semites or the Jews of Berdichev will become museum pieces. For the moment, Jews are still plentiful in Berdichev, and most of them are neither candle-burning Spinozas hunched over weighty tomes, striving to wash away seas of evil with pen and ink, nor Albert Einsteins disappearing into infinity. No, they are simple Jews trying to taste the joys of life on Earth, and they are just as likely as any anti-Semite to belch and be primevally stupid.

Take, for example, your average hardworking Berdichev Jew, whether he is named Hunzya, Elek, or Munchik. Munchik, first name Zygmunt, is actually a Pole, but when they are all together in their cobblers' aprons, banging their hammers on their lasts and stretching waxed threads in their mouths, which stink of garlic, you can't tell him apart from the others. When Israel Salomonovich, the music teacher, comes in to have his boots repaired, they laugh at him behind his back. There's class solidarity for you: the Hunzyas and the Eleks disparaging their own Jewish intellectuals, the way our Ivans and Sashas despise Russian intellectuals. "*Intelligent holt dym veidl in di händ*," the Jews will say, which means that the intellectual holds his tail in his hands. Why a tail? Clearly, the intellectual is either a dog or a devil.

Hunzya, incidentally, is one of that handful of Jews, a couple of dozen out of forty thousand, who survived the German occupation. His mother, brothers and sisters, grandfather and grandmother all died in that huge pit near the airfield. Once, when Hunzya went to Kiev and got soused, he shouted at a group of East German tourists, "Hitler kaput!" A wiry Ukrainian policeman chased him, but clever Hunzya hid in the bushes on Saint Vladimir's Hill, just as he once had hidden from the Ukrainian Polizei.

But we have strayed from our original intention, which was to take a walk around the station at Kazatin before traveling on to Berdichev. In Kazatin, a new train crew takes over, and a new diesel is hooked on so the old one can be inspected. As a result, the passengers are stuck here for thirty-five minutes, almost as long as it takes to travel from Kazatin to Berdichev. On this lap of the journey there is a three-minute stop, halfway, at Ivankovtsy, where a large number of *katsapy*—a Ukrainian epithet for Russians—have lived for centuries.

According to Einstein, a man who travels by train becomes infinitesimally heavier, and he also gets out of phase with his expected time of arrival, though I can't remember whether he's ahead or behind. My watch was no help, being ten minutes fast, because I had once dropped it. Not really dropped it; more hurled it to the floor in a fit of anger. At my wife. But that's another story.

Fortunately, the war spared the Kazatin station, which was erected at the end of the last century. It has large amounts of glass, tracery, many fine openwork windows, and walls ornamented with figures. The waiting room features a multicolored tile floor. The platforms for both the Kiev and the Shepetovka lines have roofs, which are supported by ornate cast-iron columns. They built things to last in those days. As the Romanov dynasty looked back on three centuries of rule, it thought it had an even longer time before it. The present-day crowd builds everything in haste, thinking no further ahead than the next Party congress or five-year plan.

The station greeted us with the screams of train whistles, the tramping of feet, and the slamming of doors. The loudspeaker howled, crackled, squawked out an incomprehensible announcement, then broke off in a squeal. As we emerged from our dark sleeping car onto the brightly lighted platform, our eyes burned and our knees were stiff from sitting. A cold, damp breeze washed over us. Knowing Kazatin, I expected the station square, with its undistinguished and uncherished statue of Lenin pointing at the ticket windows, to be full of people sitting on suitcases and bundles, people unable to endure the stuffy waiting rooms. And I was right. I also expected the ticket windows to be surrounded by fidgeting travelers using their hips, elbows, and eyes to express their impatience to leave Kazatin. And I was right. I was familiar too with the mosaic on the wall of the main waiting room, which portrayed young men and women in scarlet boots dancing a fast gopak. They were still there, dancing the same gopak and wearing the same scarlet boots. So many years had passed since I was last here, and I had been in so many different places, done so many different things, and had changed so much, but the dancers were as young as ever, and their boots showed no sign of wear.

When I was their age, or even younger, I sat here with Vera Kostsova, a colonel's daughter and member of a folk-dancing group. We had come from Berdichev on the evening train, and intended to take the night train to Popelnya, and then the morning train to Kiev. That was the way we used to travel, changing all the time and happy at every change. I was telling Vera stories that I made up as I went along, and stroking her knees now and then, or taking other, bolder liberties, which she rebuffed, though with little shrieks of obvious pleasure, when I felt someone's eyes fixed on us. Turning, I saw a young soldier with the shaved head of a new recruit. What a stare of hunger! It was like someone who is casually eating a sausage and suddenly senses the eyes of a starving man following every bite he takes, every chew, every swallow. Had the three of us been deep in the forest, blood would surely have flown. But even in a crowded station, I felt fear—though pity too, for the hunger in that heavy stare. I could see into the soldier's mind: he had killed me and was now, with endless moaning, slowly raping Vera Kostsova.

Although I was still an innocent, happy-go-lucky youth and knew little about psychology, I did something rather sophisticated, which even Camus would have admired, though at that time I had not heard of Camus. What I did was let go of Vera and move a little away from her. I didn't hurl myself at the soldier and sink my teeth into his throat, or whip out a penknife and stick him in the ribs. Vera, after all, was not a sausage that could be divided and shared. Nor was she my love, to win by fighting. We were not in love, only having a little fun, killing time, in the waiting room where Chubinets and I were now standing.

Amazing, how primitive life is. Hamlets of every stripe will tell you life is complex, inscrutable, but it isn't; it's primitive. In saying this, I may be contradicting some earlier statement of mine. No matter. Removed from its own context, a statement has no intrinsic value; otherwise we would have to take seriously such notions as: If someone smite you on your right cheek, turn to him the other also. A statement is like a fish in the sea: pull it out of its context, and it dies. And begins to stink. And the poisoning you can get from a statement gone bad is worse than the poisoning from any rotten fish. So if I take up arms against Hamlet and say that life is primitive, you must bear in mind the feelings that overwhelmed me as I stood, no longer young, before the happy, red-booted mosaic in the waiting room of Kazatin's station, beside Chubinets and his life story, which was so fresh in my mind.

"Let's go to the restaurant," I said to Chubinets, "and have a beer."

Chubinets shook his head, either because he was afraid of being late for the train or because of the prices. "I don't like station restaurants," he said. "Let's go to the buffet and have some cold meat."

"But you don't eat meat."

He dismissed this with a wave. "I've been eating it for years now. My life has been put through the grinder so often, a couple of slices of meat won't make any difference."

Chubinets looked tired. Our sleepless night was taking its toll. We both yawned.

"Come, let's have a beer, Sasha. Then you can get a little sleep," I said. "I'll pay. The beer here in Kazatin comes from the Berdichev brewery. It's better than pilsner. Believe me, I know my beer, and I know Berdichev."

So we entered the huge old restaurant with its luxurious bourgeois atmosphere, and sat down at a table that had a tablecloth spattered with fat and smelling sourly of tomato.

"Station restaurants," said Chubinets, "are even worse than the restaurants in hotels."

Perhaps he was still thinking about the jealous husband at the Brovki restaurant who spit in his soup.

The waiter, after receiving a good tip, changed the tablecloth and quickly brought us fresh beer. We had a little food to go with it, of course, some local salted fish. After eating and drinking, Chubinets started to talk about his family.

"In 1957, I took up with a woman from the Tax Department. Galina was her name. We got married. We're still together. My daughter, Elena, is very beautiful and well behaved. The same year as my marriage, I was called in and told that my conviction for Ukrainian nationalism had been overturned. Things improved. You can't imagine what I'd had to endure, what humiliation, because of that damned 37 on my identity papers, banning me from the big cities. Whenever our theater company went on tour to Kiev, Minsk, or Moscow—we even played once, in 1952, in a Moscow cultural center—I couldn't stay at a hotel. And rooming houses wouldn't take me either. I had to spend the night at the railway station. Sometimes I arranged with a truck driver to let me sleep in his truck while he stayed in the hotel room I'd paid for."

From salted fish, Chubinets and I went to salt pork, not local but quite good.

"I shouldn't eat this," he said. "It's bad for my blood pressure, and I have rheumatism—because of frostbite in my legs when I was in exile."

I looked at the clock; we had another twenty minutes, so I asked the waiter to bring us some Kazatin fried eggs and sausage, as described on the menu. When the eggs arrived, they were heavily peppered, but Chubinets liked them.

"Of course, things are better now," he said, eating hungrily. "Last year, my wife was given a two-room apartment near the Tax Department. The kitchen is all right, and there's a toilet and bathroom. But it's practically on top of a truck yard and a grain elevator, and there's noise all day and all night. We've tried exchanging it, but nobody wants it. I can't go on living there. My nerves can't take it."

"Finish your beer, Sasha," I said, "or we'll miss the train."

I had picked a table near the window so we could see the Kiev platform and our train's mail car, from which boxes and packages were being unloaded. We emptied our glasses and wiped the foam from our lips. When I looked out again, mailbags were being trundled away on a cart and the train was slowly moving. We jumped up and raced out. We didn't actually "race," of course. Had I run with all my might on my two sturdy legs, leaving my crippled companion to fend for himself, I might have been able to scramble onto the rear car. But I couldn't abandon him like that. I stood with him on the platform, and we watched the train recede into the distance—a scene in a hundred films. Chubinets was still clutching a fork from the restaurant. With his other hand, he shook his cane and cursed the Kazatin railway authorities.

"First of all, Sasha," I said, controlling my anger and disappointment, "lick your fork clean. You still have egg on it. Then throw it in the trash can. Second, you should thank the train thieves, because without them we'd have left our jackets, papers, and money in the sleeping car and run out for a beer in nothing but our shirtsleeves and with only a three-ruble note in our back pockets." I said this to quiet my own fear of being stranded in Kazatin.

We set off in search of an official who could help us. It took a long time to find the right one; we spoke to employees who couldn't tell us anything and peered into ticket-office windows in vain, until I found myself digging my nails into the palms of my hands. And Chubinets brandished his cane as he hobbled, at a female reservations clerk, at a station inspector, and even at a policeman on duty. I restrained him each time, but with difficulty. And cursed him under my breath for such behavior, using the most pungent Russian curses, which, in case you didn't know it, are of Chinese or Mongol origin. Before the Tatar invasion, the Russian people, supposedly, did not curse, though personally I find that hard to believe. Our word for the male sexual organ, for example, is *hooey*, which in Chinese means "man."

Eventually, wandering in weariness and despair, we

came upon a man on the platform for Shepetovka who looked truly official. The Shepetovka platform, by the way, is much more provincial, quieter and darker than the platform for trains arriving from Kiev, and it's located at the rear rather than the front of the station. He was a railway policeman, a fat and stolid-looking army veteran, and was as mild and unhurried as we were nervous and anxious.

"Now then, what seems to be the trouble?" he asked, with a languor better suited to driving an ox cart down a country lane than to the hustle and bustle of a junction that never slept. I could see Chubinets's cane starting to twitch in his hand, although the man could have flattened both him and his cane with a single blow. Fortunately for us, he did not resort to force, but explained everything calmly and coherently, in his slow Ukrainian way, and laid our fears to rest.

"So you're from train number 27? That's the night train out there now, being shunted around. In a while it'll be brought back here, to the Shepetovka track, gentlemen."

In a rush of gratitude, I pulled out a pack of American cigarettes, Camels, and offered it to him. The policeman refused, becoming less native Ukrainian and more bureaucratic Russian at the sight of the foreign brand name.

"Thank you, but I'm not allowed to," he said. Then he read out the name, pronouncing it as if it were written in the Cyrillic alphabet. "Samel cigarettes? When I was in school, I learned a little German. Samel . . ." he mused. "Is that Samuel in Russian? Is Samuel the owner of the tobacco company?"

"Actually, it's the name of his pet camel," I improvised, beginning to feel expansive as my confidence returned.

"A strange lot, these capitalists," he said, laughing good-naturedly. "They honor their animals, but ride to heaven on the workers' backs."

The man was a dray horse. We have millions of such good-natured dray horses dragging their squeaking wagonloads over the ruts and potholes of history. And who else is there to do the dragging? Certainly not the secret agents and spies with microphones in their buttons. Not the cosmonauts. No, it's not they who do the work. They're too busy up there in the driver's seat, urging on the dray horses: Giddyap! *Tsop! Tsobay!* Slow beasts, perhaps, but reliable.

At long last a train was signaled onto the Shepetovka track, and our sleeping car, number 11, was clearly identifiable by its darkened windows. Our bags had not been touched. Soon we left all our cares behind, left them at the station, which seemed to float away in our wake, its bright electric halo glowing against the night sky, as if some minor local sun were rising over Kazatin.

# 12

IT WAS ONLY after our train had passed the warehouses, sheds, and workshops outside Kazatin, and the odors of hot iron and fuel oil that wafted in through the window as they drifted by, that things returned to silence and the passengers to sleep. Chubinets nodded from weariness and beer. At first he dozed bolt upright, but gradually slipped to one side, then collapsed full length on the bench. His crippled leg was sticking out, so I slid my English suitcase under it to make him more comfortable. Let the poor man sleep, I thought. He's exhausted by life and by his journey, and by the story I made him relive.

I lowered the window more and let the wind wash my face. As often happens when you stand at the window of a fast-moving train, a speck of dirt flew into my eye, and both eyes began to tear.

I had lived in Berdichev for four years when I was an adolescent. I'd also spent eleven years in Rostov-on-

Don, and have been in Moscow for the past fifteen. Before Moscow, I lived for six years in the Chernigov district of the town of Kozelets, with its fish-filled river, the Oster, and the wonderful eighteenth-century cathedral by Rastrelli, a real gem of a building. I've been other places too. But whenever my travels take me near Berdichev, which isn't often, I am always filled with a strange emotion. Can it be that this is my historical homeland? Because Berdichev is the historical homeland of all Russian Jewry. All of us, even the old-time converts to Christianity, Saint Petersburg residents of long standing, seem to have some connection with it. And not only Russian Jews. In the tense year of 1967, his excellency Comrade Malik, then Soviet representative at the United Nations, was heard to shout at the representative of Israel: "This is not the Berdichev bazaar!"

One can understand a Soviet sneering at Tel Aviv or Washington, at Paris, Stockholm, Rome, or Berlin. But on this occasion Comrade Malik was deriding a city in his own country. He was internationalizing it, blatantly harking back to an attitude, itself international, shared by the warring ideologies of the Second World War. Malik could himself have been a red-faced, drunken anti-Semitic trader at that very Berdichev market, hawking bony fish or jars of cheap tobacco. God knows, Berdichev counts enough people like him among its inhabitants.

But Berdichev is less a place than a state of mind; it is a symbolic city spread across the country and around the world. A man can be mocked for being from Berdichev even though his feet never touched its streets, whether he's a Moscow professor, a New York lawyer, or a Parisian artist. On the other hand, there are Berdichev residents—say, of the squat old houses on Makhnovsky Street or the smart Party buildings along the boulevard—who have absolutely nothing to do with *that* Berdichev. Berdichev, then, is both a ghost and a living thing. But the ghost has more life than the living thing. Some flesh, even when pink, is dead.

Moved by these thoughts, I gazed out at the dark fields of the Berdichev countryside; I watched a row of slim fir trees that bordered the tracks. They were no less beautiful than the illuminated New Year firs around the Kremlin. The darkness reduced the trees to two dimensions, to a pen-and-ink drawing of trees. Later in the morning, when the sun rose over them, they would acquire volume as their branches spread and shook off the night, and they would turn pinkish green. I remembered watching them when I last traveled through these parts, just over a year before, in a first-class compartment on a Moscow train. It was August, and the buckwheat was in flower. I had not been to Berdichev in many years, and had no one I was close to there. Certainly not my uncle's widow, who meant less to me than Sasha Chubinets.

Chubinets doesn't live in Berdichev, but I think perhaps he should. It has a wonderful Russian Orthodox cemetery that's still in use. I'm not being ironic here. I think a man should know where his grave will be, should choose the spot long before he dies. In our day and age, it's getting more and more difficult for a corpse to rest with dignity. Though, true, it has been difficult in the past too. Under Catherine II and Alexander I, the Jews were given permission to have their own cemeteries, but the first thing Nicholas I did after throttling the Decembrists was to dissolve the Jewish Funeral Confraternity. When you want to get rid of a people, forbid them to bury their dead. Hitler's crew, on the other hand, took care of burying themselves, since they didn't plan to leave any survivors, not even Jewish gravediggers.

And Bohdan Khmelnitsky, when he joined the Ukraine to Russia in 1649, buried more than six hundred thousand Jews, including women, old men, and infants, thus cementing the friendship between Russians and Ukrainians in Jewish blood, even though after the unification, the murderous hetman lost his independence and the chance to carry out a Final Solution. The tsar, in 1655, did no killing but expelled the Jews from Russia, from lands they had lived in even before the coming of the Slavs. At the beginning of the eighth century, there was no Russia, and Slavic Kiev had not yet been founded, but Jews were already living in Sarmatian Kiev. The name Kiev has nothing to do with the Slavic legend about the brothers Kij, Shchek and Khoviv, princes of the Polyane tribe. They didn't found the city; the city existed before their arrival, and Kiev in Sarmatian means "hills." The Jews who had settled there called it Tsiev or Kiun. In the congratulatory missive they sent to Alexander II on the thousandth anniversary of Russian statehood—Alexander having abolished restrictions on Jews and stopped the persecutions of Nicholas I—they declared: "We Jews settled in Russia before it was founded."

Nations are like forests; as long as they are not totally chopped into firewood or burned to the last cinder, they go on reproducing themselves in their own disorganized fashion, dropping their seeds to the ground, which sprout into seedlings wherever they happen to fall. Each seed, a thinking seed, is subject to chance, to the vicissitudes of moisture and sunlight, food and shelter. Some fall far from the original roots, far from the nation-thicket. The Jewish seed has always felt cramped in the Russian forest, hemmed in. It is too intelligent, too impatient with idiots. For the Russian seed, it is just the opposite: Ivan the Idiot is seated in the place of honor. This makes the Russians a tightly knit nation, and they amuse themselves by allowing a phantom city to arise in Berdichev, a foreign city within Russia's walls.

My uncle Zabrodsky was a pleasant, cultured man, an expert in his field, and a highly respected member of the People's Commissariat for Foreign Trade, the Russian acronym for which was NKVT. His wife, naturally enough, enjoyed her husband's position, but made use of it in an original way. At the first sign of a problem in her daily life—such as trying to buy tickets for the Moscow train in Kazatin—she would shout, "My husband is a senior official in the NKVT!" And the T, with her lisp, would sound a lot like D. It was not her fault if people heard NKVD and ran to satisfy her every wish. When my uncle was arrested and hauled before a senior officer of the NKVD, he thought that his arrest was because of the behavior of his wife, which he was constantly reprimanding her for. But the investigator assured him that, no, that was not it at all; the reason for indictment was an article against Lenin my uncle had written in his youth, when he was a member of the Jewish Socialist party, and had worked on that party's newspaper. The arrest was in pre-Yezhov times, when interrogators were still polite and did not make trumpeting noises when they blew their noses.

"For you, to be or not to be, that is the question, and your life depends on how you answer," was the way the interrogator summed up my uncle's situation.

When it was decided that my uncle was not to be and, in fact, when he no longer was, his widow was forced to leave Moscow and make her home in Berdichev, but some of the luster of her past remained. After her husband's posthumous rehabilitation during the Khrushchev period, she took up the old refrain. "My husband was a senior official in the NKVT!" she would shout.

Berdichev people love to shout. Although I was approaching it now in the middle of the night, I knew that the city would shout a welcome. And indeed, the train had barely pulled into the station when I heard someone calling "Chichilnitsky! Chichilnitsky!" at the top of his lungs.

I know the name. A good-looking family, the girls in particular, with splendid bodies and stupid-cunning faces. The eldest was a hairdresser. On summer days she would stand outside her beauty parlor in her smock and shout at any passing man, irrespective of his age: "Young man, make me work!"

She had a pleasant voice, and was a talented singer. In the late forties, I remember, there was an amateur talent show at which she sang a song composed by her brother, Sunya Chichilnitsky. It was called "The Chestnut Trees at Berdichev" and was all about white chestnut blossoms falling upon the face of the singer. After the song, Sunya read one of his poems:

> "A full-throated laugh
> From someone on a balcony . . ."

The public applauded the Chichilnitskys warmly, but the first prize went to Nikolai Okhotnikov, a plumber at the Lenin leather factory. Okhotnikov came striding out onto the stage, face scarlet, and bellowed, as if to stun his audience:

> "The Russian countryside,
> This is my motherland."

"Chichilnitsky! Chichilnitsky!" came the shout again. Maybe it was another Chichilnitsky they wanted. There were as many Chichilnitskys in Berdichev as there were Chubinetses in Chubintsy. Where do they all come from? If Gogol had lived to write a third part of *Dead Souls*, would he have made Chichikov pass through Berdichev and father a brood of children on a beautiful dancing girl? And if so, would the name Chichikov have been changed to Chichilnitsky with the passage of time? For all I know, Chichikov too may lie in the Russian Orthodox cemetery at Berdichev. I can see him beneath a pink marble cross, his eternal rest watched over by an angel of the same pink perched upon his headstone. Or he may be lying under a stone of magnificent black labradorite with blue veins running through it, his name and dates lettered in gold. What a pity that Gogol chose to take that crude, sad journey to Jerusalem instead of going to Berdichev.

The Russian Orthodox cemetery at Berdichev is at its most beautiful in winter, when snow shrouds the graves and tombs with purest white. In summertime it is a sweet-smelling garden full of bird song. But when you go to its far end, where instead of crosses the graves have stars or strange granite parallelepipeds on their headstones, you can see the changes modern literature has wrought on our perception of the world. In the old days, death was an individual, apolitical thing; now, even the graves of privileged and wealthy individuals bear the stamp of collectivism. Take, for example, the grave of Lucy Kripak, the charming seventeen-year-old daughter of the director of the Berdichev tannery. She was slain by a club accordion player who was hopelessly in love with her. Her stone, though smothered in a sea of fresh flowers, was hewn clumsily and completely lacks personality.

Yes, even Berdichev is sometimes racked by wild passion. An everyday conversation on a street corner may suddenly ignite into violence, and its sparks may reach Kozelets or Solekamsk and be rekindled.

Our train came to a stop, and Berdichev loomed in the darkness. Though the station clock said three in the morning, the citizenry was already up; there was a swarm of people with bundles and suitcases waiting for the express from Odessa to Moscow. An hour before it was due, the platform was packed, but the train would stop for only three minutes, the same length of time allowed at Ivankovtsy, where hardly anyone got off or on. The morning Moscow-Odessa express, the other important train to pass through Berdichev, had not yet arrived either, but people were rushing around with suitcases, pushing and shoving, puffing and panting, their eyes bulging. Where will car number so-and-so be? At the head or the rear? How are the cars numbered? Sometimes, the conductors prepare the passengers already aboard for the entertainment they'll have when the train reaches Berdichev. Heads crane out of windows, laughter erupts, and ears prick up at the cries of Berdichev women and the wail of Berdichev children trying to claim the seats they have reservations for. There's an atmosphere of pogrom about the proceedings.

A former Red Army man, a Jew, recently wrote in a newspaper that train stops in Berdichev reminded him of an incident that occurred there in 1919, during the Civil War. He had been a member of the Bogunov Regiment, a cavalry unit serving under the famous Red commander Nikolai Shchors, and had somehow managed to survive the Second World War and the purges. What happened was this: an armored train secretly manned by Petlyura's Ukrainian nationalists entered Berdichev station flying a red flag, and opened fire with machine guns and artillery on the Red soldiers and the local populace, causing a general panic. Shchors personally led a counterattack on the armored train. But who, asked the Jewish veteran, will challenge today's Petlyura bandits, who wave their red flags from the safety of their office windows? The veteran's letter to the editor was ignored, and the Southwestern Railway Board continues to make even its timetable an anti-Semitic weapon. Knowing the bedlam that invariably takes place at Berdichev, it does nothing but laugh up its sleeve, and the stopover there remains as short as ever. And the people, distraught, keep pressing forward to board, shoving, shouting, and clinging for dear life to the handrails of the steps.

Those who aren't going to Moscow or Odessa but to Zdolbunov, in the Rovno district, are businesslike, stolid, and unencumbered by children, and they travel in smaller numbers. They can be aboard in a minute if necessary. So the Kiev-Zdolbunov train waits at Berdichev a good fifteen minutes or more, and the Berdichev passenger can walk through the cars calmly and with an ironic smile. Which is what happened this time. Two people entered our car, and then stepped back.

"What's wrong, Marusya?" one asked.

"It's dark. You won't be able to see to deal the cards, and there's some slob in there snoring."

He meant Chubinets, who, fortunately, didn't hear, or he'd have gone after those Berdichev Jews with his cane, and I would have had to part with another thirty rubles to smooth things over.

The citizens of Berdichev love their much-insulted city; they like to boast of the famous people born there, of the famous events in history that occurred there.

There are no Berdichev trivia unimportant to them. The highest point in Avratyn Heights lies in this district, for example, though it's nothing but a gently sloping rise between the Dnieper and the Pripyat. There is only one true hill, Bald Hill, where since tsarist times military barracks have been located.

There are always plenty of military people in Berdichev: lieutenants engaged to be married, or colonels who buy themselves little retirement homes on tree-lined side streets on the outskirts of the city. They tell jokes about Jewish chickens in phony Jewish accents but are the first to buy the fat local chickens and geese to cook for themselves. What a funny, shameful city Berdichev is, and yet how many of these white-headed old men would leave it to shuffle back to the wild cloudberries and cranberries of their native Siberia? They curse the city, and stay. These retired army people are even more anti-Semitic than the Ukrainians. Perhaps they're afraid that if they're not, the Ukrainians will make them leave.

It is common knowledge that Russians are much better behaved in Russia proper than they are in non-Russian areas, where, as foreigners, they have to keep an eye on what goes on behind their backs. In the old days the nobility's sense of class solidarity kept the lid on nationalist differences; nowadays there's an alternative way to maintain the illusion of cultural unity, a way to reconcile the red-necked retired Siberian and the fat-assed Ukrainian cottage owner: the telling of Jewish jokes. There they go now, walking down the platform: a Siberian meat pie and a Ukrainian dumpling. Notice their fishing gear, decorated woven bags, salt pork and tomatoes, as they go down to Chervonoye for some early-morning fishing for bream and pike. There they go, two culturally unified brothers staring contempt at the Berdichev Jews. The Berdichev Jews, however, have learned to ignore the contempt. Besides, they have their own problems. For example, the still-missing Chichilnitsky.

At a Berdichev wedding I once met a horde of Chichilnitskys, several families of them together. The music had scarcely begun when they launched themselves into dance, feet flying high, and they sang:

> *Gesunt sollst de sein,*
> *Gesunt sollst de sein,*
> *Ay, yay, yay, yay; ay, yay, yay, yay!*
> *Gesunt sollst de sein.*

Which is Yiddish for "To your health."

They had good voices. Quite a few Chichilnitskys are in the Berdichev Mixed Chorus. I remember a performance at the district folk festival in Zhitomir, the women in Russian costume and the men in embroidered shirts. They did a piece by Pavel Kuzmich Samokhin, principal of the Berdichev Music School:

> *My sweetheart's walking in the yard,*
> *What a fellow, in the yard,*
> *Oi, yeli, yeli yeh. . . .*

And when the Berdichev children came out for the final gopak, there were several Chichilnitskys of both sexes there in their scarlet boots singing, "Hep! my friend, don't you cry. . . ."

The Chichilnitsky being called now, by a voice like a foghorn—perhaps he was supposed to come on the night train but got held up by urgent business in Kiev or Kazatin. Wherever he is, I feel like taking a stroll through town. Though I'm uneasy about leaving the train after what happened at Kazatin. I go down a couple of steps of the car and, holding on to the handrail, take a look around and drink in Berdichev's night air. Berdichev sleeps in its houses and its cemeteries: the Russian Orthodox cemetery near the station; the Catholic cemetery next door, divided from it by a picket fence; and the Jewish cemetery at the opposite end of town, out by the tannery. When you travel by bus down the Kiev-Zhitomir Highway to Berdichev, the first thing you see upon entering the city are piles of coarse stones, a dreary field where nothing green grows. That's the Jewish cemetery. No bushes for nightingales to sing in, no lilacs blooming, only the stink of the tannery. The Orthodox cemetery is much more pleasant to walk through. On a spring day or in summertime, you can look at beautiful tombstones and sit on soft, soft grass.

"Chichilnitsky," the call goes on. "Chichilnitsky!"

A persistent people. If they want Chichilnitsky, they'll shout until he hears them, even if he's as far away as Kazatin.

Still holding the handrail, I lean out to take in more air, and I shout too: "Zabrodsky! Zabrodsky! Felix Zabrodsky!"

Let my name resound in this Berdichev air, dive into

it, swim through it, circle the station building, and come to rest on the cobblestones that stretch from the station to the city center and beyond, right up to where the old gray-brick Berdichev water tower used to stand. The old boulevards too no longer exist. The wrought-iron fences that used to skirt them, with an openwork grille that Leningrad or Odessa would have been proud of, have been removed, and large numbers of great horse-chestnut trees have been chopped down because they blocked the newly built offices of the city party committee, a white plastered box, which the inhabitants jokingly call the White House.

"Zabrodsky!" I continue shouting. "Zabrodsky!" There's no stopping me. I do not let the sound of my name die away. Perhaps it will awaken my past.

"Hey, Felix! What are you doing up there? Where are you going?"

I look down. The last time I spoke to the man who's standing on the platform below me was at least thirty years ago, but seeing him now, I feel as if it were only last night. We had escorted two village girls from the Berdichev Textile Mills back to the station, to see them off to Zagrebelie or wherever it was they came from. The man's name was Gumanyuk, and he was pure Ukrainian. But like all Ukrainians in Berdichev, he spoke Russian with a Jewish accent.

"So, Felix, where are you living now?" he asks.

"Moscow."

"Me, I'm here at the Progress Works, in the boiler shop. I came here for a beer after the night shift. The station buffet is the only place a person can get beer at this time of night. Ma salted me some pork fat; I had to have a beer to drink with it. Then I hear someone shouting your name."

Amazing, I thought. Surely his mother's not still alive. Old Gumenyuchka, as we called her, must be a hundred now. And still salting pork fat?

Ukrainian salted pork fat is the best in the world. That is one of the few universal truths I still believe in. Gumanyuk's mother came from the Vinnitsa area, which is where she learned the secret recipe. For if Ukrainian salted pork fat is the best in the world, Vinnitsa salted pork fat is the best in the Ukraine, and in Tulchin, where old Gumenyuchka comes from, the art of pork-fat salting has reached its apotheosis. If an international congress on salted pork fat is ever held, it should be held not in Geneva or Paris but in Tulchin.

I remember old Gumenyuchka's kindly red-cheeked face and her intelligent hands. If you ever try the pork fat salted by those hands, you will want to kiss them, the dry hands of an old Ukrainian woman. As one might wish to kiss the hands of Tolstoy or Gogol after reading their most brilliant pages.

"So where are you working?" Gumanyuk asks.

"Moscow."

"Moscow, I understand, but where in Moscow?"

"Right in the center. Did you ever hear of the poets of the Little Bronnaya and the prose writers of the Makhovaya?"

"You're a writer, then?"

The train begins to pull out of the station, moving

slowly, with me in the doorway holding the handrail while Gumanyuk walks alongside.

"Are you married?" he asks.

"Yes."

"I'm not. An old bachelor. It's impossible to marry women from Berdichev."

"Parisians say the same thing about their women."

"Really?"

"Greetings to your mother. Kiss Grandma Ukraine for me, and my thanks for her wonderful pork fat."

Before it's too late, I suddenly think, before the train picks up speed, I should get off, take a room in a Berdichev hotel, go for a morning walk down the boulevards, drop in on Gumanyuk in his rich peasant's cottage with its galvanized roof. I could sit around drinking homemade sugar whiskey and eating salted pork fat and fried eggplant, and pancakes, with stewed cherries for dessert. But once again I've let the chance slip by. Tonight I'll be staying in Zdolbunov, because the truth is, I could never stay in a hotel in Berdichev. In Berdichev, the only place I'd want to spend the night is in someone's home.

# 13

THE FAMOUS SOVIET satirist and humorist Zabrodsky lives
and works in Moscow. He has written theatrical skits,
reviews, features, scenarios, and television shows. He's
doing well, the darling of the public and approved by
the bosses. A man of great talent, blessed with the gift
of fantasy. Like Gogol before him, he can sometimes
be a good old-fashioned liar as well. He has a large
apartment near the Little Bronnaya and not far from the
Makhovaya; it's on the corner of Gorky Street and Tverskoy Boulevard, the same building that houses the Ar-
menia shop. The fact that his wife is Armenian is surely
a coincidence. The apartment is luxuriously furnished
and includes a white grand piano, on which Zabrodsky's
small daughter practices, and a fairly large private library. Besides the complete works of Zabrodsky, the
library has a Bible, a copy of the Cabala, the Russian
and foreign classics, and volumes of philosophy and
history by Shestov, Rozanov, Taine, Tocqueville, Ta-

tishchev, and the German psychologist and idealist phi-
losopher Wilhelm Wundt. There are even a few
Ukrainian authors: Shevchenko, Olga Kobylyanskaya,
Grushevsky.

The main problem I have is that this famous Soviet
satirist and humorist is me. You may ask how I can be
a Soviet satirist and humorist and have such deep books
in my home. My reply is that I can use the money. Yes,
many things about life in the Soviet Union become
clearer, nobler, if you regard them through the eyes of
money, listen to them with the ears of money, and think
about them with the mind of money. The morality of
a Russian individual is much more acceptable when put
in this light.

Why am I going to Zdolbunov? Not for a matter of
any great importance. A small job, the result of a letter
some troublemaker wrote to a Moscow newspaper,
complaining about the local hardware stores, which,
though they are supposed to serve the needs of the tillers
of the soil, the agricultural workers in the Zdolbunov
district, for many years now have not been stocking
babies' pacifiers, combs, razor blades, and other essential
items. The paper's editor, in an effort to respond to the
wind of change now blowing, commissioned me to
write a satirical article on the subject. Frankly, I could
write this kind of thing without leaving the comfort of
my bathroom. I have a pretty good idea of these stores,
which decades ago squeezed the village shopkeepers out
of rural areas. They stock cheap candy made from soya,
brands of stone-ground barley like Parus and Volleyball,
cans of vegetables that have sat on the shelf for five or

six years, bagels as hard as rocks, and salt and matches. There are deliveries of bread twice a week. Oh, and wine too.

Wine is an issue unto itself. The cases of poisoning that were taken for drunkenness at first. A man has a glass of wine at lunch and comes down with diarrhea the moment he climbs back onto his tractor or combine. The troublemaker's letter also said that in the busiest part of the growing season, operators were having to drive as much as seven kilometers to reach the central medical clinics at the state farms, and this on their tractors or combines. Some even had to drive their bulldozers to get there.

Anyone familiar with the world of literature will therefore know that my article on the shortcomings of rural Zdolbunov's food and retail goods distribution system would practically write itself. All I had to do was take a walk down Tverskoy Boulevard, come up with a few metaphors, add a dash of local color, and decide just how much free speech or freethinking might be accommodated by the wind of change now blowing. I could say, for example, that as one who has traveled a bit in this wide world I've seen small stores in other countries that stocked such articles as aspirin, bandages, iodine, toothpaste, and hair tonic, not to mention a magnificent selection of pacifiers. And perhaps even conclude with the question: What does the Soviet State Planning Commission intend to do about this situation?

It would have been simple to do this in Moscow, yet I found myself applying instead for a free round-trip ticket to Zdolbunov. Of late, I have been writing in the bathroom less often. I have the urge to travel. They say travel broadens the mind, but it's really for those who are spiritually ill at ease. Not long ago, I went to the Urals, in that case too because of a worker's letter. A curious place, the Urals. On a bus there I accidentally bumped into a woman, and I had scarcely begun to apologize when she called me a bastard and spat, "Who do you think I am, your girlfriend?"

Normally I am not that interested in local color and don't stay long in the places I travel to. A plane there and a plane back. But this time, for my trip to Zdolbunov, I chose to take the train. I did so for several reasons. First, because by changing in Kiev I'd be able to stop off at the archives there. And second, because I really did want to travel once more by night through the small towns of the southwest, particularly through Berdichev. No matter what people take me for, whether a Russian, a Jew, or a Ukrainian, the fact is that in the daytime I am cheerful and witty, but at night I sleep badly. Visions of disease and decay torment me. The thought that if I do die soon, my complete works might be published posthumously in three volumes by Iskusstvo Press. Then I wonder if I'll be referred to in the foreword as a "consummate master of illusion," which is how one could have described me before Stalin's rule began in the late 1920s. A poet of the twenties—whose poems are in my collection—was described, in his foreword, as being "as remarkable for his talent as for the defectiveness of his creative method." This defectiveness may be illustrated by the following example. Speaking of one of the leaders of the proletariat, Feliks Dzerzhinsky, chairman of the Cheka and then the OGPU, the poet wrote:

> *His heavy manacles like tambourines resound*
> *In the fields where children play,*
> *A bejeweled chain that weighs him down*
> *As his sentence slips away.*

In the twenties you could describe the Polish-born chief of the Cheka, the NKVD, and the Special Squad in Hasidic style, like Chagall. You could write boldly, with fantasy and gaiety, and not have to fawn or fall into foaming-at-the-mouth rages. You could make Iron Feliks stride across meadows like a goat with a chain rather than a bell.

Rosa Luxemburg asked, "How can Yuzik be so cruel?" using Iron Feliks's nom de guerre. She soon learned about cruelty, when the budding Nazis, at the other end of the political spectrum, broke her neck with the butt of a rifle and threw her corpse into a Berlin canal. Perhaps someday I'll have a chance to see that canal. But what I have before me at the moment are Feliks's meadows beginning to gleam in the dawn outside my train window.

We had already passed through Chervonoye, Lyubar, and Chudnov, the last stations in the Berdichev area, and were plunging onward into the western Ukraine. More names flashed by: Klevan, Korets, Yidichin. The Slavs of these parts were Germanized long ago, trading with Danzig rather than with Kiev. Since the dawn of history, they'd floated their wares down the western

Bug, first by raft or dugout. We were now in Volynia, which at one time was covered by forests of evergreen and deciduous trees; centuries ago, these forests were destroyed in order to promote the wheat trade with Europe, since grain prices had begun to rise and Slavic wheat could command a good share of the market. Another reason for the destruction of the virgin forest was the demand for potash, first in the West, then, in the last few centuries, in the East.

Despite the strong historic links between the western Ukraine and Europe, the disparate parts of the Ukraine were swallowed up by Russia, and this happened only because of the schism in Christianity. A schism tragic not only for the Ukraine, but for Poland too. On April 26, 1686, Poland, under pressure from Turkey, concluded a peace treaty with Russia, recognizing for all time Russian suzerainty over Smolensk, Kiev, Novgorod Seversky, and the whole of the eastern Ukraine. Poland's weakness was its Catholicism, and the Ukraine's, its Eastern Orthodoxy, because if the two had belonged to a single branch of Christianity, they might have joined together to form a strong Slavic state and so have effectively blocked off Europe from Russia and its Asiatic hordes.

The area we were now in had resisted Russia longer than anywhere else, a fact that is explained by the closeness of the Uniate Church, dominant here, to Catholicism. The people here speak differently, with the sibilance of the Poles, and their national costume is closer to that of the Poles, Hungarians, and Romanians; they even cook their salted pork differently, preparing it, in the Polish fashion, with onions, or the way the Hungarians do, with peppers—but *not* with garlic. Their fields are different as well, with barley, oats, and rye growing in predominantly sandy or loamy soils, while wheat scarcely enters the picture, surviving only here and there in thinner soils. The banks of the region's meandering and majestic rivers are fringed with bog grass and—what particularly fascinates me—mysterious clumps of heather. The same heather from which the Scots of olden times brewed liquor. It's as if the very landscape were resisting unification with Asia.

A wonderful area. I once spent two weeks here, alone, without my wife, and for a while I loved Volynia. With my wife, that would have been impossible, because had she accompanied me, all the worries and responsibilities of my everyday life would have blurred everything and made it abstract, and you cannot love an abstraction, be it political or artistic. This is why my creative collaboration with Sasha Chubinets was of such value to me. His story could not be fitted into the petty frame of everyday things. Quite the contrary, with him, the most trivial detail spawned an epic, an epic that was sometimes comic and sometimes tragic. It was a caricature of a life, but charged with feeling and passion.

So here I was, watching the sleeping Chubinets, a man who had had no childhood, no adolescence or young manhood, and might possibly have no old age either. It was his missing past that had turned him into a caricature, a creature worthy of Goya, Leonardo da Vinci, or even Holbein in *The Dance of Death*. I looked at him, at his lined and careworn face, his crippled leg, his ever-present anger. You could give the picture an ironic caption, in the style of Goya, using the words of the Ukrainian lullaby:

*Sleep little one, by the light of the moon,*
*Sleep sweet and sound, for day will come soon.*

But since Chubinets never had such a lullaby sung to him by his careworn mother, and his great-grand-mother, Tyoklya, the only person who ever loved the poor little cripple, was too ancient to sing to him, per-haps some pink marble angel in the Orthodox cemetery in Berdichev will cradle him and hum some Ukrainian melody as he takes his last breath and goes to his eternal rest.

The train braked at a grade crossing with a sudden jerk that made Chubinets hit his head against the bench. He sat up and rubbed his eyes, obviously not knowing where he was for a moment. Then he recognized me, remembered everything, and asked, "What was the last stop?"

"Berdichev," I said, although in fact we had passed many stations since then.

"Aaah"—he yawned indifferently—"I've been there once or twice. In Berdichev they know how to cook."

That was all he knew, all he thought, about Berdi-chev. Not too bad, for a Ukrainian. Most would have immediately launched into some anecdote about the town, their eyes sparkling with vicious amusement. Chubinets, however, spoke of Berdichev as if it were some run-of-the-mill place like a hundred others. But

Berdichev is not a run-of-the-mill place, and I found myself not only telling him about it, but also trying to persuade him to move there. I don't know—maybe I wanted to have someone there I'd like to visit. It was a pipe dream, of course. Still, I went on telling him he should become a Berdichev Ukrainian and that one could still get permission to be buried in the Eastern Orthodox cemetery, though there was talk of closing it down and building a new cemetery outside the city, somewhere near the site of the mass executions of Jews in 1941. This was why the Jewish monument had been removed.

"Well, I certainly need more peace and quiet," Chubinets said. "You can see I slept for only a short while and it's done me a lot of good. All I think of these days is sleep. At home, day and night, there's that grain elevator next door, howling and squealing. And when I go on tour with the theater, it's worse. We were recently in the Carpathians, not far from here. . . . The lives of our provincial repertory actors should be written up, in a book. Not by me—my health and nerves wouldn't allow it. Some people, yes, write to put money in their pockets. Of course I wouldn't mind the money, but the words I force out onto the paper keep trying to get back inside me. They're like poor orphans reproaching me for turning them out into a cold and pitiless world. Go on, be off with you, I want to tell them, live without me, meow as much as you like, be as miserable as you like. Go beg at the doors of my readers. Maybe they will take you in and look after you. Now, a word that has only been spoken but not written down—that's a safe word. It plays outside if it wants to but always comes home at night."

So long as it doesn't get picked up by some stranger, I thought, and put in his own literary orphanage.

"Actors in the provinces lead awful lives," said Chubinets, "and the life of a theater administrator is even worse. Unless you're a scoundrel and a drunken fool like our senior administrator. Once, I arrived in the town of Mukachevo in a dreadful state. I was a little late and running a fever. In the hotel lobby was Nosov, the senior administrator, with the actors. They were waiting for the room assignments. We don't get treated like celebrities from the capital, you know. So I began assigning the rooms. My head ached, my tongue stuck to the roof of my mouth. If only I could lie down, I thought, but there I was, running back and forth. If Nosov doesn't help, I thought, I won't make it, I don't have the strength. But he was as drunk as a pig and disappeared to sleep it off. Soon I was completely exhausted and my legs felt like lead weights. The actors who still hadn't been given rooms were cursing. One actress came up to me and said, 'If I don't have a room in one hour, I'm quitting the tour. In three days you'll be out on your ear, and so will Nosov. I'll go straight to the district party committee and report you to the Theater Board.' So I went to find Nosov and tell him that the actors were cursing and making threats, for which I couldn't blame them.

"Nosov, only half awake, looked up at me and smiled with his swollen red lips. He said, 'You don't know your job, Chubinets. Take her by the hand, she's a woman, talk her around, explain the situation. And if she wants to leave, make her write a letter of resignation.' This didn't help at all. My head was swimming. You know, I have a high red-blood-cell count: forty-five instead of the fifteen it should be. Just before going on tour, I had it tested at the clinic. But there was no point in dealing with a drunk. So I went back to the lobby. The same actress came up to me, with her leading man, the one who played heroes and lovers, though he couldn't hold a candle to the late Leonid Pavlovich. There may be a few good actors left in the capital somewhere, but there are none in the provinces, I can tell you. The ones we have now live badly and they act badly. And it's not surprising, seeing how they're treated.

"The actress spat the foulest language at me, and her hero-lover backed her up. He said he wouldn't go to rehearsals or to the first night of the tour either. It took me until nine in the evening to get them all settled in their rooms.

" 'What's the problem now?' Nosov asked when I went back to him.

" 'Where am *I* supposed to sleep? I don't have a room,' I said.

" 'Sleep in the drivers' room,' he said. 'There's a free bed there, because one of them is out on a trip.'

" 'I can't,' I said. 'The air in there stinks of cigarette smoke, and I'm sick. Put me in with the lighting man instead.' The lighting man is a serious person; he's studying radio at night school.

"But Nosov said: 'Maybe you want me to put you in with the cashier. She's not bad.'

"At last I found a bed in a hikers' hostel not far from the hotel. I was told I could sleep until nine in the morning, but then I'd have to leave. There were no individual rooms, only a large dormitory with people sleeping on straw mattresses on the floor. I had just dozed off and was beginning to dream when a new group of hikers came in, joking and laughing. It was one in the morning, but they were up at six and again woke me. When they finally left, I tried to go back to sleep, but at eight o'clock, not nine, the receptionist came and told me I had to leave. By now I was in no condition to do anything, even think; everything seemed so awful, I felt like crying.

" 'Why don't you get some rest?' Nosov said, seeing the state I was in. 'You're free today. You can have room 32. Just go and register.'

"So I went to fill out the form, but was told I couldn't have the room until three in the afternoon. Oh well, I thought, I'll use the time to go see a doctor at the local clinic. The doctor, examining me, gave me a medical certificate at once and told me to go to bed. I had angina, which had affected all my blood vessels. He gave me a prescription, but the nearest pharmacy was out of the medicines. They told me to try another pharmacy, way out at the edge of town. I took a bus there. All I wanted to do was sit, but it was so crowded, I couldn't find a seat. I kept seeing red spots in front of my eyes, and I also moaned from fatigue. People thought I was drunk and watched me carefully. Someone even offered me his seat, but by then there were only two stops before I had to get off. The second pharmacy had amidopirin but was out of penicillin and novocaine. I went back to the hotel, thinking that at last I could lie down, but room 32 turned out to be full of bedbugs. Also, just outside the window was an exhaust vent from the restaurant kitchen, and all the odors from the cooking penetrated the room. First thing in the morning came a smell of some kind of stinking meat, then sausage and egg, pork, onions, fish, all of it fried in fat. In addition to that, immediately below the room was a refrigerator, and every five minutes its motor would switch on or off, making noises that lasted two or three minutes each time. This went on day and night. At home it was a grain elevator, and on this tour, a refrigerator.

"From six in the morning to one at night, the entire serving staff of the hotel shouted as they went about their jobs, some of them shouting in Hungarian, some in Russian, and some in Ukrainian. And all of them, regardless of nationality, were black with dirt. They kept bursting into my room without knocking. Young people may like noise, but with what I've gone through I can't take it.

"And then there are the constant money problems that prey on your nerves. A lot of actors have other jobs on the side. But in this part of the world you need connections even for unskilled labor. Once, a friend of mine got a position in the local freight depot as an inspector, and he found work for me and a young actor:

loading and unloading containers, every day from nine in the morning. Or we move furniture, which isn't easy, particularly for a man of my age and in my state of health. But at times it pays well, depending on who you work for. You can earn five, ten, even fifteen rubles a move. You can also do house repairs, or fix sheds and barns. That's how actors in the provinces get by.

"Incidentally, six months ago Lelya Romanova came to see us at the theater. I was in the corridor when I caught sight of her. We embraced. So many years had gone by, but she still smelled of the same perfume, and of something else that was still the same. You know, the smell of a woman like that is permanent and indescribable. She still looked good, wore an astrakhan coat and a white fur hat. I had been married for many years, but I still desired her. My heart pounded. My God, I thought, I'm not dead yet; I'm a fish that's been taken off the hook and dropped in a bucket of water so it can be put fresh in the frying pan. I began to hope she'd be willing to be my leading lady for another performance of *A Ruble and Two Bits*.

"We went off together to the railway station, and my friend the freight inspector let her have a room for transit passengers at a modest price and without showing her papers. But when we went there, all we did was talk late into the night, and I ended up leaving her to get some sleep. Don't look so surprised! In the first place, when she took off her coat and hat, it was obvious that she had changed after all, and not for the better. The astrakhan coat turned out to be artificial, and the hat was only well-worn goatskin. She had come back to our town to get her retirement papers together so she could begin collecting her pension.

" 'I spent the whole day with the pension people weeping my eyes out,' she told me. 'They said that since I worked for the Germans during the occupation, the Germans could pay me my pension. Nobody was interested in how long I've been working for this new lot we've got now. All those tin-can buses with no heating, filled with so much smoke it gives you a headache. All those filthy, cold cultural centers and village halls unequipped for even the simplest kind of show. I don't know how I managed to bring culture to the people for thirty-five years and still remain more or less in good health, even if I do have high blood pressure and arthritis, particularly when it rains. And all those night journeys, when you don't get home till two, three, or four in the morning, and those big parts I played, which were always so complicated and had too many lines. Let me tell you, I earned my award as Distinguished Artist of the Ukraine. I have testimonials too, and even a medal.

" 'Yet when I apply for a pension, they drag up the German occupation—that's all they can think of. That this should happen to me now, when I have nobody to turn to for help or support. My husbands I divorced; my lovers left me for younger women. I'm sorry but I can't help crying—my nerves are in shreds. The final blow came when I was doing a sketch in a club. I was supposed to be reading a letter from a mother to her son, who's in the army, at the front. A letter brimming with tears. "I'm a hero's mother," I was supposed to say. When I reached that line, I couldn't go on; I had hysterics right there on the stage. After that, they said I should retire.'

"Lelya and I drank wine and got a little drunk. She said, 'Kiss me.' I kissed her hand. She looked at me in despair, and I could see that she realized she wasn't my wife and couldn't be my mistress.

" 'What a pity we didn't get together for keeps that time,' she said. 'I would have waited for you till you came out of prison. We could have helped each other. That's why people live together, to help each other. I didn't understand that until it was too late.' "

The sun was rising. Our long travelers' night had come to an end. Chubinets and I were no longer alone in the car. We could hear people talking in the dialect of the western Ukraine, the language in which Olga Kobylyanskaya wrote poems like "Valse Mélancolique," in which she made Ukrainian words twist and turn and glitter in the European fashion. Chubinets and I continued talking, but now it was the reluctant talk of people who do not know each other very well.

Sometimes there are chance meetings between bodies, when unknown hands encounter hands in the dark, and unknown lips meet lips. But then the sun comes up— that primal source of realism and skepticism in the universe—and the romance of night melts away like the pale morning moon. Thus, too, chance meetings between minds. Some laugh at such occurrences, but I treasure them. For all their brevity and embarrassment, there is something wonderfully natural, unprofessional, about them, like an unannounced poetic game. It's obvious why they occur more often at night, when we are all closer to our old roots. And the abruptness with which they cease leaves us with a sense of something unfinished, and therefore alive, because things finished are dead.

# 14

---

OUR TRAIN ARRIVED at Zdolbunov almost on time. I helped Chubinets retrieve his briefcase and string bag from the rack and handed him his cane, and together we descended onto the platform and walked out of the station into the square. We made an odd couple. There I was, a well-to-do passenger from the big city with an English suitcase in my hand, and there was Chubinets, liable, in the full light of day, to be taken for a village idiot who panhandles in passageways and station entrances. Both of us felt this incongruity, and felt the surprise and disapproval of those who saw us.

"Where are you staying?" I asked Chubinets.

"I'll try the Zvezda."

"You'd be better off at the Volynia," I suggested. "I have a reservation there; I can help if you have any problem. Wait for me here—I'll get a cab."

"No, it's too much trouble," said Chubinets. "The bus is quicker."

"Don't worry. I'll get a cab and be right back."

He was right; I did have trouble getting a cab. It was only by holding out a ten-ruble note that I was able to flag one down at the opposite end of the square.

"The Volynia?" the cabdriver asked, running an experienced eye over me and seeing an expense account.

"Yes, but first I'd like to pick up someone at the bus stop."

"And where is this person?" the cabdriver asked impatiently as I vainly searched the area around the bus stop.

Chubinets was nowhere to be seen. There were all kinds of people there, but no sign of him. The spot where only five minutes ago he had been standing, clutching his cane, string bag, and briefcase, was now empty. I was irritated by the crowd milling at the bus stop, crisscrossing the square, all of them looking, waiting. No, I was not irritated by the crowd but because I knew that I no longer needed Chubinets. He had given me all that he had to give, and his physical presence now would have prevented me from making use of that gift. This made me seem a scoundrel in my own eyes, an exploiter and abandoner. Even though it wasn't I who did the abandoning but he, and here I was looking for him.

Not true, Zabrodsky, said a voice within me. You knew he would go if you left him, and that was exactly what you wanted: for him to disappear, an old cripple with a string bag and a briefcase. Having him around now would be demeaning. And inhibiting—as a soft-hearted cook is inhibited by the sight of a sheep, alive and bleating, when he has to make a mutton stew.

In my room at the Volynia Hotel, I phoned the Zvezda, where Chubinets had said he would try to stay. I was told that there was nobody of that name registered. So the deed was done, for better or worse. The sheep was gone, and the cook could start cooking. All that remained was to choose the recipe and the sauce.

But first I had some chores to attend to, so I got to work, and by late morning I had finished taking notes—facts, figures, names—for my article. Back in Moscow I would rework it, add a few poignant touches and acerbic asides, and type the thing out. Then I could return to my real writing: the saga or odyssey of Chubinets, the story of the horrors we have gone through and those that are still with us. A blasphemous, profound, observant, lyrical story, about how a man is scorned every day by the country he lives in, and how the country is scorned by the state, and the state by the tyranny over us all.

It would take time, I realized. Even the first draft, which I would have to do immediately, while the impression of the journey was fresh, would take ten days at least. So I went to the post office to send a telegram to my wife, who was expecting me back on Monday so we could leave for Sochi together. I wrote: MAMA STOP DELAYED URGENT BUSINESS STOP FRENCH KISSES STOP IRON FELIKS. I thought the telegram amusing, perhaps even on the level of the one I had sent from Sochi the previous year: MAMA STOP LYING ON BEACH STOP LOSS

OF WATER FROM SWEAT CAUSES DEBILITATION STOP ZA-
BRODSKY. The girl at the window in Sochi had giggled,
like any experienced consumer of semi-Soviet humor.
She even sang, under her breath, some lyrics I had written. They had been on television the day before:

> *So I took the floor and danced,*
> *While the people stood entranced,*
> *And watched the harvest hero paw*
> *His partner on the threshing floor.*
> *Ay yay yay! Ay yay yay!*
> *Those who brought the harvest in*
> *With the dancers all join in!*

That was how the post office clerk at Sochi had reacted. But her Zdolbunov counterpart was of a different
generation, between forty and fifty, and her face seemed
familiar. She took the telegram from me, read the words
with a professional eye, read them again more slowly,
then handed back the form.

"No," she said. "This won't do."

"What's wrong? Did I fill it out incorrectly?" I tried
to be humble, as one is with an editor at a publisher's.

"The form is all right. It's the words that won't do."

"The words are my affair. It's a private telegram."

"That's where you're wrong, citizen," she replied,
and I winced at the word *citizen*. "This is written on
state paper and is subject to approval by a servant of the
state."

It was *she*, of course. Not she in person, but her carbon

copy, her double—the double of the editor to whom I had lost my virginity a long time ago.

"How can you write such obscenities to your mother?" she asked.

"In the first place, it's not my mother but my wife."

"Then why do you say 'Mama'?"

"That's really none of your business."

Don't lose your temper, I told myself. To paraphrase Lenin, Soviet reality turns its citizens, day by day, into hysterical neurasthenics, and some of them call their wives Little Piglet, some Penny Bun, and others Mama.

"And why say 'French kisses' and be filthy? Why not simply write 'kisses,' like any normal person?"

Her eyes were the color of dark cherries. She was that type of woman who looks wanton into old age. The type you can make a pass at and know she'll come to your hotel room. But she sensed that in my hotel room there was another waiting for me, and jealousy made her implacable.

"Cross out 'French' or I can't accept this telegram. And what does 'Iron Feliks' mean? Feliks is your first name, I take it. Why the 'Iron'?"

No, I decided. I won't let her have the iron.

" 'Iron' is my pen name. Like Gorky for Peshkov. My real name is Zabrodsky." And I pulled out my card. Not the scarlet card of the Party but the dark blue membership card of the Writers Union. It did the trick.

"I don't need to see that. I know who you are. Tell me, what are you working on now?"

"I'm writing a screenplay for a Russian-Ukrainian film called *People*."

"Oh, how interesting!"

She melted. She allowed the Iron Feliks, and I dropped the French kisses. Experience has taught me how much I can get away with. In any case, as has happened more than once before, after thinking the matter over carefully later, I realized that my editor was right and had saved me from making a fool of myself in print.

Once, when I was working at Moscow's Institute of Marxism-Leninism, I occasionally had lunch with a lecturer in Marxism at the restaurant there, which was nearly as opulent as the restaurants in the Kremlin. This lecturer scarcely ever washed his hands, either before or after eating, but he always washed his mouth out carefully, both before and after, and took a long time about it. Noticing my questioning look, he explained.

"What is the most unclean thing in man? His mouth. The mouth is a pullulating mass of bacteria."

He was right, just as the editor was right. Editors may not be well grounded in the world of Gogol and Bunin, but they know that you should use your mouth only for eating, because otherwise, if you aren't careful, you can say something that will never be washed away, no matter how thoroughly you gargle afterward.

I sent off the telegram, had a quick lunch in a local restaurant, rinsed out my mouth, and hurried back to my hotel room, because I was awaited there by my mistress: a stack of writing paper.

There was a time when writing paper was to me simply stationery, a necessary tool of my trade, which in turn was necessary to bring in money, so I could buy the little things that make life pleasant. There was always virgin paper lying around, in different shapes and sizes, for me to impregnate so it could give birth to the usual sketches, skits, and scenarios. The paper I used was good quality, purchased at a shop not open to the general public, but I did not care about the quality as I opened up each pack and swiftly filled page after page in a sloping longhand, using a good fountain pen and dark blue ink. Sometimes, for variety, I tried green or red, but always returned to blue.

There were lots of commissions, and I wrote a great deal, because my dacha needed new plumbing or my wife needed a new fur coat. But I was not sleeping at night, I had stomachaches after eating, kidney problems, tachycardia, even palpitations of the liver. This was because the more time passed, the more I felt the chains on me. I wanted to rip them off, particularly at night, even if it meant tearing out pieces of my own flesh, because the chains had fused with my skin. The older I get, the more my will struggles to break free and run off into the forest, perhaps to die under the eyes of wolves, but at least with heart and soul naked and unchained.

That was why I raced back to my hotel room, where I was awaited, as a groom is awaited by his bride, by virgin sheets of top-quality writing paper. I now pay great attention to paper. Somewhere there may be a free but impoverished genius who has never used his pen to acquire a two-story dacha. He writes his masterpieces on wrapping paper, on paper made from rough fiber, oakum, and pressed hay. And somewhere there may be a poet who lives on a diet of plain sausage or mortadella and uses newsprint made from inferior timber by-products. But I require high-grade vellum for my bride. Smooth and springy paper, like a young woman's skin. Paper of the purest cotton or linen fiber. It must be strong, and able to contain the ink. I can't stand spreading lines and blotches. Now I have in front of me a sheet of paper imported from a Nordic land and made in strict accordance with an old Scandinavian formula. It is paper that might have been used by Knut Hamsun, a man who hated intellectuals and wisdom, and praised freedom and madness. These last few days, I have realized how great are the joys of madness, and how strong the temptation to turn the chained laborer into a pink-cheeked, irresponsible child.

Sometimes, in the morning, I went to the window and watched Zdolbunov roll before me, as if it lay outside the porthole of an ocean liner. Buildings, houses, pedestrians, and vehicles pitched and yawed. Nothing remarkable. A standard-issue Soviet city. In the evenings, a few neon lights shone provincially in the dark, in Ukrainian: a green sign that said CLOTHES, a red that promised HAIR STYLING, and a blue advertising BUTTONS. My nights were restless. In the middle of a snore, I would jump up, turn on the lamp, and catch in the dark air a fleeting idea, an idea as evasive as a mosquito, and put it on paper. That was how I lived. With clenched teeth, I groaned from the nightmares that visited me by day and the joys that visited me by night. I uttered words punishable by law and thought the inhuman things that have tormented man since time immemorial. And the white-skinned, silken Scandinavian paper kept on absorbing the words, sucking them in. At last I finished. And, finishing, knew that I would be impotent for a long time now, unable to make love to paper, able only to turn it into money.

The bags under my eyes were dark blue, the color of my ink. Exhausted but calm, I took a cab to Rovno, where I caught the plane that stops there on its way from L'vov to Moscow.

I love trains. For me, they have always symbolized change, hope. An airplane, for all its devilish speed, provides only the externals of change—the mere geography of change. But on a journey by rail, the small gardens and towns and the smells of coal and diesel blend with the gleaming tracks that stretch away into endless space and time. What passes us is everything we hold so dear on parting but which is so terribly boring and inescapably gray up until the day we leave it. What passes us is everything we wanted to escape in our childhood and meaningless youth, yearning for a larger world of resounding words and great events. That world, once sweet in our imagination, is now a lost paradise. This is where train stations come in handy, for there the disappointed present and the hopeful past coexist, in a balance that is disturbingly shaky but which holds for all that.

When I dream it is usually of stations, whistles, hooting locomotives, of changing trains at night and sitting with people I either know very well or do not know at all. But if I do not know them, why do I see them in my railway dreams? For example, not long ago, I dreamed about a Spaniard. We were traveling together and talking. He was someone I hardly knew; we may have met a couple of times in Moscow. He told me about his home in Spain, said that there was an old monastery there, over whose gates was written "Every hour wounds, and the final hour kills." And then the old Spaniard looked like Chubinets, a Chubinets painted by Picasso. And picturing a Picasso Chubinets, I thought it was logical that Spain was the inventor of the auto-da-fé. I thought that, yes, with every passing hour we are consumed by fire, but invisible fire. It's only the final hour that burns us with the familiar flame of hell. Because all of us, even the just, pass through the flame of hell before the offices of the hereafter decide whether or not we can move onward to the mansions of heaven. Where there are no nations. A man leaves his nation behind, along with his rotting cadaver. Everything is consumed, and what remains of each of us is a small heap that would resemble ashes if it took material form. This small incombustible heap is our most valuable essence. I don't know about Chubinets, but I would prefer not to be dumped into an ashtray. Let them gather me carefully, instead, in an urn.